MARYANNE LINCOLN'S COMPREHENSIVE DYEING GUIDE

by Maryanne Lincoln

EDITOR
Virginia Stimmel

BOOK DESIGNER
CW Design Solutions, Inc.

ASSISTANT EDITOR
Lisa McMullen

PHOTOGRAPHY
Impact Xpozures

CHAIRMAN
M. David Detweiler

PUBLISHER
J. Richard Noel

Presented by

RUG HOOKING

1300 Market St., Suite 202
Lemoyne, PA 17043-1420
(717) 234-5091
(800) 233-9055
www.rughookingonline.com
rughook@paonline.com

PRINTED IN CHINA

EDITO

Colorist Maryanne Lincoln began writing "Recipes From the Dye Kitchen" as a regular department for *Rug Hooking* magazine with the January/February 1994 issue. During the next 10 years she provided a comprehensive dyeing lesson for every issue, providing valuable tips, instruction, and countless formulas to thousands of readers. Now for the first time, *Rug Hooking* is pleased to compile all 50 of Maryanne's lessons in this easy-to-read reference guide. *Maryanne Lincoln's Comprehensive Dyeing Guide* explains everything you need to know to create beautiful hand-hooked rugs—different methods of dyeing, basic and complementary colors, plus a myriad of dyeing formulas. Novice as well as experienced dyers will love this book for its easy-to-follow format.

Maryanne takes the mystery out of dyeing and makes it seem easy. After reading this book, you, too, will want to try the various formulas to see how many different color combinations you can create. No longer will the idea of dyeing your own wool be intimidating. Her step-by-step directions on measuring, mixing, and dyeing wool are so easy to follow that anyone can do it.

Now relax and enjoy this wonderful book that highlights Maryanne's many years as a professional colorist. May it help to broaden your horizons and stretch your imagination beyond your borders.

—Ginny Stimmel

TABLE OF CONTENTS

CHAPTER SIX

The Great Outdoors

CHAPTER SEVEN

Creatures Great & Small

CHAPTER EIGHT

Circus

ABOUT THE AUTHOR

Maryanne Lincoln's passion for color and dyes began in 1964 when she learned to hook. Not only did she take a basic class to learn how to dye, but she also gathered information on dyeing from a variety of sources and experimented with color extensively on her own. Today, her expertise as a professional colorist makes her a leading authority on color and dyeing.

Maryanne has been associated with the McGown Teachers Workshop since 1971, and has been teaching at camps and workshops throughout the United States for the past 23 years. She is a member of *Rug Hooking* magazine's editorial board, where her love of dyeing and color inspired her to write a regular column, "Recipes From the Dye Kitchen" for 10 years. Maryanne has created a line of mail-order hand-dyed swatches for rug hookers and has developed her own line of Country Colors for dyeing. She can be contacted by writing to her at, 10 Oak Point, Wrentham, Massachusetts 02093, (508) 384-8188.

WHAT IS RUG HOOKING?

Some strips of wool. A simple tool. A bit of burlap. How ingenious were the women and men of ages past to see how such humble household items could make such beautiful rugs?

Although some form of traditional rug hooking has existed for centuries, this fiber craft became a fiber art only in the last 150 years. The fundamental steps have remained the same: A pattern is drawn onto a foundation, such as burlap or linen. A zigzag line of stitches is sewn along the foundation's edges to keep them from fraying as the rug is worked. The foundation is then stretched onto a frame, and fabric strips or yarn, which may have been dyed by hand, are pulled through it with an implement that resembles a crochet hook inserted into a wooden handle. The compacted loops of wool remain in place without knots or stitching. The completed rug may have its edges whipstitched with cording and yarn as a finishing touch to add durability.

Despite the simplicity of the basic method, highly intricate designs can be created with it. Using a multitude of dyeing techniques to produce unusual effects, or various hooking methods to create realistic shading, or different widths of wool to achieve a primitive or formal style, today's rug hookers have gone beyond making strictly utilitarian floor coverings to also make wallhangings, vests, lampshades, purses, pictorials, portraits, and more. Some have incorporated other kinds of needlework into their hooked rugs to fashion unique and fascinating fiber art that's been shown in museums, exhibits, and galleries throughout the world.

For a good look at what contemporary rug hookers are doing with yesteryear's craft—or to learn how to hook your own rug—pick up a copy of *Rug Hooking* magazine, or visit our web site at www.rughookingonline.com. Within the world of rug hooking—and *Rug Hooking* magazine—you'll find there's a style to suit every taste and a growing community of giving, gracious fiber artists who will welcome you to their gatherings.

–*Ginny Stimmel*

ABOUT THE PUBLISHER

Rug Hooking magazine, the publisher of *Maryanne Lincoln's Comprehensive Dyeing Guide,* welcomes you to the rug hooking community. Since 1989 *Rug Hooking* has served thousands of rug hookers around the world with its instructional, illustrated articles on dyeing, designing, color planning, hooking techniques, and more. Each issue of the magazine contains color photographs of beautiful rugs old and new, profiles of teachers, designers, and fellow rug hookers, and announcements of workshops, exhibits, and gatherings.

Rug Hooking has responded to its readers' demands for more inspiration and information by establishing an inviting, informative website at *www.rughookingonline.com* and by publishing a number of books on this fiber art. Along with how-to pattern books, *Rug Hooking* has produced the competition-based book series *A Celebration of Hand-Hooked Rugs*, now in its 15th year.

The hand-hooked rugs you'll see in *A Celebration of Hand-Hooked Rugs XV* represent just a fragment of the incredible art that is being produced today by women and men of all ages. For more information on rug hooking and *Rug Hooking* magazine, call or write us at the address on page 1.

DYE EQUIPMENT & SAFETY

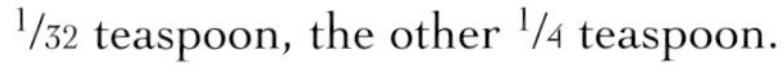

Like any cook about to follow a recipe, you must assemble your tools, pots, and ingredients before you follow a dye recipe. Here's a list of what every wool dyer's kitchen should contain. (Please note: When you're done with these implements, don't throw them back in your kitchen cabinets lest someone pull them out to cook food. Dyeing utensils and pots should be for dyeing only. Don't use them for food preparation, as you may end up ingesting the dyes. Green eggs andham may be fine for Dr. Seuss, but not for rug hookers.)

As you can see by reviewing the list, the majority of these tools can be found at any kitchen shop. The dye spoons, however, are unique to dyeing and will have to be obtained through a rug hooking supplier (see the glossary for addresses). What makes these spoons so special?

A TOD brand dye-measuring spoon is one with calibrated scoops at both ends. One end measures 1/32 teaspoon, the other 1/4 teaspoon. This spoon is what I learned to dye with 30 years ago. I now use and prefer the Grey brand of spoons because a set of three double-ended spoons has scoops that measure 1/128, 1/64, 1/32, 1/16, 1/8, and 1/4 teaspoon.The TOD spoon is adequate for most published formulas. The Grey spoons make it easier to cut formulas down and to dye formulas that have been written after these spoons were introduced. Keep in mind that the fraction with the largest denominator (1/128) is actually the smallest spoon. Likewise, the one with the smallest denominator (1/4) is the largest spoon.

The spoons from both manufacturers are made of polished aluminum. Wash and dry them after every scoop of dye. I don't recommend dipping aluminum spoons in salt to clean them because the salt may eventually corrode the spoons.

ASSEMBLE YOUR TOOLS

- An apron, protective smock, or lab coat.
- 2 pairs of rubber gloves. Wear surgical gloves when handling dyes and loose-fitting, heavy, lined rubber gloves for handling hot wool.
- A mask to cover your nose and mouth when you're measuring dry dye.
- Tongs for poking and lifting wool in the dye bath.
- 1- and 3-quart enamel, glass, or stainless steel pots (don't use aluminum, as it will affect the dyeing process).
- An enamel, glass, or stainless steel soup pot (for scrunch dyeing).
- An enamel, glass, or stainless steel roasting pan or canner big enough to hold 6 to 8 quart-size jars (for jar dyeing).
- Small enamel pan to dissolve dyes in.
- 6 to 8 wide-mouth quart-size jars (for jar dyeing).
- 1- and 2-cup glass measuring cups.
- A teaspoon.
- Assorted long-handled spoons for stirring the dye solution in the jars and pots.
- Heavy aluminum foil.
- Dye spoons (see above for more information).
- Plain, uniodized salt.
- White vinegar (5 percent).
- A wetting agent, such as Synthrapol SP (see Chapter 3).
- Wool.
- Dyes.
- A notebook and pen.

OTHER MEANS OF MEASURING DYES

There are other ways to measure dry dyes and dye solutions besides special spoons and other glass cups. If you measure large amounts of dye for backgrounds and other large pieces of wool, you can get the job done faster and with greater accuracy by weighing the dyes, wool, salt, vinegar, and wool on a scale. Scales are available from PRO Chem (the address is in the glossary). To accurately measure liquid dye solutions, you will have great success with the use of different pipettes, beakers, graduates, and syringes (also available from PRO Chem). PRO Chem has four different glass pipettes for liquid metric measuring: 25ml (milliliters), 10 ml, 5 ml, and 1 ml. The pipettes each have lines marked out to measure small amounts so that you can be precise down to the drop if need be.

I use the largest pipette when I want accurate large amounts; in the 25 ml I can measure anything up to 25 ml and then do multiples of it. For instance, if I need 50 ml, I fill the 25 ml pipette twice; and if I need 63 ml, I fill the 25 ml pipette twice plus 13 ml. You can measure accurately less than 25 ml in it, but it is difficult to measure amounts less than 5 ml with the 25 ml pipette. The 5 ml and the 1 ml pipettes are handier for small quantities. For instance, 1.25 ml could be obtained by either filling the 1 ml pipette once plus .25 ml more; or you could use the 5 ml pipette and fill to the 1.25 ml line.

Take time to learn how to use pipettes, beakers, graduates, and syringes before starting to measure dye solutions. Practice with water a time or two to become familiar with them. See the appendix for metric equivalency charts.

Liquid measurements come in handy when trying to accurately develop substitute formulas. Once you mix up the basic liquids that you will be measuring from, you won't have to handle the dry dyes again until the solution is used up.

SAFELY USING CHEMICAL & NATURAL DYES

The dyes we use to color our wool are not toxic, but they are chemicals and should be handled with respect. All of us use laundry and dish detergents, bleach, ammonia, drain cleaners, furniture polish, and the like. They are all chemicals. You should handle dyes with the same amount of respect and care that you use when handling those products.

If you know or even suspect that household cleaning products irritate your lungs, always wear a mask when measuring the dry dyes and doing the actual dyeing. Don't have a fan running or a window open when measuring the dry dyes, as the fine particles fly about easily. Do, however, work in a well-ventilated area when actually dyeing to cut down on fumes and steam, and have a damp paper towel or newspaper covering your work table to catch errant particles.

If you know or even suspect that household cleaning products irritate your skin, always wear gloves. The dye manufacturers encourage us to use gloves—and masks—when handling these chemicals.

Neither Cushing nor the PRO Chem dyes come with skull and crossbones symbols on them. But if you have safety concerns, get in touch with the dye company and request a Material Safety Data Sheet.

Ironically, natural dyes may well be more dangerous than synthetic dyes. Some dye plants and mordants (a substance that fixes color in fabric) are poisonous, so be cautious when handling them. There is no company to fall back on for information; it is up to you to learn about them. Don't assume that just because a dye is natural, it can't hurt you. Be an informed user: Take the time to read about these dyes before using them.

There are many different classes of synthetic dyes that are used to color textiles. Some are specifically designed for certain fibers. Others are a blend of ingredients so they can be used on a wide range of fibers, from protein fibers like wool to cellulose fibers like cotton. Sacrifices are made when you choose one of these mixtures—sometimes you may not be able to get the color fastness or depth of shade that you want.

Acid dyes are used for dyeing protein (animal) fibers such as wool. Both PRO Chem wash-fast acid dyes and Cushing acid dyes are called acid dyes because they need an acidic dye bath to work effectively.

WATER, SALT, & VINEGAR

Using the proper equipment and procedures will help you dye with perfectly predictable results—if we lived in a perfectly predictable world, that is. We work with a great many variables. Water quality and composition differ from season to season and region to region. Wool varies from sheep to sheep. Dyes have not been consistent over the years. So don't expect consistent results and you won't be disappointed.

The dye bath starts with a certain amount of water, to which we add small quantities of a wetting agent (discussed in Chapter 3), salt, vinegar, and of course the dyes. All water pretty much looks the same, nice and clear, but the interesting part about it remains hidden, despite that clarity.

Water is not the same from state to state, town to town, or even house to house. It is not the same from season to season—during the wet season the concentration of minerals in it is different from the concentration during the dry season. We can't depend on the potability of water to mean it's acceptable as a dyeing ingredient. In some parts of the country chemicals are added to community water supplies to alter them for human consumption; those same chemicals (chlorine, for example) can work against us when we dye wool. Then there are those parts of the country where acid rain affects the ground water from which tap water is derived.

Cushing and PRO Chem dyes work best in acidic water, which allows them to attach themselves to wool fibers. We change the acidity of the water and thus encourage that attachment by adding vinegar to the water. We retard the attachment by adding a small amount of salt.

I have always used both salt and vinegar to dye gradation swatches. I add salt to the dye bath before adding the wool to help keep the dye from spotting the material. I add vinegar about three fourths of the way through the dye process or at its end because I like to have dark values that are different from each other, and I don't seem to be able to get those results unless I do. Vinegar, or a suitable substitute such as citric acid crystals, is a necessary ingredient in the dye kitchen, not an optional one, when dyeing with acid dyes.

KEEPING RECORDS

With all your equipment lined up by your stove, you are almost ready to begin dyeing. But before you start, make sure you have pen and paper nearby to record your successes so you can repeat them another day. I have a simple spiral notebook to make notes in as I work in my dye kitchen. From those notes I write out a record card and file it so I can quickly retrieve the formula with all its particulars to duplicate later.

I assign a simple name or number to each formula, and then I include all the important information about the swatch: the size and color of the wool, the dye formula,the procedure, a small sample of the results, and any other appropriate comments. I use the back of the card for additional information. Dyeing a lovely color without recording these facts about it reduces your chances of ever dyeing it again.

CHAPTER ONE

BASIC COLORS

Basic Red

Shaded Rose, *6" x 5 1/2", #3 cut wool on rug warp. Dyed and hooked by Maryanne Lincoln, Wrentham, Massachusetts, 1993. For this flower, Maryanne dyed eight values of basic red using Pro Chem wash fast acid dyes.*

RUG HOOKERS LOVE TO SEE NEW COLORS AND TO COLLECT SAMPLES AND FORMULAS FOR ACHIEVING THEM. SO EACH TIME I TEACH MY THREE-DAY COLOR COURSE, WE SPEND SOME TIME PASTING SAMPLES INTO A NOTEBOOK AND DISCUSSING POSSIBLE COLOR VARIATIONS. WE ALWAYS HAVE A GREAT TIME. EVEN THOUGH I AM THE ONE ACTUALLY CREATING THE COLORS IN MY DYE POTS, WE ALL GET EXCITED ABOUT EACH NEW COLOR, AND WE CAN'T WAIT TO PULL OUR NEW CREATION OUT OF THE DYE POT.

I would like to invite you to join me in developing a new group of colors from just four dyes. If you follow my step-by-step instructions, you should easily be able to achieve the colors on your own. We will make one color, gradually working our way around the color wheel. If you keep sample swatches of each color, eventually you can construct your own color wheel of dyed wool.

W. Cushing and Company offers more than 90 different dyes; Pro Chem has about 20 different colors of wash-fast acid dyes. However, if you want to join me in these projects, you only need either four Cushing dyes (Canary, Cherry, Peacock, and Black) or four Pro Chem dyes (#119 yellow, #338 red, #490 blue, and #672 black).

When I formulate a color for the first time, I like to use white wool because it allows me to see the true color unaffected by the color of the wool. After I see the color over white, I can confidently dye it over any color and accurately visualize the final results. You can save yourself this step if you wish and move directly on to dyeing over other shades of wool. [*Editor's Note: I caution against skipping the white step because the color reproduction does not exactly match the color of the dyed wool.*]

BASIC RED

Yellow is the lightest color on the color wheel, so it is the first color I teach in my course. However, since red is my favorite color, I thought we'd start with red. Use either the Cushing

Shaded Rose, *7" x 6", #3 cut wool on rug warp. Dyed and hooked by Maryanne Lincoln, Wrentham, Massachusetts, 1993. For this flower, Maryanne dyed eight values of basic red using Cushing dyes.*

formulas or the Pro Chem formulas unless you want to do both and compare the results as I have done. Cushing dyes: 5/32 teaspoon Cherry; 3/16 teaspoon Canary; 1/128 teaspoon Peacock. Mix all three dyes together in 1 cup boiling water (CBW). Dye a gradation of values on a 3" x 24" swatch of white or natural wool. Pro Chem: 3/8 teaspoon #338 red; 1/8 teaspoon #119 yellow; 1/128 teaspoon #490 blue. Mix all three dyes together in 1 CBW. Dye a gradation of values on a 3" x 24" swatch of *white* or natural wool. Use the jar method on page 44.

Both of these basic reds make great swatches for hooking a realistic red rose. Use any of the darker values alone for background colors for a special oriental. I have hooked these flowers using each version of basic red so you can see the results without hooking. Remember, I dyed white wool.

After you dye these red gradations, you will begin to devise your own shortcuts. If you use my jar method, note that the first value poured is the darkest value, and it uses half of the total amount of dye solution. Therefore, you can eliminate the darkest value by just preparing half of the formula. On the other hand, if you want a value darker than the darkest value, simply mix up twice as much dye solution and pour as usual. Or, if you don't want the two lightest values, stop pouring after the sixth value.

FOR EXPERIENCED DYERS ONLY

If you want to make the Pro Chem red but you think it is a little too bright, increase the #490 blue to 1/64 teaspoon and the #119 yellow to 5/32 teaspoon (1/8 teaspoon + 1/32 teaspoon). This doubles the blue but not the yellow. Part of the yellow in the mixture goes toward making the red, and part of the yellow combines with the blue to form green, which will dull the red a little.

If you want to make the Cushing red but you want it as bright as the Pro Chem red, increase the Cherry to 10/32 teaspoon and the Canary to 1/4 teaspoon. This doubles the red and increases the yellow by 25 percent, offsetting the green part of the formula which is what dulls the red color. The color will be redder and brighter. I increase the yellow portion of the formula because it keeps the red from becoming too pink. Since dye spoons will not measure less than 1/128 teaspoon, I cannot reduce the green in the formula without changing over to liquid measuring, which we will discuss elsewhere.

Two primary colors, when combined, create different colors around the color wheel. Opposite colors on the color wheel combine to form duller colors. If you mix a combination of red and yellow, you need to add at least a small amount of the opposite color, green, to tone the color down. Therefore, any formula can be dulled, if necessary, by adding a bit of its complement to the mixture. (A professional color wheel makes achieving the desired result much simpler.)

DYEING OTHER FABRICS

Pro Chem dyes will dye wool, silk, and nylon. Cushing

Perfection dyes will dye wool, cotton, silk, linen, viscose rayon, and mixtures thereof. Be sure to choose a dye that will work on the fiber that you are interested in.

If you want to dye a fiber other than those listed above, you need to use a different class of dye. Fibers are different; some are natural, others are synthetic. Among the natural fibers, protein fibers include wool and silk, and the most common cellulose fiber is cotton.

There are many different classes of dyes. Some are specifically formulated to work on certain fibers. Other dyes are a combination of several dyes and are designed to be used on a wider range of fibers. Sometimes you may not be able to achieve the depth of shade you want, or the color fastness may be sacrificed to some extent with these combination dyes.

If you want to dye woolen yarn instead of fabric, substitute 1/2 ounce of yarn for the 3" x 24" woolen swatch specified in the formulas. The yarn can then be hooked traditionally in the rug or punch hooked from the backside. Yarn dyed to match the rug can also be used to whip the edge when finishing the rug.

If you have a lot of miscellaneous strips for traditional rug-making or short pieces of yarn that you want to dye, put them into a section of an old nylon stocking before plunging them into the dye pot. Don't forget to securely fasten the nylon so that the little pieces don't swim loose when you move the nylon around in the dye bath.

Basic Green & Dip-Dyed Variations

In rug hooking, we use many different shades of green for a variety of subjects. Therefore, I'll teach you how to make basic green from either Cushing or Pro Chem wash-fast acid dyes. Then, we'll get our creative processes going and discuss variations on these two greens that you might want to try. Work out some variations of your own, and try them, too.

Basic Green from Cushing dyes: 3/32 teaspoon Peacock; 5/32 teaspoon Canary; 1/64 teaspoon Cherry; 1/128 teaspoon Black. Mix all four dyes together in one cup boiling water (CBW). Dye a gradation of values on a 3" x 24" swatch of white or natural wool using the jar method on page 44.

Basic Green from Pro Chem dyes: 3/16 teaspoon #490 blue; 3/8 teaspoon #119 yellow; 1/64 teaspoon #338 red; 1/128 teaspoon #672 black. Mix all four dyes together in one CBW. Dye a gradation of values on a 3" x 24" swatch of white wool using the jar method.

Notice that in my examples the two swatches of green are not exactly alike. The Pro Chem version contains about double the amount of green (yellow and blue together). If we decreased the yellow in the Pro Chem green to 5/16 teaspoon, the color would match the Cushing version more closely.

I have used greens like these to hook beautiful realistic rose leaves. However, if you are planning to hook leaves with either of these greens, I suggest dying the formula over beige, light gray or celery-colored wool to soften the colors. When jar dyeing, as the dye solution is diluted in progressively lighter values, the color of the wool shows through more. By starting with darker wool, the lightest dyed values will not look so white because the original color peeks through.

I have been dyeing realistic colors for vegetables. The five darkest values of this Pro Chem green are perfect for hooking realistic sweet bell peppers. The Cushing green also makes a good pepper if you increase the Canary to 6/32 teaspoon.

After I dyed the basic gradations over white, I decided to dip-dye several different solid and checked materials into the formulas. I dip-dyed two batches each of assorted plain colors (beige, yellow, apricot, and white) and checks (black-and white, lavender-and-gray, and apricot-and-gray) all at once into each of the two undiluted formulas. The

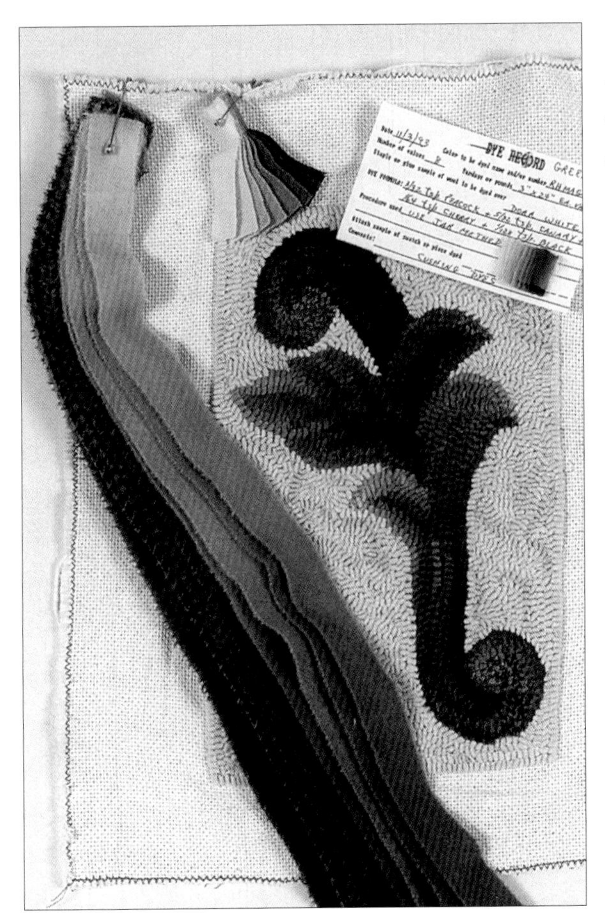

Textured Scroll, *7" x 11 1/2", #6-cut wool on rug warp. Designed, dyed, and hooked by Maryanne Lincoln, Wrentham, Massachusetts, 1993. For this scroll, Maryanne dip-dyed basic green over assorted plain colors (beige, yellow, apricot, and white) and checks (black-and-white, lavender-and-gray, and apricot-and-gray) using Cushing dyes. Note the lavender checks from the light end of the strip peeking through on both knobs of the scroll. The background is a #6-cut, mottled-ecru wool.*

results were just what I was looking for to hook the scroll shown here (Cushing version) and the border for the leaf piece (Pro Chem version).

Shaded Leaf, *5 1/2" x 5 1/2", #3-cut wool on rug warp. Designed, dyed, and hooked by Maryanne Lincoln, Wrentham, Massachusetts, 1993. For this leaf, Maryanne dyed eight values of basic green using Pro Chem wash-fast acid dyes, but she did not use the two lightest values. The border is a #6-cut, black-and-white checked wool, dip-dyed in the Pro Chem green and hooked in a chain stitch. The background is a #3-cut, mottled-ecru wool.*

FOR EXPERIENCED DYERS ONLY

The dyes shown here are bluish-greens; another time when I make them I am going to increase the yellow in each formula to make truer greens. Think it through with me. The blue and yellow in the formula create the green. If we increase the amount of yellow and keep the amount of blue the same, we create a different type of green. Another way to achieve the same change would be to keep the amount of yellow the same and decrease the amount of blue.

As we covered previously, to dull a color, add some of its complement (the opposite color on the color wheel) to the formula. For a duller green, add its complement, red. If you add a tiny bit of a complement, it dulls the color a little. If you add a lot of the complement, it makes the color muddy. Adding a complement effectively dulls a color, yet the new color still has life.

For example, to dye a dull, yellowed version of our greens, increase the yellow and the red in the formulas. Increasing the yellow changes the basic green to a yellowed green. The increase in red dulls the yellowed green a bit because red is the complement of green.

DYE RECORD

Date

Number of values

Yardage or pounds

Dye formula

Procedure used

Comments

Color to be dyed (name and number)

Attach a sample of the pre-dyed wool.

Attach samples of dyed wool.

PRO CHEM SAFETY TIPS

In addition to the information Maryanne provided in her article, we've included these important safety tips from Pro Chemical & Dye Company. Pro Chem publishes a free catalog of its products that includes the following common-sense practices. Pro Chem encourages dyers to use its products safely.

1. Do not smoke, eat, or drink in areas where dyes and chemicals are in use.
2. Cover work areas with dampened newspaper that can be carefully rolled up and discarded.
3. Keep dye and auxiliary containers closed except when in use.
4. Avoid exposure to dye powders, auxiliary chemicals, and vapors during pregnancy or lactation.
5. Wear goggles if corrosive chemicals are used.
6. Always add acid to water.
7. Always add lye to cold water.
8. Quantities used by home dyers rarely exceed limits set for disposal in municipal or septic systems. Therefore, disposal should not be a problem.

Adding black to a formula also dulls the color, but you end up with a different kind of dull than by adding the complement. Black "turns the light off" in a color. Sometimes we want a smokey or "dead" look, so adding black is effective. However, don't automatically reach for black when you want to dull a color; first, try to dull the color by adding its complement.

KEEPING RECORDS OF YOUR RECIPES

Maintain records of each dye session. I keep a spiral notebook handy as I work in my dye kitchen so I can keep track of my work. Afterwards, I transfer the information onto "dye record" cards and keep them together. When I want to duplicate a specific color, I refer to the appropriate card with all the particulars about the formula.

In order to easily retrieve the correct card, assign a simple name or number to each formula and keep the cards in order. Include all pertinent information: the size and color of the wool; the dye formula; the dyeing procedure (dip dye, jar dye, etc.); small samples of the dyed wool; and any appropriate comments. You can use index cards, create your own cards, or use preprinted cards.

A TIP FOR HANDLING DYES

Many rug hookers have problems with spotting and colors separating when using Pro Chem or the new Cushing dyes. To alleviate the problem, raise the heat of the dye solution very slowly and stir often. Start with very low heat, then raise the heat slowly at ten-minute intervals, stirring often to distribute the heat evenly. When the heat is evenly distributed throughout the dye solution at the highest level, the dyes absorb evenly into the wool.

Basic Orange

Butterfly, *10" x 7 3/4", #3- and #6-cut wool on cotton rug warp. Designed, dyed, and hooked by Maryanne Lincoln, Wrentham, Massachusetts, 1994. Maryanne dyed the wool for this bright butterfly with Pro Chem wash-fast acid dyes, but she used only the darkest six values of the eight-value swatch. She hooked the outlines and accents with dark antique brown and the body with a scrap of medium brown. The butterfly is #3-cut, and the background is reverse-stitched in #6 cut.*

FOR THIS LESSON ON BASIC ORANGE, I DYED TWO SWATCHES OF WHITE WOOL—ONE WITH A PRO CHEM WASH-FAST ACID DYE FORMULA, THE OTHER WITH A CUSHING FORMULA. BUT, WHENEVER I DYE A COLOR, I ALWAYS THINK OF WAYS TO VARY IT, EITHER BY ALTERING THE DYE PROCEDURES, ADJUSTING THE FORMULA OR DYEING OVER DIFFERENT MATERIALS. AFTER YOU DYE THESE TWO COLORS ON WHITE WOOL, TRY DYEING THEM AGAIN OVER YELLOW OR PINK WOOL FOR INTERESTING VARIATIONS.

Basic Orange from Cushing Dyes: 1/2 teaspoon Canary; 1/16 teaspoon Cherry; 1/128 teaspoon Peacock. Mix all three dyes together in one cup boiling water (CBW). Dye a gradation of values on a 3" x 24" swatch of white or natural wool using the jar method.

Basic Orange from Pro Chem dyes: 3/4 teaspoon #119 yellow; 1/8 teaspoon #338 red; 1/128 teaspoon #490 blue. Mix all three dyes together in one CBW. Dye a gradation of values on a 3" x 24" swatch of white or natural wool using the jar method.

The two swatches of orange are quite different from each other. The Pro Chem orange contains more yellow and red than the Cushing orange, but the blue in each is the same. Because the yellow and red make orange, the Pro Chem version is brighter than the Cushing.

As soon as I pulled these two orange swatches from my dye-pots, I began thinking of ways to change them to make them even more appealing. At the same time I was thinking about all the interesting things to hook with them. Besides the obvious pumpkins and tabby cats, shades of orange can be used to create faces, fields of grain, and bright centers for flowers.

The vivid Pro Chem orange is perfect for a poppy or tiger lily. Summer is the season for butterflies and bright garden flowers, so I decided to hook a butterfly with it. The Cushing colors are softer, so I hooked a moth with them, but they would also make beautiful flowers. Either orange formula dyed over checks, tweeds or plaids will produce beautiful soft apricot, rust, or orange shades, depending on the color of the material.

FOR EXPERIENCED DYERS ONLY

Orange is a mixture of red and yellow. If the amount of red in

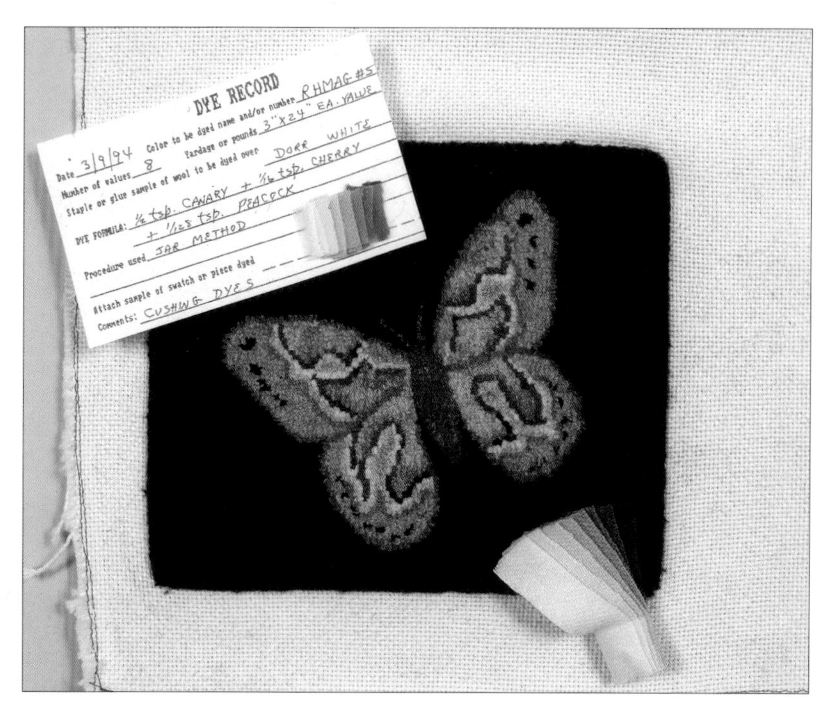

Moth, *7 1/4" x 6 1/4", #3-cut wool on cotton rug warp. Designed, dyed and hooked by Maryanne Lincoln, Wrentham, Massachusetts, 1994. Maryanne dyed an eight-value swatch orange with Cushing dyes but used only the darkest six values to hook the moth. She outlined and accented the moth with scraps of medium brown. The large areas of medium to light brown are hooked with material that Maryanne originally dyed for brown pears. The background is navy.*

the formula is equal to or greater than the amount of yellow, the color will be reddish orange. If the yellow is at least twice as strong as the red, the orange will be yellowish. Note that the yellow dye in the Cushing formula is eight times the amount of red dye. In the Pro Chem formula, the yellow is only six times as much as the red, so the Pro Chem orange is brighter.

Remember that complementary colors dull each other when mixed together. Check your color wheel to understand why the blue dye plays a complementary role in these formulas; it's opposite orange on the wheel. Similarly, if you dye these oranges over blue wool, the colors will become muted. If you dye them over pale green, the colors will also be muted because green is a combination of yellow and blue.

Now that you understand how each of the three primary colors plays individual roles in these formulas, spend some time at the dye pots to familiarize yourself with the colors separately. Dye similar values of each color (red, yellow, and blue) on white wool, and keep the samples for reference. Use a standard measure for each color, and keep in mind that the dyes are not all the same strength, measure for measure, as they come out of the package.

SAFETY TIPS FOR THE DYE KITCHEN

Common sense, not children or pets, should be your constant companion while you are dyeing. Keep all dyes and other chemicals well labeled and safely stored away. And remember, the most dangerous part of dyeing is boiling water. Natural dyes may actually be more dangerous than chemicals because some plants and mordants are poisonous. Take the time to learn about them before using them.

The dyes themselves are relatively non-toxic, but they are industrial chemicals and should be handled with caution. Do not ingest or inhale them or allow them to come in contact with your eyes. Generally, exercise the same amount of caution as when handling other household products like bleach and ammonia.

Avoid prolonged or repeated contact with skin. Dye companies encourage the use of gloves and masks when handling dyes. When measuring dry dyes, do not open a window or use a fan, especially the exhaust fan on your range, because the particles fly about easily. But, perform the actual dyeing in a well ventilated area to help reduce odors and steam buildup. Clean up spills immediately before liquids turn into powder. Clean up dry spills with a vacuum, not a broom.

Always use implements to stir dye solutions, but do not use food utensils as dyeing tools. Once a pan or utensil has been used for dyeing, never use it again to cook food. If you plan to dye regularly, consider creating a separate dye kitchen, complete with range, work space and utensils.

If you have any other concerns about dyeing, request a Material Safety Data Sheet from the dye company. If one is necessary, the company is required by law to supply it.

Basic Blue

Morning Glory, *6 3/8" x 6 3/8", #3-cut wool on cotton rug warp. Designed, dyed, and hooked by Maryanne Lincoln, Wrentham, Massachusetts, 1994. Maryanne used all eight values of Cushing blue to hook this flower. The leaf and stem are hooked with a dip-dyed swatch ranging from dark to medium green. The background is hooked with a dyed piece shaded to resemble a sky. The outer borders are hooked from leftover pieces of wool from the blue and green swatches. After she hooked the morning glory, Maryanne drew in a "deepening line" to separate the throat of the flower from the background using a draftsman's micro-fine pen.*

IN THIS DYEING LESSON, I WILL TEACH YOU HOW TO CREATE BASIC BLUE FROM PRO CHEM WASH-FAST ACID DYES AND CUSHING DYES OVER WHITE WOOL. I HAVE CHOSEN A MORNING GLORY AND BLUEBERRIES TO ILLUSTRATE THE COLORS. DYE OVER LIGHT-COLORED WOOL FOR VARIATIONS OF BASIC BLUE: OVER YELLOW, THE BLUE BECOMES GREEN; OVER PINK YIELDS SLIGHTLY PURPLE, ESPECIALLY THE LIGHTER VALUES; OVER BEIGE MAKES SOMEWHAT DULLER BLUES.

Basic Blue from Cushing dyes: 1/128 teaspoon Canary; 1/128 teaspoon Cherry; 1/8 teaspoon Peacock; 1/64 teaspoon Black. Mix all four dyes together in one cup boiling water (CBW). Dye a gradation of values on a 3" x 24" swatch of white or natural wool using the jar method.

Basic Blue from Pro Chem dyes: 1/64 teaspoon #119 yellow; 1/128 teaspoon #338 red; 1/2 teaspoon #490 blue; 1/4 teaspoon #672 black. Mix all four dyes together in one CBW. Dye a gradation of values on a 3" x 24" swatch of white or natural wool using the jar method on page 44.

Notice that the two swatches of blue are quite different from each other. The Pro Chem swatch contains twice as much blue and 16 times more black. Therefore, the Pro Chem version is darker and bluer. I created the Pro Chem formula with much more dye because I wanted darker values to hook the blueberries.

FOR EXPERIENCED DYERS ONLY

Both blue formulas are created primarily with the blue dyes. The black makes the blue darker; the yellow and red combine to make orange, the complement of blue. (Remember that the opposite color on the color wheel acts as a complement and tones down the color.)

In the Cushing version, the blue (Peacock) is predominant because it is present in a relatively larger amount than in the Pro Chem formula. Compare Cushing blue to a sample of the primary Peacock. Notice that the Cushing blue is duller or softer because of the addition of orange (Cherry red and Canary yellow), the complement of blue.

To make a greener blue, add more yellow; for a purple blue, add more red. If the new colors are too bright, don't create a different formula. Rather, add more of the complementary color to

Blueberries, *6 1/2" x 5 1/2", #3-cut wool on cotton rug warp. Designed, dyed, and hooked by Maryanne Lincoln, Wrentham, Massachusetts, 1994. Maryanne hooked the blueberries with the five darkest values of the Pro Chem blue swatch. The leaves are hooked with a medium-dark green dip-dyed swatch. Maryanne used white wool for the background and leftover bits of dark blue for the outer edge.*

> ***"To measure large amounts of dye for backgrounds and large pieces, consider weighing the ingredients rather than measuring."***

dull what you already have. Orange is the complement of blue, so add red and yellow to dull the blue.

MEASURE FOR MEASURE

Dyeing recipes call for small amounts of dry dyes (as little as 1/128 teaspoon), so standard kitchen measures are not suitable. Two brands of measuring spoons are available for dyers. The TOD spoon has measures on both ends: 1/32 and 1/4 teaspoon. Grey spoons come in a set of three double-ended spoons that measure 1/128, 1/64, 1/32, 1/16, 1/8, and 1/4 teaspoon. A set of four Grey spoons includes one that measures 1/2 and 1 teaspoon. The TOD spoon is adequate for most published dye formulas. The Grey spoons allow the dyer to easily cut formulas down.

Both of these brands of dye spoons are made of polished aluminum. Wash and dry them between dipping them into different packets of dry dye. I do not recommend dipping aluminum into salt for cleaning.

When measuring dry dyes, follow appropriate safety procedures as outlined in the section on Dye Equipment & Safety, page 5. Dry dyes have a tendency to float away from the spoon, so cover the measuring area with a damp paper towel or newspaper to hold the particles.

To measure large amounts of dye for backgrounds and large pieces, consider weighing the ingredients rather than measuring. To measure liquid solutions, use pipettes, beakers, and syringes.

The liquid measures use the metric scale, so practice with water before using them for actual dyeing. Learning the metric system will help you develop formulas that you can use in the future.

When using formulas with liquid solutions, mix up a batch of the liquid solution and you won't have to work with the dry dyes again until the solution is used up. Liquid solutions also allow you to measure accurately or to "dye by eye."

Pansy Purples

Pansy & Peach Mat, *22" x 15", #3-cut wool on burlap (actual size of red-purple pansy is 3" x 4 1/2".) Designed by Florence Petruchik. Dyed and hooked by Maryanne Lincoln, Wrentham, Massachusetts, 1994. The top pansy is blue-purple and is hooked with values from Maryanne's Cushing swatches. She created a red-purple swatch with Pro-Chem dyes for the lower pansy. Maryanne hooked the back petals of the red-purple pansy with the dark values of the blue-purple swatch. The light face of the blue-purple pansy is the lightest values of the blue-purple swatch, not white. The centers of the pansies include yellow wool in addition to green from the leaves, a gray-green dip-dyed piece.*

WHEN I WENT TO THE DYE POTS FOR THIS DYEING LESSON, I KNEW I WANTED TO HOOK TWO DIFFERENT PURPLE PANSIES. I DEVELOPED THESE TWO FORMULAS, AND AS I PULLED THE PURPLE SWATCHES OUT, I KNEW THEY WOULD BE PERFECT TO HOOK BLUE-PURPLE AND RED-PURPLE PANSIES.

My friend Florence Petruchik designed a small rug called *Pansy & Peach Mat* onto which I hooked the swatches.

As I've said before, whenever I dye a new color I always think of ways to alter it, either by varying the dyeing procedures, by adjusting the formula, or by dyeing over different materials. These two purple swatches are dyed over white wool. For slightly different results, dye them over pale blue or pale pink wool. For a softer version of the Pro Chem formula, dye it over pale green or celery colored wool.

PURPLE FORMULAS

Blue-Purple from Cushing dyes: 3/16 teaspoon Cherry; 3/16 teaspoon Peacock; 1/64 teaspoon Canary. Mix all three dyes together in one cup boiling water (CBW). Dye a gradation of values on a 3" x 24" swatch of white or natural wool using the jar method.

Red-Purple from Pro Chem dyes: 3/8 teaspoon #338 red; 1/8 teaspoon #490 blue; 1/64 teaspoon

"All water may appear the same, but the interesting parts of water are the parts you cannot see."

#119 yellow; 1/128 teaspoon #672 black. Mix all four dyes together in one CBW. Dye a gradation of values on a 3" x 24" swatch of white or natural wool using the jar method.

Notice that the Cushing measurements for red and blue are written in 16ths of teaspoons and the Pro Chem measurements are written in eighths (2/16 = 1/8). The red and blue dyes in the Cushing purple add up to 6/16 (3/8) teaspoon; those in the Pro Chem purple equal 4/8 teaspoon. Therefore, it is easy to see that the Pro Chem formula has 1/8 teaspoon more of the red-blue combination.

PLAYING WITH PURPLE

In very simple terms, purple is a mixture of red and blue. The way you alter the color is to control the mixture of these two basic ingredients. The resulting purple can also be varied with the addition of its complement, yellow.

The two swatches of purple are quite different from each other because the formulas are very different. The Pro Chem formula calls for more total dye: 1/128 teaspoon black and 1/8 teaspoon more of the red-purple combination. That's why the Pro Chem purple is so much brighter.

In the Cushing formula I used equal parts of red and blue dyes, but in the Pro Chem formula I used three times as much red. That's why the Pro Chem purple is so much redder. I wanted to hook two different but related purple pansies, so I played with the purple formulas to achieve red-purple and blue-purple.

If you use Cushing dyes, add more red to the formula to get closer to the Pro Chem red-purple. You can even substitute the Cushing dyes in the Pro Chem formula to achieve similar results. The color won't be exactly like the Pro Chem version, but it will be close. Play with the formulas yourself to get even closer.

WHY ADD YELLOW

On a color wheel, yellow is opposite purple, so we call it the complementary color of purple. When dyeing, a complementary color dulls down the opposite color. Therefore, the yellow dye in each of these formulas is the complement of the resulting purple, and it dulls the purple a bit.

The amount of yellow dye in each purple formula is the same: 1/64 teaspoon. The Pro Chem formula has more purple in it (4/8 teaspoon red and blue combined compared to 3/8 teaspoon in the Cushing formula). It makes sense that the yellow dye won't dull the Pro Chem purple as much as the Cushing.

DYEING ASSISTANTS

Dyeing assistants are ingredients other than the dye solution itself that comprise the dye bath. Some dyeing assistants are essential; others are optional. To understand this section on dyeing assistants, first read the step-by-step jar-dyeing instructions on page 44.

WATER

The dye bath starts with water, obviously an essential component. Small amounts of Synthrapol, salt, vinegar, and the dye solution are added. All water may appear the same, but the interesting parts of water are the parts you cannot see.

Water differs from state to state, town to town, and house to house. The water in your area is not even the same from season to season. During the wet season, the concentration of minerals in water is different than during the dry season. Some water supplies have chemicals added to make the water safe for consumption, and those chemicals may work against you when dyeing. Chlorine, for example, can drastically affect your results.

The water in your dye bath needs to be within a certain pH and hardness range in order for dyes to attach themselves to the fibers of wool. Most water supplies, including well water, fall easily into the desired ranges. Both Cushing and Pro Chem dyes are acid dyes and therefore like an acidic dye bath. Adding vinegar decreases the pH, so you may need to experiment with the amount of vinegar it takes to enable wool to soak up all the dye from your water.

SALT AND VINEGAR

I use salt and vinegar to dye gradation swatches with Cushing and Pro Chem dyes. I add salt to the dye bath before adding the wool; I add vinegar about three quarters of the way through the dye process or closer to the end. I like to have dark values that are different from each other, and I can't get those results unless I add vinegar at the end and check the wool for value corrections.

Vinegar is necessary; it is not an option. Salt, on the other hand, is not an essential ingredient in the dye bath. However, if you leave out the salt, you may get more spotting. In some cases, such as dip-dyeing for fruits, vegetables, and leaves, I leave out the salt because I do not need it to achieve the desired results.

SYNTHRAPOL

I use Synthrapol, a liquid detergent from Pro Chem, to pre-wet my wool. I also recommend that you add a small amount of it right to the dye bath, too. Add the Synthrapol to the water before you add the dye solution.

If you are happy with the results of your dyeing, and the colors are consistent and repeatable, don't worry about your water or any of the other dyeing assistants. However, if you are having problems creating the colors that you want, you may need to pay more attention to the water that you use. Consider having it analyzed or use an alternate water source. For answers to your technical questions, call Pro Chem's hotline: (508)-676-3838.

Basic Yellow

Detail of **Pansy & Peach Mat**, *22" x 15", #3-cut wool on burlap. (Actual size of yellow pansy is 3 1/2" x 3 1/2".) Designed by Florence Petruchik. Dyed and hooked by Maryanne Lincoln, Wrentham, Massachusetts, 1994. Maryanne used only the Pro Chem swatch to hook the yellow pansy.*

WITH THIS LESSON, WE COMPLETE OUR FIRST TRIP AROUND THE COLOR WHEEL. YELLOW IS THE LAST OF THE BASIC COLORS: RED, ORANGE, YELLOW, GREEN, BLUE, AND PURPLE. IN FUTURE CHAPTERS, WE WILL CREATE NEW COLORS TO FILL IN BETWEEN THE BASIC COLORS. WE WILL ALSO TRY DIFFERENT DYEING TECHNIQUES IN ADDITION TO THE JAR-DYEING METHOD, WHICH WE HAVE USED EXCLUSIVELY THUS FAR.

YELLOW FORMULAS

Basic Yellow from Cushing dyes: 3/4 teaspoon Canary; 1/128 teaspoon Peacock; 1/128 teaspoon Cherry. Mix all three dyes together in one cup boiling water (CBW). Dye a gradation of values on a 3" x 24" swatch of white or natural wool using the jar method.

Basic Yellow from Pro Chem wash-fast acid dyes: 1 teaspoon #119 yellow; 1/128 teaspoon #490 blue; 1/64 teaspoon #338 red. Mix all three dyes together in one CBW. Dye a gradation of values on a 3" x 24" swatch of white or natural wool using the jar method.

When I set out to formulate these two yellows, I planned them for the *Pansy & Peach Mat*. I aimed for a bright yellow to hook a pansy face and ended up using only the Pro Chem version. (The back petals are outlined with one of the light blue-purple values

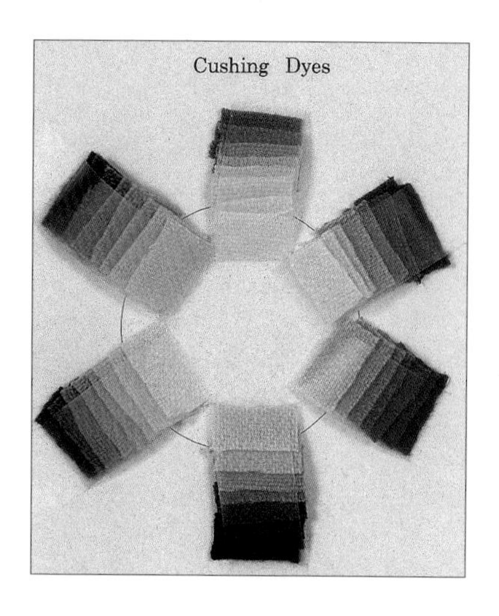

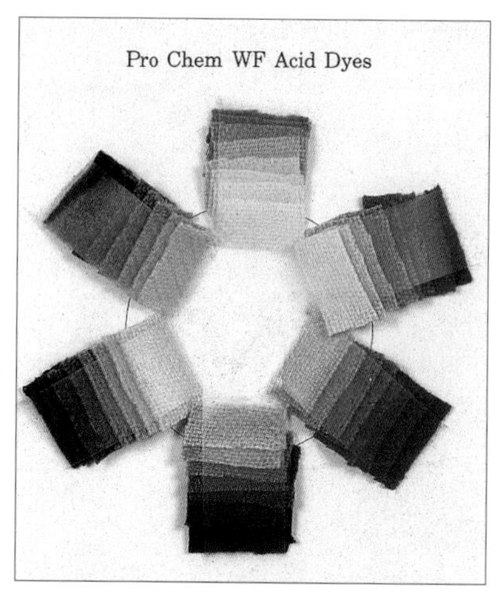

A color wheel is a valuable tool for color-planning rugs. It shows at a glance how colors relate to each other.

from page 17.) Either yellow would have worked well; both are beautiful, clear basic colors. But, the Cushing version is slightly greener, so I decided not to use it for a pansy.

In the detailed photo of the mat you can see pieces of elements other than the yellow pansy, our present topic. The checked border is a combination of reddish brown and off-white. The inner line of color next to it is a medium-dark gold. The inner background will be black. I have started to hook it around all the edges of the detail.

FOR EXPERIENCED DYERS ONLY

Think about the basic-yellow formulas in this lesson. Because I wanted clear, bright pansy yellows, I was very careful to add only tiny amounts of the complement, purple, to tone down each swatch just a bit. (Remember, opposite colors on the color wheel are complementary. When mixed together, they dull each other down.)

In the Cushing version, the 1/128 teaspoon Cherry plus 1/128 teaspoon Peacock combine to create purple, our complementary color. The Cushing yellow swatch is slightly greenish because the blue component of the complementary purple is a little heavy. Therefore, not only is our yellow dulled, but it is also shifted around the color wheel to a slightly greenish yellow.

When I formulated the complementary component of the Pro Chem version, I intentionally added more red than blue, rather than equal parts as in the Cushing yellow. I wanted the Pro Chem yellow to be different, and I knew that the blue would overpower the color if I didn't double the red. Consequently, the extra red makes the yellow warmer.

To make the Cushing yellow more like the Pro Chem yellow, increase the Canary to 1 teaspoon and the Cherry to 1/64 teaspoon. The colors won't match exactly, but they will be very similar. Conversely, to make the Pro Chem yellow more like Cushing, decrease the yellow to 3/4 teaspoon and the red to 1/128 teaspoon.

Keep in mind the relationship of complementary colors and how they work and mix together. When you mix complementary colors together in the dye pot, they dull each other. This theory also comes into play when you are deciding what color wool to dye over. If you want to dye these yellow formulas and retain the brightness, dye them over yellow or natural wool. However, if you want to dull the colors down, dye the yellow formulas over a light version of the complement: light purple or lavender.

The theory of complementary colors extends into color planning, too. Hooked next to or near each other like the yellow and purple on these pansies, complementary colors make each other look brighter, rather than duller as when mixed together in the dye pot. Brighter is only appropriate if that is your goal. If it isn't, be careful when you color plan with complementary colors.

For some interesting variations, dye the yellow over analogous colors like pale green or apricot. (To understand the term "analogous," read the information about the color wheel below.) Also try dyeing it over pale versions of the other two primary colors: light blue and pink. Yellow over light blue will reward you with a green, and yellow over pink will give you an orange-like color.

THE COLOR WHEEL

If you have been dyeing along with me, you have dyed Cushing and Pro Chem versions of the three primary colors (red, blue, and yellow) and the three secondary colors (purple, green, and orange). Finally, we can arrange them in a color wheel to which we can add and refer in future issues. Some of our colors are bright and others are dull, but nonetheless, it is still worth our while to arrange the colors in a circle.

Simply glue or tape the swatches in a circle as shown in the photo. In future sections, I will add colors until our color wheel includes 12 basic colors. To do this, we need to add just one color between each of the existing colors. Therefore, leave a little space between the six basics so you can add new swatches as we go along.

A color wheel shows at a glance the basic colors and how they relate to each other. We can also see each color and its complement (the color that lies directly opposite on the circle). Here are some other terms to which we will refer when using our new color wheels.

Primary colors are the three basic colors (red, blue, and yellow) used to create other colors. (We also use black, the absence of color, which doesn't appear on the color wheel.) **Secondary colors** are the three colors derived by combining two primaries at a time. Red and blue combine to form purple; red and yellow combine to form orange; yellow and blue combine to form green. **Complementary colors** are opposite each other on the color wheel. In the group of six colors that we have dyed, red and green, yellow and purple, and blue and orange are complements. **Analogous colors** are neighbors on the color wheel—colors on either side of the color being used. Refer to the color wheel to see that the analogous colors of yellow are green and orange; for purple, blue and red. Study the wheel to determine other analogous combinations.

A New Blue

Maryanne often uses a gradation swatch that is more than just a dark-to-light strip of color. These samples show that the light ends of the dip-dyed strips look blue, but the dark ends are various shades of dull blue and gray. The swatches go from bright to dull as well as medium to dark instead of just light to dark.

A NEW BLUE IS THE FEATURED DYE COLOR FOR THIS ARTICLE. I EXPLAINED HOW TO CREATE A BASIC BLUE ON PAGE 15. UNLIKE THAT BLUE, THIS BLUE CONTAINS NO YELLOW; ONLY BLUE, RED, AND BLACK ARE IN THE FORMULA. I USED THIS NEW HUE TO HOOK A TROPICAL FISH AS I PREPARED TO EMBARK ON *RUG HOOKING* MAGAZINE'S CARIBBEAN CRUISE.

Prepare white, natural, or very light blue wool for dyeing by presoaking it for about 20 minutes in a basin of hot tap water and a drop or two of PRO Chem's Synthrapol detergent. You will need two 9" x 24" strips for the dip dyes—one for the Cushing formula and one for the PRO Chem—and twelve 3" x 24" strips for the jar (gradation) dyes.

DIP DYEING

To dip dye, mix the prescribed amounts of Peacock and Cherry in 1/2 cup of boiling water, and pour the mixture into a 2-quart saucepan along with the 4 cups of hot water, 3 tablespoons of vinegar, and one 9" x 24" piece of wool. Place the pot on a stove burner set at a medium-high temperature and stir the wool, keeping it under the water as best you can. Bring the solution just to a boil, then simmer the wool until the water clears (usually about one minute). This will dye the wool a medium value of blue.

Remove the wool, add the

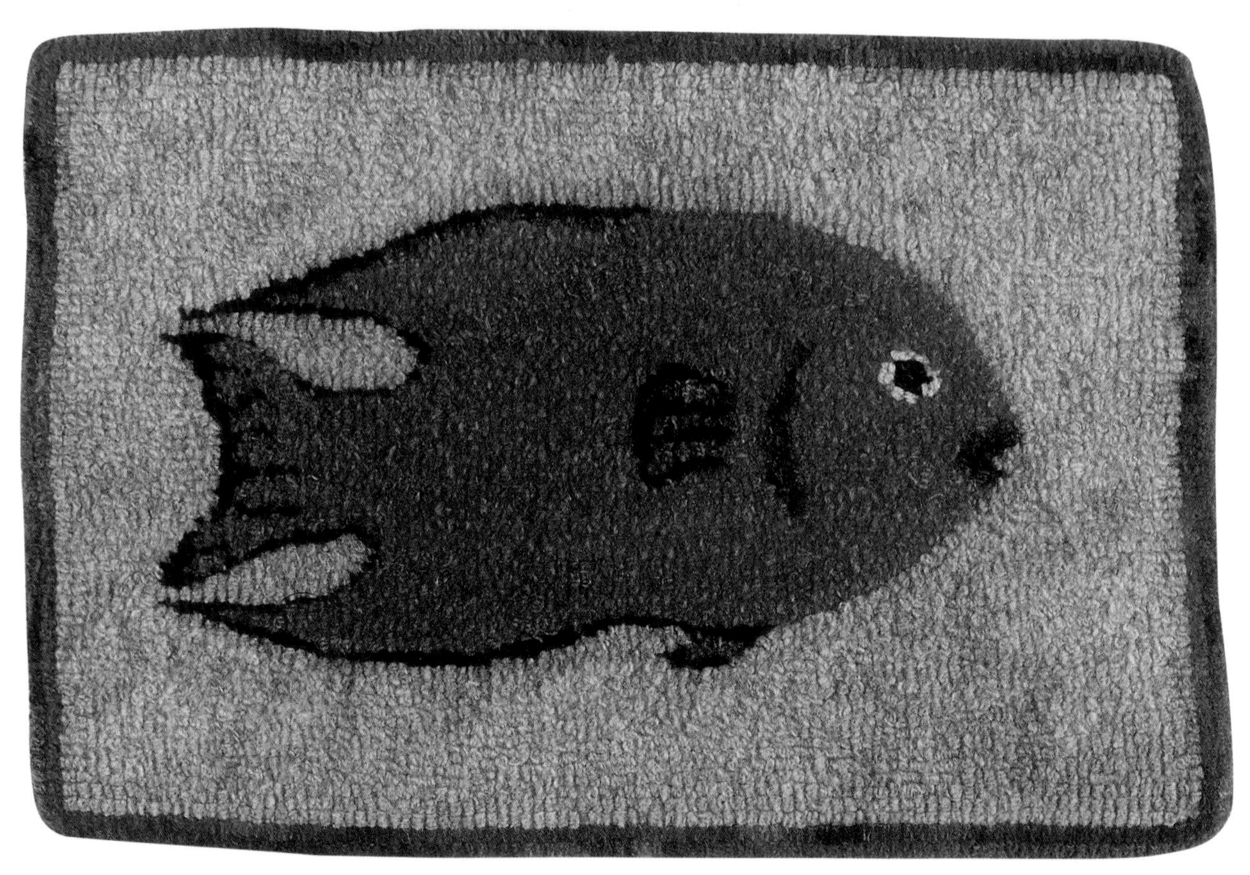

Fanciful Fish, *8" x 5 1/2", #3-cut wool on cotton rug warp. Designed and hooked by Maryanne Lincoln, Wrentham, Massachusetts, 1995. Maryanne used wool dip-dyed in PRO Chem dyes to achieve her blue. The background is a smoky light blue-green.*

black dye and 2 tablespoons of vinegar to the dye bath, and turn the heat up again to boil. Dip one end of the blue wool into the pot. Dip the wool up and down so the dye will be distributed along the bottom half of the strip gradually. If you just hold the wool half in the dye bath and half out without dipping it repeatedly, the color will attach to the wool in a choppy manner, so that instead of getting a piece of wool that is bright blue on one end gradually shading into black on the other, there will be a definite line between the blue and black.

When the dye solution is almost clear, submerge the entire strip into the dye bath. Cover the pan loosely, and let the wool simmer for 5 to 10 minutes. Rinse the wool several times in tepid water. Squeeze out the excess water and hang the wool to dry.

For my little fanciful fish I used PRO Chem dyes. (Refer to the ingredient list for the PRO Chem dyes and amounts.) I used the above procedures to achieve a strip that goes progressively from bright blue into grayed tones.

DIP-DYEING RECIPES

Cushing Dyes

Step 1

3/32 tsp Peacock
3/64 tsp Cherry
1/2 cup boiling water
4 cups hot water
3 Tbsp white vinegar

Step 2

1/128 tsp Black
2 Tbsp white vinegar

PRO Chem Dyes

Step 1

1/16 tsp #490 blue
1/64 tsp #338 red
1/2 cup boiling water
4 cups hot water-
3 Tbsp white vinegar

Step 2

1/64 tsp #672 black
2 Tbsp white vinegar

"Dip the wool up and down so the dye will be distributed along the bottom half of the strip gradually."

JAR-DYEING RECIPES

Cushing Dyes

Step 1

1/16 tsp Black
1 cup boiling water

Step 2

3/32 tsp Peacock
3/64 tsp Cherry
1/2 cup boiling water
6 tsp plain (noniodized) salt (1 tsp per jar)
6 Tbsp white vinegar (1 Tbsp per jar)

PRO Chem Dyes

Step 1

1/16 tsp #672 Black
1 cup boiling water

Step 2

1/16 tsp #490 blue
1/64 tsp #338 red
1/2 cup boiling water
6 tsp plain (noniodized) salt (1 tsp per jar)
6 Tbsp white vinegar (1Tbsp per jar)

JAR DYEING

I tried each of the formulas as dip dyes, and then I adjusted them so they could be used for transitional gradations of six values. I like to hook fine-cut flowers with a gradation swatch, as I feel that I have better control over the application of the color when I have several different values and each value is by itself on one piece of wool.

If you have some experience at dyeing rug wool, the formulas will not seem difficult to understand and execute. Reread the jar-dyeing instructions if you are uncertain about the size of wool to prepare, what to add, and how long to process the dyed wools.

For the Cushing gradation swatch, start by mixing the black dye in 1 cup of boiling water and use the jar method to distribute this solution into six jars. Then mix the Peacock and Cherry in 1/2 cup of boiling water and add 3 1/2 teaspoons of this solution to each of the jars. Add extra water to each jar plus the salt and wool. See the jar-dyeing instructions for how and when to add the vinegar.

Use the same procedures for the PRO Chem swatches as you did with the Cushing ones. However, with PRO Chem you need to add only 3 teaspoons of the blue and red solution to each of the jars. Don't forget to add water and salt, and read the jar-dyeing instructions for how and when to add the vinegar.

For a swatch that is light to dark, combine all three dyes into 1 cup of boiling water and use the jar method to dye six values. For a bright blue, use twice the amount of blue and red dye in 1 cup of boiling water and omit the black.

GRADATION TECHNIQUES

In these swatches I chose to add black to dull the blue. Sometimes it is more desirable to add the complementary color, which in this case would be orange (orange is opposite blue on the color wheel, and opposites dull one another). If I had substituted a mixture of orange for the black in all of these formulas, the dark end of the swatch would look brown, yet the lighter values would still be blue.

Mahogany Red

Hooked picture frame, *12" x 11", #3 cut wool on burlap. Designed and hooked by Maryanne Lincoln, Wrentham, Massachusetts, 1995. The shading in the scroll work that twines around the center reveals the different values Maryanne obtained with the Cushing dye formula she discusses here. Maryanne will fill the center space with a photograph of an old fashioned girl and then frame this hooked piece.*

A NEW MAHOGANY RED IS THE FEATURED COLOR FROM THE KITCHEN IN THIS CHAPTER. YOU CAN USE ALL THE VALUES TO SHADE A BEAUTIFUL SCROLL OR JUST THE MIDDLE-DARK TO MIDDLE-LIGHT VALUES TO CREATE A FACE. I HAVE DEVELOPED THE FORMULAS WITH RED, YELLOW, AND BLUE.

Many people would not call this red—it is a dull red that could be called mahogany in the dark values and flesh pink in the light values. It is important to understand this so that you can place it properly on the color wheel. In relation to primary red, it has yellow in it, but not enough yellow to make it orange. It also has blue in it, which is obvious because it is duller than a clear red (the blue combines with the yellow to make green, which dulls the red). If you were to decrease the blue and yellow, the result would be a brighter red, and if you were to increase them, you would have a browner red. Increasing just the yellow would give you a rusty orange, and increasing the blue would result in a red-purple tone. Remember that color can be changed by adding more of one of the dyes, or by decreasing the amount.

SELECTING WOOL COLORS

Prewet all the wool in a pan or basin of hot tap water with a drop or two of PRO Chem's Synthrapol detergent added. You will need sixteen 3" x 24" strips of white or natural wool (eight for each formula). I dyed both formulas over white wool so that the true color of the dye formula would show, but you can also overdye pastel colors of wool for many interesting variations. For example, if you dye over beige, gray, pale green, or celery wool, the color will be duller. If you dye over pale pink, yellow, or apricot, the light values will show a shift to slightly brighter, warmer tones instead of just lighter ones.

When deciding which color of wool to dye, consider the possible complementary and analogous relationships between the dye formula and the wool color. I like to dye over several different colors of wool for several variations of a swatch. This is an easy way to manipulate color and add variety to a color plan without preparing a lot of different dye formulas.

The formulas provided for Cushing and PRO Chem dyes have the same measurements for the dry dyes. The results are slightly different but not as different as you might expect. The Cushing swatch is slightly pinker, and I used it to hook the scroll. The PRO Chem swatch is a bit browner and would be more suitable for flesh. If you wish to make the swatches more alike, you can adjust the formulas by adding more or less of one of the ingredients to get the desired color. The difference between the two formulas is slight, and therefore any change in the measurements should be in small increments, no more than 1/128 or 1/64 teaspoon.

INTERMEDIATE AND ADVANCED DYE TECHNIQUES

If you are an experienced dyer you may wish to overdye different colors to use for flesh tones. To do so, mix the PRO Chem formula at half-strength and dye over white, natural, celery, and beige wool. Prewet a 3" x 12" strip of each of those colors of wool and put one of each in each jar of dye solution (four strips in each jar). By using the half-strength solution and twice as much wool, the results will be lighter than the original gradation swatches described above. Experience will guide you as to how many values you need. You can also use this half-strength solution with the open-pan dye method to dye a variety of light-colored wools for flesh tones. If you have some shell-pink wool, dye a small piece for a pinker cheek blush.

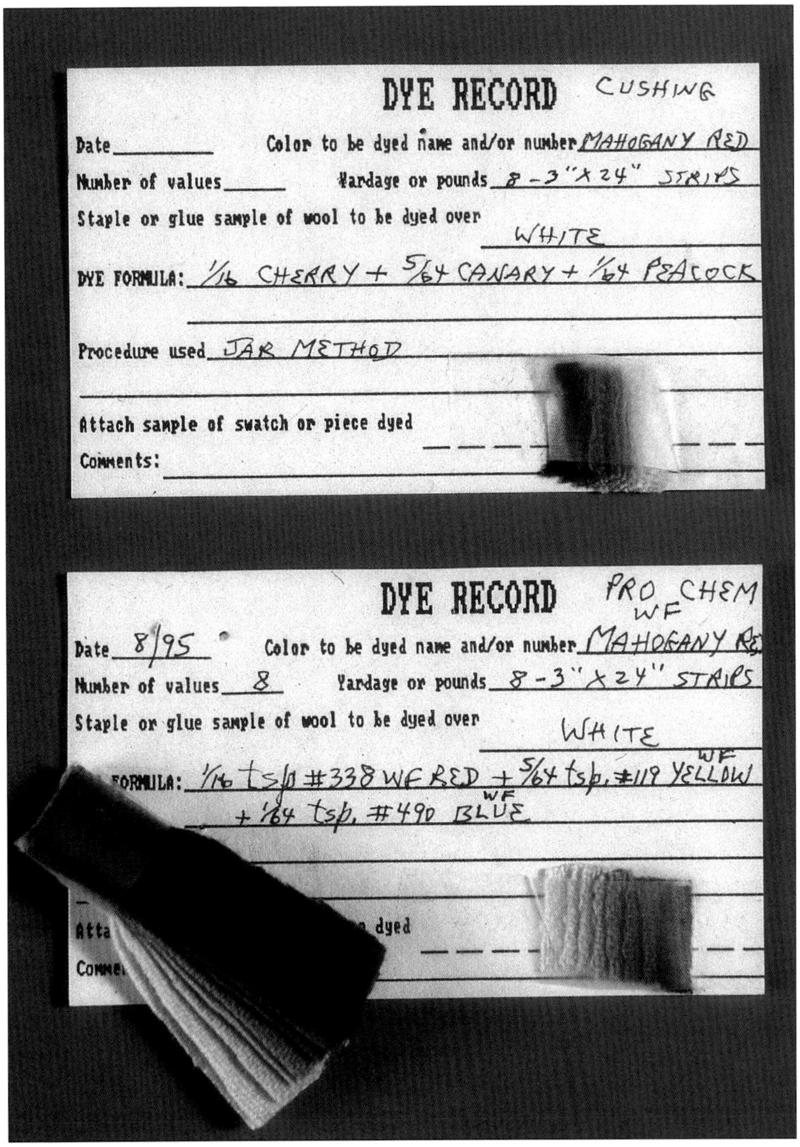

JAR-DYEING RECIPES

Cushing Perfection Dyes

1 cup boiling water
1/16 tsp Cherry
5/64 tsp Canary
1/64 tsp Peacock
8 tsp plain salt
(1 tsp for each jar)

PRO Chem WF Acid Dyes

1 cup boiling water
1/16 tsp #338 Red
5/64-tsp #119 Yellow
1/64 tsp #490 Blue
8 tsp plain salt
(1 tsp for each jar)
8 Tbsp white vinegar
(1 Tbsp for each jar)

DIP DYEING

The scroll pictured on page 24 was hooked with a jar-dyed, 8-value swatch, but it can also be hooked with a dip-dyed swatch. Use the formulas I've presented here to dip dye over several colors so that the different arms and knobs of the scroll will be varied. The light ends will keep the basic color of the wool while the dark ends will take on the mahogany color. If you have never done this type of dyeing, experiment a little to get the results you want.

Mix one of the formulas given above and add 1/4 of the solution to a 3- to 4-quart pan, along with

A DYEING TIP

When I'm jar dyeing I never pass the stove without stirring my dye bath. The stirring keeps the temperature uniform in the solutions, much as you'd stir a stew to keep the heat evenly distributed among its ingredients. Tongs make the stirring easy, but I must confess my tongs are rather special: They are surgical tongs obtained by my husband at his medical supply company (he's always finding new ways to make my hooking and dyeing easier).

You don't have to raid a hospital to find such useful gadgets as tongs, forceps, and sponge sticks. Try a flea market. These instruments are used by electronics hobbyists, and the price you pay for them will be worth it for their years of use (I've used mine for more than a decade, and they are still rust-free).

1/4 cup of white vinegar and enough water to make 1 1/2 quarts. Increase the heat under the pan and dip eight 3" x 24" strips the full length. When the water clears, add 1/4 more of the dye solution and dip 2/3 of the length of the strip so that the light ends don't get any darker. When the water clears again, add the remaining dye solution and dip the bottom 1/3 of the strips in the solution. Judge by eye if the strips need more color, and repeat the process if necessary. When the water clears the final time, cover the pan and simmer for 5 to 10 minutes. Rinse the wool, squeeze out the water, and dry it. This method will give you subtly graded swatches that will add variety and interest to your hooked scrolls.

Two New Greens

THIS CHAPTER'S FEATURED COLORS ARE TWO NEW GREENS: A SOFT GRAY-GREEN MADE WITH CUSHING DYES AND A NICE GRAYED YELLOW-GREEN MADE WITH PRO CHEM DYES. THE DRY DYE MEASUREMENTS ARE THE SAME FOR BOTH FORMULAS, BUT THE COLORS OF THE TWO SWATCHES ARE NOTICEABLY DIFFERENT. BOTH COLORS ARE VERY APPEALING, AND THEY CRIED OUT TO ME TO BE HOOKED INTO LEAVES. I AM A PUSHOVER WHEN IT COMES TO GREEN LEAVES; I LOVE TO HOOK THEM. I HAVE DEVELOPED THE FORMULAS USING RED, YELLOW, BLUE, AND BLACK.

Both of these greens are duller than secondary green on the color wheel, and they both lean toward the yellow side of green. Therefore, they are located between yellow and green on the color wheel. If you had a three-dimensional, spherical model of the color wheel, the Cushing green would be located between yellow and green and be very close to the neutral axis, because it is grayish. The PRO Chem green would also be located between yellow and green, but because it is brighter than the other green, it would not be as close to the neutral axis. A good, basic reference text on color is *Principles of Color* by Faber Birren (Schiffer Publishing Ltd., 1987).

JAR DYEING

To dye your wool using these formulas, pre wet all wool in a pan or basin of very hot tap water with a drop or two of PRO Chem's Synthrapol detergent. Synthrapol is a wetting agent that helps the wool absorb the dye.

Because of their subtle tones, these colors work best when dyed over white or natural wool. I dyed both formulas over white wool so that you can see the true colors of the dye formulas. However, you might try dyeing the PRO Chem formula over pale yellow to brighten it up and to make it even more yellow, especially in the lighter values. Dye the Cushing green over pale blue for a beautiful, soft blue-green. Both of the greens would also be attractive dyed over pale green or celery.

INTERMEDIATE AND ADVANCED DYE TECHNIQUES

To make the Cushing green more yellow like the PRO Chem green, add more Canary to the formula. To make the Cushing swatch more of a dull blue-green, add more Peacock to the formula. To make either of them brighter, just decrease the amount of red in the formulas. Red is the complementary color in these formulas. Add more of it to dull the color.

Leaf Square, *7 3/4" x 9 3/4", #3-cut wool on cotton warp. Designed and hooked by Maryanne Lincoln, Wrentham, Massachusetts, 1995. Maryanne used two dye formulas, one a yellow-green and the other a gray-green, to hook these autumn leaves. The medium-rust wool of the background and the dull purple in the leaf veins and border complement the green leaves.*

The Cushing green is already quite dull, and if you add more red the color will begin to take on a brown look. Add still more and the color will no longer be green—it will definitely be a red-brown. When I am dyeing by eye and I want to create brown, first I combine blue and yellow(Cushing or PRO Chem) to create green, and then I start adding red. At first, the green will just keep getting grayer and duller. But as I add more red, the color becomes brown. You may want to experiment with this sometime.

CONTRAST WITH COLOR

I used both of the green swatches to hook these leaves. The duller one is hooked with the Cushing green swatch. The larger, brighter leaf is hooked with the PRO Chem swatch. I used a rust color that I had on hand to hook the background. It makes me think of pine needles covering the forest floor in the fall. I added a bit of a dull purplish color for the veins of both leaves and then used it again in the stripe around the border.

Look at the picture of my hooked leaves and notice especially how they contrast with the medium-rust background. The brighter leaf is hooked with lighter values on the edge of the leaf, and it stands out better against the background. The duller of the two leaves seems to almost fade into the background in a few places, because the value

JAR-DYEING RECIPES

Cushing Perfection Dyes

1 cup boiling water
3/128 tsp Cherry
1/4 tsp Canary
1/32 tsp Peacock
1/128 tsp Black
8 tsp plain salt (1 tsp for each jar)
8 Tbsp white vinegar
(1Tbsp for each jar)
Eight 3" x 24" white or natural wool strips (1 piece for each jar)

PRO Chem WF Acid Dyes

1 cup boiling water
3/128 tsp #338 Red
1/4 tsp #119 Yellow
1/32 tsp #490 Blue
1/128 tsp #672 Black
8 tsp plain salt (1 tsp for each jar)
8 Tbsp white vinegar
(1 Tbsp for each jar)
Eight 3" x 24" white or natural wool strips (1 piece for each jar)

of the green on the edge of the leaf is very similar to the value of the background. Remember, value refers to the lightness or darkness of a color.

In some cases you may want to have the edges of a motif blend with the background in places. That motif then becomes secondary to others that are brighter or have more contrast to the background color

Use this color placement technique when you want to play down an edge or even a whole motif. Be sure to watch how the values of your motifs combine with the background (as with my leaf) or you may have difficulty telling where the background ends and the motif begins. If you find that this is happening, try changing the value of your background—making it either lighter or darker—to bring out the edges of details like leaves and flowers so they won't get lost against the background. When you work hard to shade leaves and flowers or other motifs, you want to be able to see them clearly. Medium-value backgrounds are difficult to work with because you have to pay attention to this possible problem.

If you have never tried to hook leaves with a swatch of six or eight values, I encourage you to do so. Leaves can be fun to hook if you take the time to shade them. Prepare the two dye formulas described here, and use some real leaves as patterns, tracing around them onto paper. After arranging the shapes in a pleasing manner, draw them on your favorite backing. Use a #3- or 4-cut of wool and enjoy creating a beautiful leaf rug.

Dye Beautiful Browns from the Basics

Maryanne provides the formulas in the accompanying section for the swatches seen here. Top row, left to right: Basic Browns #1A, 2, 3, and 4, all dyed with PRO Chem dyes. Bottom row, left to right: Basic Browns #5, 6, and 7, all dyed with Cushing dyes.

MOST OF THE FORMULAS I PRESENT ARE DERIVED FROM JUST A FEW BASIC DYES: RED, BLUE, YELLOW, BLACK, AND SOMETIMES ORANGE. WITH THESE FEW DYES YOU CAN CREATE A RAINBOW OF COLORS, IN EVERY SHADE AND TINT IMAGINABLE. IN THIS CHAPTER, I WILL DISCUSS HOW TO DYE BROWNS RANGING FROM WARM TO COOL, DEPENDING ON THE COMBINATION OF DYES USED.

As you probably know, the color wheel is divided into warm and cool colors. The warm colors are red, orange, and yellow, and the cool colors are green, blue, and purple. Red-purple and yellow-green act as transitions between warm and cool colors and can appear either warm or cool, depending on how they are used.

In color language, brown is not a separate color. It is a descriptive term for a dull, warm color. There are red-browns, orange-browns, yellow-browns, and red-purple-browns. There are also browns that tend toward the cool side of

Chair seat,
16 1/2" diameter,
#3-cut wool on burlap.
Designed by Pearl McGown.
Hooked by Maryanne Lincoln,
Wrentham, Massachusetts, 1973.

the spectrum, such as gray-browns and slightly greenish browns, but they are still considered warm colors.

On the other hand, when we dull the cool colors of green, blue, and purple, we create grays. Gray is a term used to describe dull, cool colors. For instance, we talk of purplish grays, gray-greens, and blue-grays. Of course, gray also refers to true neutral values, which are mixtures of black and white.

BROWN DYES

Both Cushing and PRO Chem wash-fast dyes have brown dyes that are already mixtures of several hues. Some of my favorite Cushing browns are Seal Brown, Golden Brown, Medium Brown, and Dark Brown. PRO Chem also has a few mixed browns. The newest one, #504, is a nice neutral brown. The others don't seem really brown to me, however.

These days, whether I plan to use Cushing or PRO Chem dyes, I try to stick with the basic colors to achieve brown. My favorite method is to start with mixtures of the complements blue and orange. Then I add small amounts of the other dyes (red, yellow, and black) to tint the color toward red, yellow, or orange, or even to dull it more. I could use a mixture of red and yellow for orange, but I have found that I have less color separation (spotting of different colors) by starting with orange dye, rather than by mixing the two colors to get orange.

As I compared the results of the two different dye brands, it was obvious that Cushing Orange is brighter in comparison to Cushing Peacock than PRO Chem #233 orange is to PRO Chem #490 blue. You will see in the photograph on page 28 that the three browns dyed with Cushing dyes look like variations of orange, depending on what else was added. But in all the browns I dyed with PRO Chem dyes, no orange can be seen. You could cancel out some of the orange look in the Cushing formulas by using less Orange or adding more Peacock, its complement.

If you are not familiar with what the basic colors (red, blue, yellow, black, and orange) look like, dye a small sample of each before you mix them for the brown formulas listed below. Mix $^1/_{128}$ teaspoon of each color in 1 cup of hot water and dye a 1" x 12" sample of each over white wool. Add the dye to a small open pan with 2 to 4 cups of water, $^1/_8$ teaspoon of salt, and 1 teaspoon of vinegar. Add wool that has been soaked in hot water and a wetting agent, and simmer it over medium heat until the water clears. If the water doesn't clear, add more vinegar and continue to simmer the wool (you may know by experience that you'll need more vinegar than a recipe recommends).

I arbitrarily chose the initial quantities in these formulas, making an educated guess what would be a good starting point. This is often the way I work out muted colors like these browns. I begin at a logical starting point and then refine the amounts until I get the color I want. With these formulas I am showing you how close all these colors are to each other and how it takes only very small changes in the dye measurements to make a difference.

It all comes down to understanding complementary color mixing. When I get close to the color I want, sometimes I dissolve one or more of the dyes ($^1/_{128}$ teaspoon in 1 cup of boiling water) and add from a few drops to $^1/_4$ or $^1/_2$ cup of the solution until I get the color I am looking for. You may look at one of these colors and see that it is just what you want for a particular project, except you wish it were a bit brighter or duller. Take my formula and adjust it to get the exact color you need.

These formulas are just the beginning of a study of browns and how to create browns with formulas from a few basic colors. Read on for suggestions on how to change each formula to create more interesting variations.

PRO CHEM FORMULAS

The following formulas use PRO Chem dyes. Each formula was dyed over 3" x 12" white wool in 4 values.

Basic Brown #1A

$^1/_{32}$ tsp #233 orange
$^1/_{128}$ tsp #490 blue

I would describe this hue as a gray-brown. Isn't it surprising that a combination of two bright colors gives us this gray color? Shift the balance of dyes, however, and the swatch could become either a dull blue (more blue than orange in the formula), or a dull orange (double the amount of orange). The color, as we see it, is fairly close to neutral (neither orange nor blue). Therefore, adding more of one or the other color will tip the color toward blue or orange.

Basic Brown #2

$^1/_{32}$ tsp #233 orange
$^1/_{128}$ tsp #490 blue
$^1/_{128}$ tsp #338 red

This brown is really more of a dull red. Compare this color to Basic Brown #4 to see what happens when you add $^1/_{128}$ teaspoon of #119 yellow.

Basic Brown #3

$^1/_{32}$ tsp + $^1/_{64}$ tsp #233 orange
$^1/_{128}$ tsp #490 blue
$^1/_{128}$ tsp #119 yellow

This recipe creates a yellow-brown. I would like to see the color that would result from adding $^1/_{128}$ teaspoon #338 red to this formula. I would expect it to become slightly more orange.

CUSHING FORMULAS

None of these Cushing formulas should really be classified as browns. They are pretty colors, but each one needs something more to dull it. Each formula was dyed over 3" x 12" white wool in 4 values.

Basic Brown #5

1/32 tsp Orange
1/128 tsp Peacock

To bring this orange closer to a brown, I would add another 1/128 teaspoon Peacock, and maybe even 1/128 teaspoon Black. So the new, browner formula would be 1/32 teaspoon Orange + 1/64 teaspoon Peacock + 1/128 teaspoon Black.

Basic Brown #6

1/32 tsp Orange
1/128 tsp Peacock
1/128 tsp Cherry

To make this red-rust color browner I would add 1/128 teaspoon Peacock and 1/128 teaspoon Black. The new formula would be 1/32 teaspoon Orange + 1/64 teaspoon Peacock + 1/128 teaspoon Cherry + 1/128 teaspoon Black.

Basic Brown #7

1/32 tsp Orange
1/128 tsp Peacock
1/128 tsp Canary

To make this yellow-orange color browner I would add 1/128 teaspoon Peacock, or, better yet, decrease the amount of Orange to 3/128 teaspoon and add 1/128 teaspoon Peacock. Thus the new, browner formula would be 3/128 teaspoon Orange + 1/64 teaspoon Peacock + 1/128 teaspoon Canary.

Basic Brown #4

1/32 tsp #233 orange
1/128 tsp #490 blue
1/128 tsp #338 red
1/128 tsp #119 yellow

I'd call this color a red-brown. Note that the difference between this formula and the dull red formula (Basic Brown #2) is that this one has 1/128 teaspoon yellow added. The yellow combines with the blue that is already in the formula to make green, which makes the resulting red duller (because green is red's complement). Also, the added yellow shifts the red a bit around the color wheel toward a more orange-red.

BROWNS IN THE ROUND

The hooked round table mat on page 29 is a chair seat pattern by Pearl McGown that I hooked in conjunction with Pearl's correspondence color course in the early 1970s. One of the assignments was to dye certain types of swatches and then use them to hook this particular mat. I could choose any color I wanted, and I just happened to choose brown. This chair seat is the only piece I have hooked in all browns. One of the browns is a dark dull to a light bright, and another is a dark bright to a light dull. Can you tell which is which?

CHAPTER TWO

COLOR COMPLEMENTS

Here Comes the Sun

Swatches of wool created using the four formulas Maryanne presents here.

AS I BEGAN PLANNING A GIANT SUN MAT, I REALIZED THAT I NEEDED SOME NEW YELLOWS TO GIVE A BOLD NEW LOOK TO MY RUG. AND OF COURSE, NO YELLOW FORMULA IS COMPLETE WITHOUT ITS COMPLEMENT: PURPLE.

In preparation for hooking this mat, I have developed several of the following yellow formulas. The accents and the background of the rug will be hooked in purple, the complement of yellow. These formulas were developed using PRO Chem wash-fast acid dyes. You may notice that for the yellow and the purple formulas I used a combination of the same dyes (#119 yellow, #338 red, and #490 blue), but I put them together in different proportions. In the yellow formulas, the amount of yellow dye is predominant, with only small additions of purple. On the other hand, in the purple formulas I let the amount of purple

> *"It is not a mistake that I first diluted the purple solution before adding to the yellow formulas, or that I did not dilute the yellow solution before adding it to the purple formulas. If I hadn't diluted the purple, the results would have been too harsh since purple is so much stronger than yellow."*

(the red and blue mixture) predominate, with only small additions of the yellow dye.

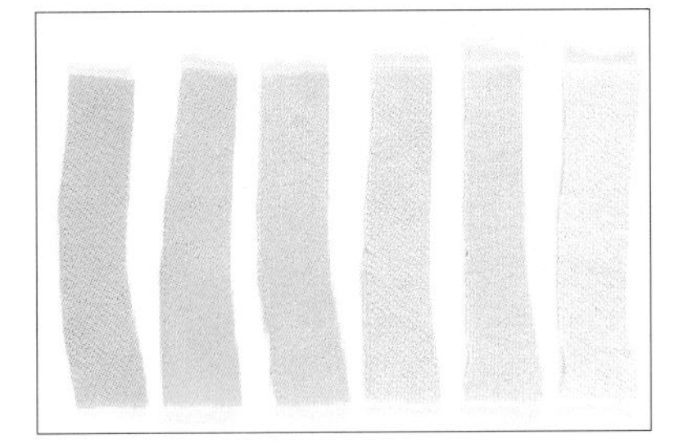

Daffodil (bright yellow)

Step 1

3/32 tsp #119 yellow

Dissolve this dye in 2 cups boiling water and distribute to 6 jars by pouring off half the solution until all 6 jars have solution. Then go ahead with the second part of the formula as per my jar dyeing method (as outlined in chapter 44). Before adding extra water to each jar, mix up the following and add the listed amount to each jar.

Step 2

3/128 tsp #490 blue

3/64 tsp #338 red

Mix these two dyes in 2 cups boiling water. Spoon out 2 teaspoons from this 2 cups of purple solution into 1 cup water and stir. Measure from this diluted purple solution and add to the jars that have the yellows as per the following list:

- Jar with the lightest yellow—add no purple
- Next lightest—add 1 tsp of the diluted purple solution
- Middle light—add 2 tsp purple
- Middle value—add 3 tsp purple
- Middle darkest—add 4 tsp purple
- Darkest yellow—add 5 tsp purple

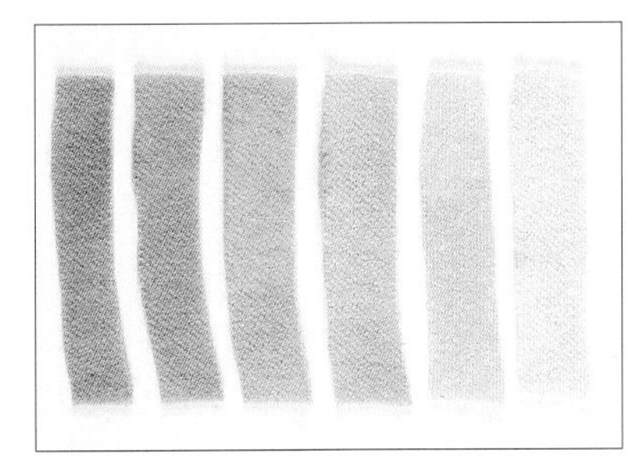

Gold (slightly duller yellow)

3/32 tsp #119 yellow

Dissolve dye in 2 cups boiling water and distribute to 6 jars as per the jar dye method.

Mix up the same purple as above in 2 cups boiling water and spoon off 4 teaspoons of the solution into 1 cup of water to create a weakened solution of purple. (NOTE: This weakened solution is twice as strong as the one used for the brighter yellow.)

Now add this purple solution to the yellow in jars as per the following amounts:

- Lightest yellow—add 2 tsp purple
- Next lightest—add 4 tsp purple
- Middle light—add 6 tsp purple
- Middle—add 8 tsp purple
- Middle dark—add 10 tsp purple
- Dark—add 12 tsp purple

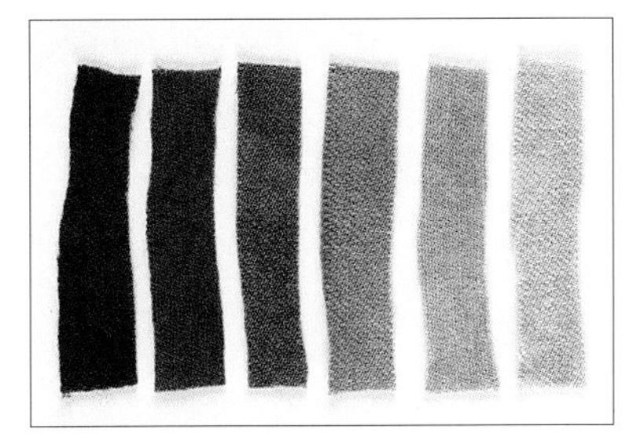

Purple Mountains (soft purple)

3/64 tsp #338 red

3/128 tsp #490 blue

Dissolve dyes in 2 cups boiling water and distribute to 6 jars as per the jar dye method.

Next, mix up 3/32 tsp #119 yellow in 2 cups boiling water. From this solution, add to each of the jars that contain purple as follows:

- Lightest—add no yellow
- Next lightest—add 1 tsp yellow
- Middle light—add 2 tsp yellow
- Middle—add 3 tsp yellow
- Middle dark—add 4 tsp yellow
- Darkest—add 5 tsp yellow

ADVANCED DYERS

I suggest that you try different combinations of this yellow-purple mixture. Why not dye my formulas over different colored wools? How about substituting Cushing dyes to see the slightly different results that you will get? Also perhaps try combinations of other complementary colors and see what you can come up with.

Also, with the help of a color wheel, match up pairs of complementary colors. These are the colors that are opposite each other on the wheel.

Once you have picked a pair of complements, try to create a formula that demonstrates how a duller color will occur when opposites are added to one another.

In addition, keep in mind that jar dye formulas are just one way to combine complementary colors. Try creating a dip-dye formula or maybe a mottled background formula. For instance, you might dye a piece of wool with one of the complementary colors and then dip the dyed piece into its opposite color.

Here's an example: Measure out a combination of blue and yellow to make a green. Dye your chosen piece of wool by dip-dyeing so that the end result will be a wool strip that is dark green on one end, gradually shading up to a light green on the other. When the dye bath clears, remove the wool and add red to the dye bath. Then dip-dye the dark end of the green strip in the red dye bath. Watch the color as it develops. Remove the strip when you are pleased with the color. If the dye bath isn't clear when you want to remove the strip, put the strip in a bath of boiling water with vinegar added for a few minutes to be sure that the dye sets properly.

I haven't given any set amount of dye to use to make up the green that you start with. Nor have I given the amount of red to add. I strongly encourage you to experiment with different amounts of dye and differently sized pieces of wool.

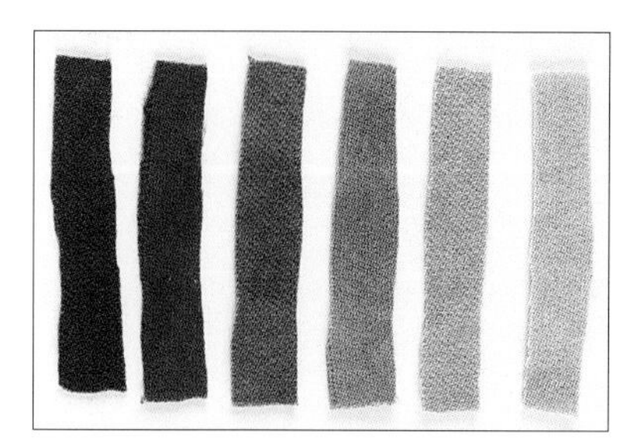

Purple Shadows (darker purple)

7/128 tsp #338 red
4/128 tsp #490 blue

Mix up the purple by combining in 2 cups boiling water. Distribute to 6 jars. Then mix up 3/32 tsp #119 yellow in 2 cups boiling water, and add to the jars that you have purple in as follows:

- Light—add 1 tsp yellow
- Next light—add 2 tsp yellow
- Middle light—add 3 tsp yellow
- Middle—add 4 tsp yellow
- Middle dark—add 5 tsp yellow
- Dark—add 6 tsp yellow

FOOD FOR THOUGHT

It is not a mistake that I first diluted the purple solution before adding to the yellow formulas, or that I did not dilute the yellow solution before adding it to the purple formulas. If I hadn't diluted the purple, the results would have been too harsh since purple is so much stronger than yellow. The purple dye solution does not have as much dry dye as the yellow solution has, but because purple as a color is stronger, the yellow would look duller and not suitable for the sun.

On the other hand, in order for the yellow to have any effect on the purples, I had to add the yellow without diluting it first. If I had diluted the yellow, the purples would be too bright for what I wanted to use them for.

If you read the formula instructions closely, you will see that there will be leftover dye in all four formulas. When I worked out these formulas, I knew that I would be experimenting with different combinations. I mixed up the purple that would be needed for the first formula, Daffodil. Then for the second formula, Gold, instead of mixing up the purple again, I just used what I needed from the purple solution left over from the first formula. If I had not achieved pleasing results and had decided to try for another version of the yellow formula, I would have continued using purple from the amount already mixed up and left over from the other two formulas.

New Colors Under the Sun

Sun Mat, *20" in diameter, #5-cut wool on linen. Designed by Pris Buttler. Hooked by Maryanne Lincoln, Wrentham, Massachusetts, 2002.*

IN THE LAST SECTION, I TOOK YOU THROUGH THE STEPS FOR DYEING WOOL FOR MY *SUN MAT* SHOWN HERE. TO HOOK THE SUN, I COMBINED THE TWO YELLOW SWATCHES, DAFFODIL AND GOLD. TO HOOK THE EYES AND BACKGROUND, I USED THE SWATCH PURPLE SHADOWS WITH SMALL BITS FROM THE SWATCH PURPLE MOUNTAINS. NOW THAT I HAVE COMPLETED THIS PROJECT, LET ME EXPLAIN HOW I WILL FINISH IT.

THE SUN ALSO RISES

I intend to mount this mat on a piece of Foamcore™, as this will allow me to hang it on the wall with no frame. Foamcore™ is a layer of foam sandwiched between two different sheets of paper and is available in craft stores in different colors and thickness. The foam layer creates a stiff surface on the Foamcore™, and the product sometimes has a sticky side used for mounting posters, as well as needlework for framing. It is very lightweight yet sturdy, and it can be cut to size with a ruler and X-ACTO® knife.

To prepare this mat for mounting, it is necessary to stitch around the outside about 2" from the hooking before cutting away the excess backing. Actually, to prevent the edge of your round mat from raveling, it is advisable to stitch one row of straight stitching and one row of zigzag stitching very close to each other.

In order to cut my Foamcore™ to the exact size needed, I first cut a piece of heavy brown paper to the exact size of the finished hooking. This is an important step, so take your time and be as accurate as possible. Get a tracing of the mat first from the reverse side after it has been steam pressed. Then, transfer the tracing to the brown paper. Finally, trace around this paper pattern directly onto the

Foamcore™. After carefully cutting the backing on the traced line, you can continue mounting the hooked mat.

ONE MORE COLOR PLAY WITH PURPLE AND YELLOW

Before I move on to talk about the two new formulas I developed, I want to expand on just one more possibility from yellow and purple outlined in the previous issue.

You may be a rug hooker that shies away from using bright sun yellows in your hooking, but you just love to use warmer golds and mustard-type colors. If we take the Daffodil formula and adjust it by using less yellow, adding red, and toning it down with a different amount of purple, the new formula will be a warmer yellow. The possible color variations are almost endless. When I adjust a formula to try and make a particular color, I have a tendency to take small steps at first. Then after I dye a small sample of the new formula, I am more confident about adjusting the new color further.

The Daffodil formula calls for $^{3}/_{32}$ teaspoon #119 yellow PRO Chem wash-fast acid dye. For a new warmer yellow, let's use $^{2}/_{32}$ teaspoon #119 yellow plus $^{1}/_{128}$ teaspoon #338 red. This will give us a very bright color because we are combining two primaries. Dissolve this in 2 cups boiling water and distribute to four jars as per the jar dyeing method.

To tone this down we must add some of the complement, which in this case is purple. Since we have only changed our yellow by a small amount, its complement would also change very little. I am choosing to keep it the same basic mixture, but I will add more to the jars.

Swatches of Squash and Seal Point Brown

Purple

$^{7}/_{128}$ tsp #338 red

$^{4}/_{128}$ tsp #490 blue

Mix dyes in 2 cups boiling water. Then, spoon the full strength solution directly into the jars with the yellow according to the following:

- Lights—add 3 tsp purple
- Next lightest—add 4 tsp purple
- Next darkest—add 5 tsp purple
- Darkest—add 6 tsp purple

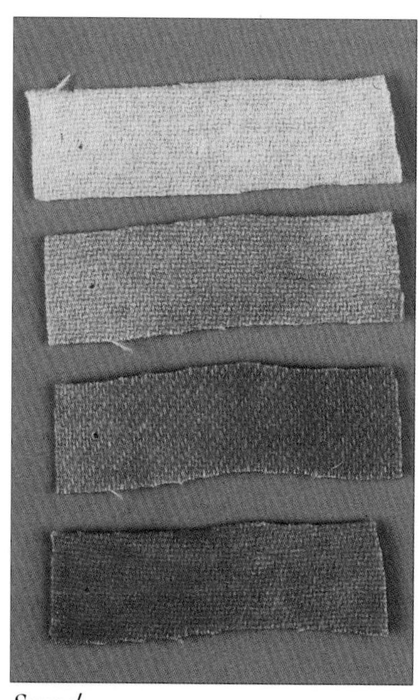

Squash

TWO NEW FORMULAS

As a slight spin on the Daffodil formula detailed above, I invented my Squash formula to produce a lovely orange color. Please note that I produce gradations of Squash using the same Purple formula outlined above.

Squash

Step 1

$^{2}/_{32}$ tsp #119 yellow

$^{1}/_{128}$ tsp #338 red

Combine the two colors in 2 cups boiling water and pour in four jars as per my jar dyeing method.

Step 2

After yellow mixture is in the jars, mix up Purple (see recipe above), and add to the four jars as outlined. Add 3" x 24" pieces of natural wool to each jar.

The new color will look quite orange. I feel that I could have used the same amount of yellow, as in Daffodil, and the results would have still definitely been a yellow, not a yellow-orange. To tone this new color down so that the dark value isn't quite as bright, I might have added more purple in the second step.

As I always do, I dyed a gradation of Squash over natural wool. If you like softer colors, however, dye over beiges, light plaids, or other off-white wools.

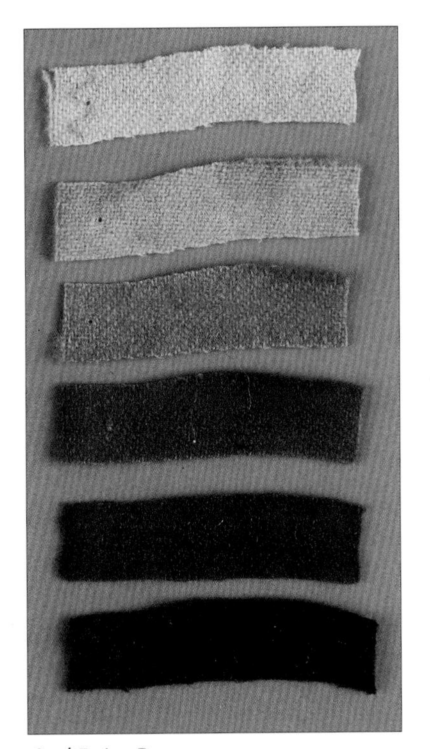

Seal Point Brown

SEAL POINT BROWN

Recently, I came up with a new PRO Chem wash-fast acid dye color that I would like to share with you. The name describes the color, and the different values in this swatch would be nice background choices.

Since this formula is written for a piece of 6" x 24" wool instead of 3" x 24" wool, can you see how you might translate this formula into amounts to dye 1/3 yard pieces of the four darkest values?

The wool accommodated by this new formula will be twice as much as with the Squash formula, so you take the amounts of formula used for Squash in the sidebar and cut those amounts in half for Seal Point Brown. For instance, to dye 1/3 yard of the darkest value of Seal Point Brown, just multiply the formula by four instead of eight.

YARDAGE FORMULAS FOR SQUASH

For those of us who dye large pieces instead of gradation swatches, these formulas can be used in many different ways.

- One complete formula as written on page 36 will dye: 1/3 yard of wool the same color as the lightest of the four values.
- Two times the formula will dye: 1/3 yard of wool the same as the next lightest of the four values, or 2/3 yard the same as the lightest value.
- Four times the formula will dye: 1/3 yard of wool the same as the next darkest of the four values, or 2/3 yard of the next lightest value, or 1 yard of the lightest value.
- Eight times the formula will dye: 1/3 yard of wool the color of the darkest of the four values, or 2/3 yard of the next darkest value, or 1 yard of the next lightest value, or 2 yards of the lightest value.

CHANGING YOUR MEASUREMENTS

Two times the formula means double the dry dye measurements in **Step 1** and double the liquid measurements (teaspoons) in **Step 2** (page 36). Four times the formula means four times the dry dye from **Step 1**, and four times the liquid measurements in **Step 2** and so forth for the other values.

Keep in mind that these formula multiples for yardage dyeing are not exact. What this means is that the strength of the dye solution that you mix up may be a little more than you need. As a result, when adding the dye solution to the dye bath, add only 3/4 of it at first. Add more as the wool takes up the color, but if the color becomes dark enough before you have added all the dye; just set aside the extra dye solution. Don't add it all just to use it up. Label it, cover it tightly, and you can use it later if you need to dye just a little more of the same color.

Usually, I end up adding it all, but it is much easier to add it a little at a time than to get it darker than you want because you were impatient and just dumped it all in.

All the formulas that I develop can be used to dye gradation swatches, or they can be used to dye larger pieces of the different values. The above list only applies to the Squash formula, however, or other formulas asking for 3" x 24" (or 72-square inch equivalents) pieces of wool in each value.

Seal Point Brown

1/8 tsp #672 black
1/4 tsp #233 orange
1/64 tsp #490 blue
3/32 tsp #119 yellow

- Dye in 6 jars as per my jar dyeing method.
- 6" x 24" piece of natural white wool in each jar.

I want to encourage you to try to create your own new yellow swatch by using the complementary colors yellow and purple. Furthermore, I hope that I have encouraged you to try some yardage dyeing by using the two jar dye formulas that I have included in this section.

An Eye for Complements

Sunny Green

WE HAVE SPENT QUITE A BIT OF TIME WITH THE COMPLEMENTARY COLORS YELLOW AND PURPLE. NOW I'D LIKE TO MOVE ON TO DYEING COLORS WITH THE COMPLEMENTS RED AND GREEN.

It is very helpful to memorize the three basic sets of complements: yellow and purple, blue and orange, and red and green. For those of us who are new to this discussion, complementary colors are those that lie opposite each other on the color wheel.

KNOWING YOUR COMPLEMENTS

In the dye pot, it doesn't matter whether you add a little bit of red to green or a little bit of green to red; the new color in each case will be duller than what you started with. As you spend more time dyeing, you'll discover that this is the case regardless of which complementary colors you mix together.

As you become familiar with how complementary colors work with each other, your dyeing adventures will become more rewarding on several levels. No longer will you feel helpless when your dyed wool turns out too bright. You will know that you should add a little of the complementary color to dull it—always remembering to add just a little at a time.

On the other hand, if the wool you dyed is too dull, it may be possible to brighten the color by dyeing the wool again with some of the complementary color removed from the formula. Maybe the wool was supposed to dye a dark red, and it came out too dark or too brown. Look at the formula for any signs of green (which could be a single green dye or a combination of blue and yellow dye). Once you find it, decrease the amounts of those dyes, and try the formula again. Use more of the complement to darken and dull the color. Use less of the complement to lighten and brighten the color.

Keeping these simple tenets in mind, you will feel more confident about dyeing the colors you want. Maybe you will look at one of the colors you have a sample for and decide to change it by manipulating the complementary color relationships in the formula. You might discover a brand new formula that is just right for your project.

Sunny Green

Combine the following three PRO Chem wash-fast acid dyes in 1 cup boiling water, and distribute to jars according to the jar dyeing method. Add 9" x 12" pieces of natural white wool to each jar.

1/8 tsp #119 yellow
1/32 tsp #490 blue
1/32 tsp #672 black

This is a beautiful green suitable for all sorts of floral leaves, as well as other foliage. Green is the combination of yellow and blue, but notice that I have added as much black as blue, and the color is still a lively green.

When creating this color, I knew that I couldn't just use an equal combination of #490 blue and #119 yellow. First of all, yellow is a weaker color than blue, and this particular blue is

ADVANCED DYERS

More often than not, you will have more than one pair of complements at work within any given dye formula. The predominant pair of complementary colors, however, are typically the ones with the largest measurement in the formula. Thereby, we can predict how to properly manipulate these complements, and what will happen when we do. Let's look at our new Rose Leaf Green to see if there are any secondary complementary combinations at work.

The formula has 1/8 teaspoon #119 yellow and 1/64 teaspoon #338 red. These two dyes combine to make a yellow-orange. Don't discount the influence of this combination on the formula simply because the red is such a small amount. Pure yellow is easily affected by the addition of any other color. The formula also has 1/32 teaspoon #490 blue. Blue and orange are complements, and as with all complementary colors when you mix them together, they will dull each other. Within this same formula, we can also see the combinations of the other two complements—yellow and purple. When you take these new complements into account along with the red and green we started with, we can be pretty certain that the color will be duller than the original Sunny Green formula.

If you look at the formula and think about it, the Sunny Green formula is a combination of two primary colors, yellow and blue. By adding a small amount of the third primary color, we have introduced the interactions of all three sets of complements.

Keeping this in mind, you can see what would happen if we increased the blue, decreased the yellow, and kept the amount of red the same. The red in the Rose Leaf Green color would begin to play a slightly different role. When the yellow is decreased, the same amount of red will have more effect on the yellow to create a bolder orange. At the same time, this bolder orange will help to dull its complement, the increased blue. Similarly, while the orange is working to dull the blue, the red and blue (purple) are acting on its complement (yellow) to dull it as well.

As you can see, adding red to our formula caused a lot more color interactions than we may have originally anticipated. Whenever you have a color that has all three primaries in it, any change in one of the three has more than just the obvious effect, and steps should be made gradually to ensure you get just the color you want.

especially strong. Therefore, to compensate for the weakness of yellow in general and the strength of #490 blue in particular, the green mixture has four times as much yellow as blue.

I also added black because #672 black makes a great gray companion to #490 blue in small amounts. I knew this blue/black combination would combine with the yellow and blue to make a beautiful green that would be easy and fun to hook with. I wasn't exactly sure what it would look like, but I was confident that I would like it and that it would be easy enough on the eyes (not too bright) to hook. Black in a color smokes it up and darkens it a little, but black's influence on a color is not as subtle as its complement. Black turns the lights off in a color and softens it.

Rose Leaf Green

Combine the following four PRO Chem wash-fast acid dyes in 1 cup boiling water, and distribute to jars according to the jar dyeing method (see page 44). Add 9" x 12" pieces of natural white wool to each jar.

1/8 tsp #119 yellow
1/32 tsp #490 blue
1/32 tsp #672 black
1/64 tsp #338 red

Rose Leaf Green

> *"In the dye pot, it doesn't matter whether you add a little bit of red to green or a little bit of green to red; the new color in each case will be duller than what you started with."*

Transitional Green

Compare this formula with Sunny Green. The formula is almost the same, but I have added 1/64 teaspoon #338 red. By adding green's complement, the color is definitely duller. As a result, this new color will be a great choice for leaves to go with many different flowers, not just roses.

Transitional Green

First, mix up the following in 1 cup boiling water, and distribute to jars as per the jar dyeing method. This part of the formula is the same as for the Sunny Green on page 20.

Step 1

1/8 tsp #119 yellow
1/32 tsp #490 blue
1/32 tsp #672 black

Step 2

After this Sunny Green formula has been distributed to the jars, mix up 1/64 teaspoon #338 red in 1/2 cup boiling water, and distribute 4 teaspoons of the solution in each jar.

Compare samples of the three swatches. What is noteworthy about them?

1. Sunny Green without any of the complement (red) is brighter than Rose Leaf Green.
2. Rose Leaf Green and Transitional Green are not only duller than Sunny Green, but they are also darker. Compare the values. When you add the complement, the color not only becomes duller but darker as well.
3. The lightest, slightly pink value of Transitional Green is the only value that even hints that red has been added.

THE LAST WORD ON COMPLEMENTS

What do you think the results would be if I had increased the red to 1/32 teaspoon #338 in the Sunny Green formula and dyed it as a straight gradation also?

I can keep adding red a little at a time, but until the red measurements are greater than the green (blue and yellow), the color will still not look red. In fact, it may never look truly red unless I not only add more red, but also decrease the amount of green.

If I continue increasing the red while keeping the Sunny Green part of the formula the same, however, we inevitably will begin to see some beautiful brown tones. Try this approach for your next autumn scene, or to hook the bark and branches of an elegant tree.

More with Red and Green

Country Cabin, *15" x 11", #6-cut wool on burlap. Designed and hooked by Maryanne Lincoln, Wrentham, Massachusetts, 2001.*

PREVIOUSLY I COMBINED GREEN AND RED TO CREATE THREE NEW GREEN FORMULAS. THIS TIME, LET'S EXPLORE SOME NEW COLOR CONCOCTIONS BASED ON THESE COMPLEMENTS, WITH THE EMPHASIS ON RED.

To refresh your memory, complementary colors are those that lie opposite each other on the color wheel with the three basic sets being yellow and purple, blue and orange, and red and green.

Two of the formulas that follow are examples of different ways to combine red and green to create dip dyes. Five of the formulas are for dyeing yardage and one is for dyeing a gradation.

The dyes used in all the formulas are PRO Chem wash-fast acid dyes: #338 red, #490 blue, #119 yellow, and #672 black.

I used 1/8 yard of natural or white wool for all formulas. Prepare the wool for all these formulas by first tearing 1/2-yard pieces off a bolt of natural or white. Then cut each 1/2-yard piece into four pieces by tearing it at the fold and then tearing each of those pieces in half. This gives you four pieces per 1/2 yard. Each of the pieces of wool is to be 18" (1/2 yard) long and about 14" wide.

Red Dip

Step 1

1/8 tsp #338 red

Dye in an open 4- to 5-quart enamel pan with 1/4 cup white vinegar and about 3 quarts of water. Add all the dye before adding the wool. Dye at a very high heat until the water clears. Bring to a boil, but don't let it boil too hard. Stir often to keep the wool submerged and somewhat circulated. When the water clears, remove the wool while you add the green complement.

Step 2

1/32 tsp #119 yellow

1/64 tsp #490 blue

Mix dyes in 1 cup boiling water and add to the dye pot. Hold the red wool by one end and dip dye the piece in the green dye. It will get dark very quickly. Therefore, pick one end, and only dip that one end about halfway up the strip. Don't dip the piece all the way into the dye pot every time. You want a gradual color change from bright red to medium dull red to very dull on the opposite end of the wool. Process until the water clears. Add more vinegar if needed. Remove the wool and add this final color.

Step 3

1/128 tsp #672 black

Add dye to the dye pot. Dip just the darkest end of the strip in the black dye.

Red-Orange Dip

Step 1

1/16 tsp #338 red

Add dye to a dye pot with about 3 quarts of water and 1/4 cup of white vinegar. Submerge the wool completely until the red dye has set. Remove the wool. This time, instead of mixing the yellow and blue together, we will add the yellow first and then the blue.

Step 2

1/32 tsp #119 yellow

Add dye to the dye pot, and dip dye the red wool in it. Continue until the water clears. Dip the strip 2/3 to 3/4 of the way into the pot.

Step 3

1/128 tsp #490 blue

Remove the wool, add the dye, and dip dye just the bottom 1/3 of the wool strip.

BROWNS FOR BACKGROUNDS

The following browns would make great background colors.

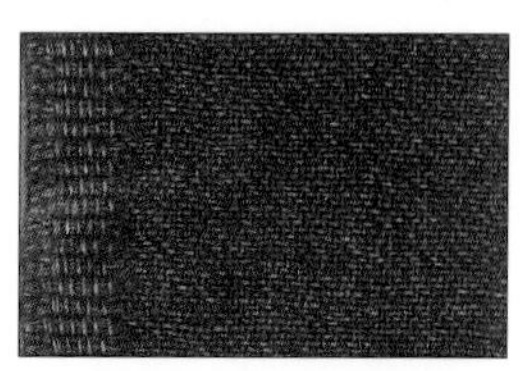

Background Brown

1/32 tsp #338 red
3/64 tsp #119 yellow
1/128 tsp #490 blue

Combine dyes in 1 cup boiling water, and add it to a dye pot with 3 quarts of water and 1/4 cup white vinegar. Add the wool and dye it until the water clears. Stir to keep wool submerged and circulated. For this color I shifted the green to a yellow-green. Instead of a ratio of 2 parts yellow to 1 part blue, I used 6 parts yellow to 1 part blue.

Gray Brown

1/32 tsp #338 red
3/64 tsp #119 yellow
1/128 tsp #490 blue
1/128 tsp #672 black

Combine dyes in 1 cup boiling water, and add it to a dye pot with 3 quarts of water and 1/4 cup of white vinegar. Add the wool and process until the water clears. Stir to keep the wool submerged and agitated.

Multiply the dry dye in the formula by four to get enough dye for 1/2 yard of wool instead of 1/8 yard. (1/2 = 4/8)

Multiply the dry dye in the formula by eight to get enough dye for 1 yard of wool instead of 1/8 yard. (1 = 8/8)

THREE GREAT GRAYS

These three warm grays are examples of light values that can be created by combining the complementary colors of red and green.

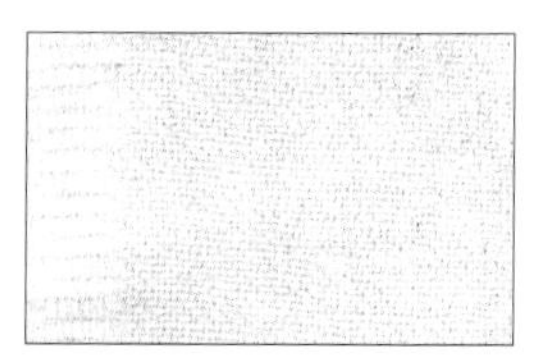

Light Warm Gray

Mix up two separate cups of dye:

- One with 1/128 tsp #338 red in 1 cup boiling water.
- Another with green (1/128 tsp #490 blue + 1/64 tsp #119 yellow).

Add 8 teaspoons of the red solution + 4 teaspoons of the green solution to a dye pot with 3 quarts of water and 1/4 cup of white vinegar. Add the wool and process until the water clears.

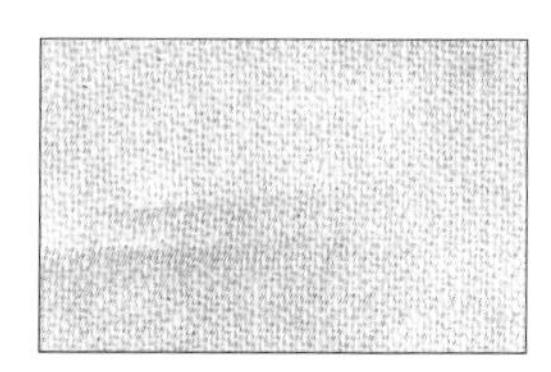

Medium-Light Warm Gray

From the 2 cups of dye that we have left (see "Light Warm Gray" above), add 16 teaspoons of the red solution + 8 teaspoons of the green solution to a dye pot with 3 quarts of water and 1/4 cup of white vinegar. Add the wool and process until the water clears.

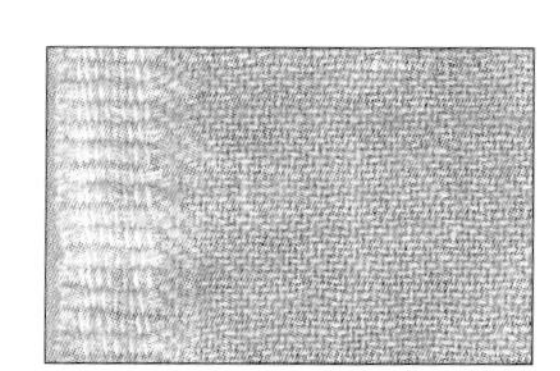

Medium Warm Gray

From the 2 cups of dye that are left, add 1/2 cup red + 1/4 cup green to the dye pot as before. Process until the water clears.

> *"If you practice looking at things in terms of the color and keep your thoughts simple, it will help you create combinations to start with when you want to come up with a new formula or adjust an existing formula."*

BEAUTIFUL BURGUNDY

The last red formula that I am going to share with you is a straight gradation of six values. It is a lively yet soft red that I can't wait to hook with. The values that I dyed emphasize the medium to dark values. I would like to dye at least four additional lighter values. Combined with the medium-light values that we have here, the color range would be perfect for wild roses and apple blossoms.

Burgundy

(Each value is dyed over 1/8 yard of white or natural wool.)

3/4 tsp #338 red
1/8 tsp #119 yellow
1/16 tsp #490 blue

Mix in 1 cup boiling water. Pour six values as per the jar dyeing method. (I dyed each value in an open pan, however, starting with the lightest.)

To a very hot dye bath of 3 quarts of water and 1/4 cup of white vinegar, I added a jar of dye and then a 1/8-yard piece of wool. I stirred often to keep the wool underwater and to agitate the bath. When the water cleared, I removed the wool, set it aside, and proceeded by adding the second lightest jar of dye to the bath. After adding the wool, I processed it until the water cleared. I removed the wool and set it aside with the first.

Before adding the next jar of dye, I added another 1/4 cup of white vinegar. I continued in this manner until I had dyed six values.

I poured the values for jar dyeing, even though I knew I wouldn't be dyeing the swatch that way, because it saves time, as I only have to measure the dry dye once. After that I am dealing with pouring out the different values.

KEEP IT SIMPLE

Sometimes when I am trying to match a particular color or create a new color by using the complements of red and green, I use a different combination of blue and yellow for the green. For instance, it may be advantageous to use a yellow-green to get the color I want. Often times I have to try different combinations until I find the one that works best for the challenge at hand.

If you practice looking at things in terms of the color and keep your thoughts simple, it will help you create combinations to start with when you want to come up with a new formula or adjust an existing formula.

For instance, practice looking at the ordinary things around you and describing them in rainbow colors like red, orange, yellow, green, blue, and violet. Also look at colors and describe them as combinations. For instance, instead of thinking of orange, think of it as a combination of red and yellow. Instead of thinking of green, think of it as a combination of blue and yellow. Instead of thinking of purple, think of it as a combination of blue and red.

If you do this (and memorize the three sets of complements), you will begin to see the interrelationships of colors within formulas. Consequently, you will be better able to predict what will happen if you add a bit of this or that. After a while this thought process will become automatic, and you will be able to determine more subtle color combinations.

I hope these formulas that focus on red and green will get you excited to try some different ideas of your own.

CHAPTER THREE

METHODS OF DYEING

Jar Dyeing

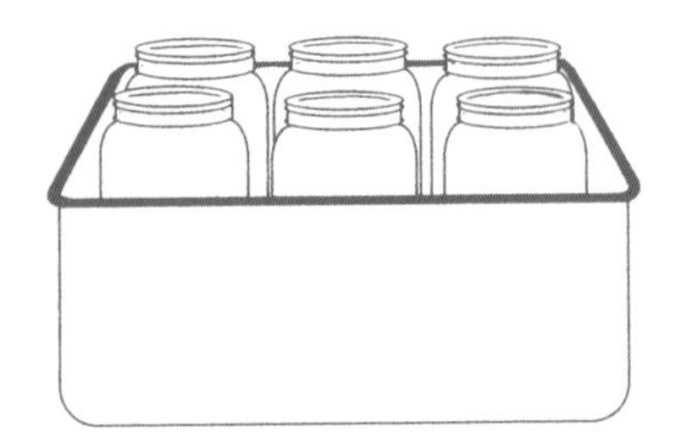

BEFORE I JOINED AN ADULT EDUCATION RUG HOOKING CLASS IN 1964, I HAD ABSOLUTELY NO EXPERIENCE DYEING ANYTHING. DURING THE THIRD CLASS EDNA CALLIS, OUR TEACHER, GAVE A LIVE, COMPLETE JAR DYEING DEMONSTRATION. WE WERE EXPECTED TO GO HOME FROM THAT DEMONSTRATION AND DYE 8-VALUE SWATCHES RIGHT AWAY. WE COULD BECAUSE ON THE FIRST NIGHT OF CLASS EVERYONE HAD RECEIVED A NOTEBOOK OF LESSON PAGES THAT INCLUDED A JAR DYEING INSTRUCTION SHEET. BY THE TIME THE DYE LESSON WAS PRESENTED, WE WERE PREPARED TO START DYEING AT HOME. IT WAS THE BEGINNING OF A LONG ADVENTURE OF COLOR DISCOVERY FOR ME.

Interestingly, jar dyeing is not the simplest way to dye a piece of wool. However, it is an easy way to dye a gradation of values. At the time none of us in the class even thought to question the procedure. As I recall, I was just excited to be learning how to dye wool for my rugs as well as how to shade flowers and leaves with the swatches that I dyed. if you just want to dye different colors, not gradations, open-pan dyeing is an easier approach (see page 51).

JAR DYEING INSTRUCTIONS

1. Soak 6 to 8 pieces of 3" x 12" wool strips in hot water with a drop of Synthrapol. If you have hard water, use a bit more Synthrapol. Let it soak while you are preparing the dye bath.
2. Measure your recipe's dry dye formula into a small enamel pan. Add a small amount of cool water to the pan to make a paste. Add 3/4 cup of hot tap water and bring it to a quick boil. Stir. Pour the mixture into a 1-cup measuring cup. Add hot tap water to make 1 cup of solution.
3. Arrange the jars in the roaster. Add hot tap water around the jars until they begin to float.
4. Stir the dye solution and pour 1/2 cup of it into the first jar.
5. Refill the cup with hot tap water to the 1-cup level. Stir and pour 1/2 cup into the next jar. Repeat this process (pouring off half the solution and adding more hot water to the 1-cup level) until all the jars contain solution. You will end up with 1/2 cup of lightly tinted solution after pouring the last value. Don't pour it into the jar with the lightest solution. It is not needed for this procedure.
6. Add 1 1/2 teaspoon of salt to each jar. Then add warm tap water to each jar until each is about 2/3 full. Put a drop of Synthrapol in each jar.
7. Gently squeeze some of the water out of the wet wool. (It is not necessary to rinse it unless you have used a wetting agent other than Synthrapol.) Use tongs to stir the wool into the jars of dye solution. Squish the wool up and down to force the dye solution through the wool. Move the tongs as you work to avoid leaving spots where the tongs grip the wool. Stir the wool often in this manner while the swatches are processing.
8. Cover the roaster, not the individual jars. If you don't have a cover, loosely cover the pan with heavy foil.
9. Put the roaster over low heat. After about 10 minutes, remove the cover and stir each jar. Turn the heat up to a simmer only—don't let the water heat to a rolling boil. Stir the wool every, 15 to 20 minutes. You can't stir too much. Make sure each piece of wool is completely submerged before you put the cover back over the jars.
10. Simmer for 1 hour. (When using

"I add as much water as I possibly can without overflowing the jars; it is important to add approximately the same amount to each jar."

THE JAR DYEING METHOD

Before you begin to dye, read through the section on Dyeing Equipment and Safety to have the right equipment on hand and to take the necessary safety precautions. As a practice run, try the project listed at the end of this chapter.

DYEING MULTIPLE SWATCHES

To dye more than one swatch at a time increase the following: the number of pieces of wool in each jar, the strength of the dye solution, the amount of salt per jar, the amount of vinegar, and the amount of extra water that you add to each jar. For example, to dye one swatch in each jar you'd use the above directions. For two swatches per jar you'd double the dye formula, vinegar, and salt per jar, and have enough water in the jar to allow you to stir the wool easily. For five swatches per jar you use 5 times dye formula, 5 tablespoons of vinegar, and $2\frac{1}{2}$ teaspoons of salt, plus sufficient water to keep the wool submerged.

The amount of extra water is not as important as the size of the material, the strength of the dye formula, or the amount of the salt. I add as much water as I possibly can without overflowing the jars; it is important to add approximately the same amount to each jar.

Until you gain experience, follow my jar dyeing instructions to the letter. As you do more dyeing, you will find yourself questioning things and more willing to experiment with dyeing methods.

PROJECT

To hone your jar-dyeing skills prior to dyeing wool for a rug, use this dyeing method to try one of these formulas on six pieces of 3" x 12" natural wool. You'll get a nice orange hue for your efforts.

Cushing

$\frac{3}{32}$ tsp Cherry
$\frac{3}{32}$ tsp Canary

PRO Chem

$\frac{3}{32}$ tsp #338 Red
$\frac{3}{32}$ tsp #119 Yellow.

---

acid dyes, remove the wool after 30 to 40 minutes and stir 1 tablespoon of white vinegar into each jar. Then put the wool back into the jars. Simmer the wool for 30 minutes longer, stirring it often. Remove the roaster from the heat, let the wool stand in the jars until it cools, then follow the rest of these steps.) Rinse the wool, starting with the lightest value and working toward the darkest. When the water rinses clear, hang the wool to dry. If the water does not rinse clear, put the wool in a small pan with 2 to 4 cups of water and 1 or 2 tablespoons of vinegar. Bring the water to a quick boil. Simmer it for a few minutes or until the water that drips from the wool is clear. If the piece is not one value darker compared to the previous strip, add some of the dye from its jar to the vinegar bath. Be careful, though—it is easy to get it too dark. If you use the vinegar bath for one value, you must do it for every value after that.

11. Clean the jars thoroughly after you've used them to avoid contaminating your next dye project.

Scrunch Dyeing

Pansy Mat, *22 3/4" x 15 1/4", #3-cut wool on burlap, Designed by Flo Petruchik. Hooked by Maryanne Lincoln, Wrentham, Massachusetts, 1995. Maryanne scrunch dyed the peach, leaves, cherries, and brown of the checkered border. Her dye techniques for the black background and pansies were described in other chapters.*

I DIDN'T USE ANY STRAIGHT GRADATION FORMULAS TO FINISH DYEING THE *PANSY MAT* BECAUSE I LIKE TO HOOK FRUITS (AND SOME LEAVES) WITH A TYPE OF DIP DYEING I CALL SCRUNCH DYEING. (I CALL IT THAT BECAUSE THE WOOL GETS SCRUNCHED IN THE PAN.) THEREFORE, I WILL MAKE A SLIGHT VARIATION IN THE PRESENTATION OF COLORS. INSTEAD OF SHARING FORMULAS FOR GRADATION SWATCHES, I WILL TELL YOU HOW TO SCRUNCH DYE AND THEN GIVE YOU THE FORMULAS FOR THE PEACH, THE CHERRIES, THE LEAVES, AND THE BROWN CHECKS ON THE *PANSY MAT*.

SCRUNCH DYEING

To scrunch dye, you only need one small enamel pan; a 1- or 2-quart size will do. Bigger is not better because you want the wool to be crowded when you dye. Use Cushing dyes or PRO Chem wash-fast acid dyes with Synthrapol as your wetting agent. You will need tongs and lined rubber gloves. You will also need a 1-cup measure, white vinegar, and 9" by 24" strips of wool.

Pre-wet the wool in hot tap water with enough Synthrapol added to saturate the fabric. Mix

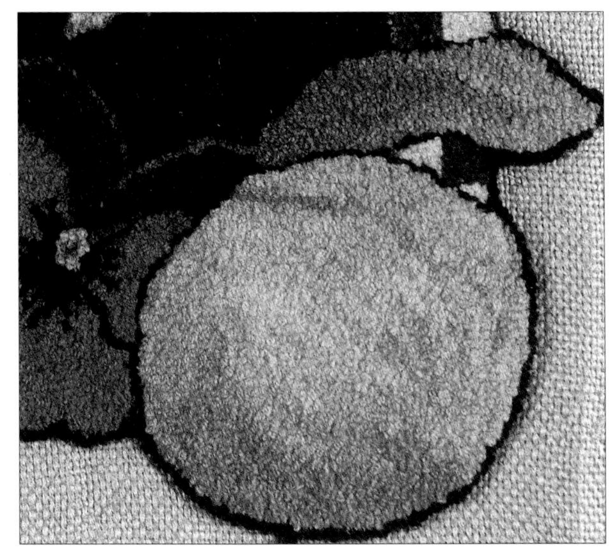

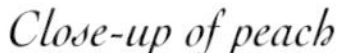

Close-up of peach

Close-up of cherries

the dye formula in 1 cup of boiling water. Fill the dye pan about 1/3 full with hot tap water. Pour 1/4 cup of the chosen dye solution into the pan. Add 1 tablespoon of white vinegar to the dye bath each time you add 1/4 cup of dye solution. Bring the dye bath to a boil and keep it simmering.

Without rinsing it, remove the wool from the presoak. Squeeze out a little of the water so the wool doesn't drip all over the place. Grip the wool with tongs about halfway down its length so both ends will enter the dye bath at the same time.

Gradually lower the wool into the simmering (not rolling boil) dye bath, going deeper and deeper as you would do in regular dip dyeing. When the wool will not go deeper into the bath, twist it and, at the same time, scrunch it down until it is completely under the water. The water should have begun to clear as you do this.

The most important thing to remember when scrunch dyeing is simple: Don't allow enough dye bath for the pieces of wool to be easily submerged. At the same time, there must be enough water so that when you scrunch down hard, you can force the wool under the water without having it overflow. You know you have enough dye bath when you release the downward pressure on the wool and it springs back to rise above the surface of the water.

If you want darker wool, add another 1/4 cup of dye and repeat the process. For interesting effects, add two or three different dyes to each batch. I like to use three related colors. Don't mix them together; add one, dip and scrunch, then add another, and so on. Cover the pan and simmer the wool until the color is set. Dark colors must simmer longer than light colors. Rinse and dry.

PANSY MAT COLORS

Peach

The peach bridges two areas on the color wheel. The light values are in the yellow section between yellow and orange, and the dark values reach over into the section between orange and red.

To scrunch dye peach, I used medium light maize yellow Dorr wool, color #83. Pre-wet two 9" by 24" strips of wool in the manner discussed above, then mix 1/32 teaspoon of #338 Red (PRO Chem wash-fast acid dyes) in 1/2 cup of boiling water. Don't forget to add vinegar to the dye bath.

If the peach starts to look too pink or if you don't have yellow wool to dye over, add 1/32 teaspoon of #119 Yellow (PRO Chem VII), dip and scrunch all the way to the top of the piece.

After the water clears, mix 1/128 teaspoon of #490 Blue (PRO Chem) in 1/2 cup of boiling water. Add half of it to the dye bath and then dip the red ends of the wool into this blue solution. Dribble a little of the leftover light blue over the light yellow ends for some greener accents. If your peach isn't dark enough or if you want more than two pieces of wool, repeat the red and blue steps.

Cherries

The cherry dye solution is a strong mixture of red and yellow. On the color wheel, it will lie just on the orange side of red, yet it is still a red.

To dye the cherries, mix equal parts—1/32 teaspoons each—of

"To scrunch dye, you only need one small enamel pan; a 1- or 2-quart size will do. Bigger is not better because you want the wool to be crowded when you dye."

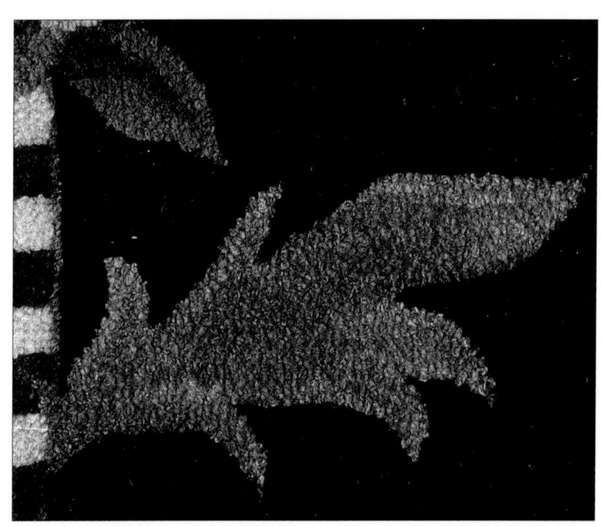

Close-up of leaves

Close-up of border

Cushing Cherry and Canary dyes. Scrunch a piece of yellow wool 3" by 24". Make sure the red dye comes all the way up over the lightest ends of the wool so you end up with a strip that is light red in the middle to dark red on both ends. (Remember to hold the wool in the middle and dip both ends at the same time.)

Next, mix 1/128 teaspoon of both Peacock and Canary in 1/2 cup of boiling water. Add half to the dye bath and dip just the dark ends of the red piece. Add only enough to darken the red on just the ends.

Leaves

The leaves are a green mixture with more yellow than the basic green. This green is a color between yellow and the green that we dyed before, but it is still very green.

To dye the leaves, I used 9" by 24" natural wool and 9" by 24" yellow wool at the same time in a mixture of 1/32 teaspoon of #490 Blue, 1/16 teaspoon of #119 Yellow and 1/128 teaspoon of #338 Red (PRO Chem). Follow the scrunch method as described above and repeat this green mixture again if necessary to get pieces that are darker at one end and lighter on the other. Then, add 1/128 teaspoon of #338 Red and 1/128 teaspoon of #672 Black (PRO Chem) to the dye bath and dip just the dark ends to dull them.

Brown-Check Border

The brown check that appears with off-white in the border is a mixture of red, yellow, and blue. I describe this color as a brown-red (red mixed with a lot of yellow and enough blue to make it a brown instead of a red). After all, browns are just warm colors (reds, oranges, and yellows) that have been dulled down.

To dye the brown, mix 1/8 teaspoon of Cherry, 1/8 teaspoon of Canary, 1/32 teaspoon of Peacock, and 1/32 teaspoon of Black (Cushing dyes) and dye over a 1/4 yard of Dorr #83 yellow.

Dyeing Tips

Fruit Placemat, *20 1/2" x 14 1/2", #3-cut wool on linen. Designed by Florence Petruchik. Hooked by Maryanne Lincoln, Wrentham, Massachusetts, 1988. Maryanne used scrunch dyeing to prepare the wool for this piece. She used only red, yellow, and blue dyes for all the motifs except the grapes, which also required some black. All the wool was dyed by eye, using no formulas.*

WHEN YOU NEED TO DYE MORE THAN ONE YARD OF THE SAME COLOR AND YOU WANT CONSISTENCY OF COLOR FOR THE WHOLE LOT, BREAK THE DYE JOB DOWN INTO AMOUNTS THAT YOU AND YOUR POTS CAN HANDLE. FOR EXAMPLE, TO DYE THREE YARDS OF WOOL THE SAME COLOR, DYE ONE YARD AT A TIME IF THE FORMULA IS WRITTEN FOR ONE YARD. MEASURE OUT ENOUGH DYE BEFOREHAND FOR EACH YARD IN THREE SEPARATE BEAKERS. THIS WAY YOU CAN DYE ONE YARD AT A TIME, ONE AFTER ANOTHER, WITHOUT HAVING TO STOP TO MEASURE DYE.

However, if the formula can be easily divided in half and your dye pots will hold more wool, instead of dying three, 1-yard batches to get 3 yards, you can dye two 1 1/2-yard batches. This close up will allow more time for other dye projects.

MEASURING WATER

The amount of water for the dye bath depends on the size of the wool and of the dye pot, and which dye procedure you are using. For evenly dyed wool, use plenty of water so that the wool is completely submerged and moves around in the dye bath easily. If you want an unevenly dyed swatch, use less water so that the wool is harder to stir and keep submerged. This is my favorite way of dyeing a background because I like the variegated look when it is hooked in.

MEASURING DYE

If you wish to dye more or less wool than the formula specifies, you'll have to adjust the amount of dye used. If the formula is written for 1/2 yard of wool and you want to dye 1 yard, double the amount of dye. Conversely, if you want to dye only 1/4 yard and the formula is written for 1/2 yard, then use only 1/2 of the formula.

Some fractions in dye formulas

"Keep in mind that water is the mystery ingredient in our dye baths. It may be safe to drink, but it definitely varies in its suitability for dyeing."

are harder to measure than others. The dye spoons that most rug hookers use do not measure 1/3 teaspoon. But if you want to dye only 1/3 yard and the formula is written for 1-yard pieces, what can you do? The easiest thing to do is to consider what you are dyeing and see if you can dye either 1/4 yard or 1/2 yard (a little bit less or more than what you need). This way, you will be able to divide the formula evenly and measure it with the Grey Dye Spoons. (Grey Dye Spoons are polished aluminum, double-ended spoons, measuring 1/128, 1/64, 1/32, 1/16, 1/8, 1/4, 1/2, and 1 teaspoon.)

Use liquid measures if you need to divide formulas unevenly. For example, mix the dye formula for 1 yard of wool in 1 cup of water and use 1/3 cup of it to get the proper amount of dye for 1/3 yard. For those of you familiar with metric measurements, you can mix the dyes in 240 milliliters (ml) of water and use 80 ml of the solution. Using these methods means that you will have dye solution left over. Cover it tightly and label it to use later for more of the same background or another dye project.

EXPERIMENTING WITH COLOR

If you dye using just the primary colors—red, yellow, and blue—it's fun to develop new colors and to experiment with color changes. For example, if you use only one primary color or a combination of two primary colors, the results will be very bright like the colors on a color wheel. However, if you use all three primaries, the results will be duller, depending on how much of the third primary you add. Dye a simple combination to see if the results are what you expected.

The complement of a color is the color that lies opposite on the color wheel: Green is opposite red, blue is opposite orange, yellow is opposite purple. If you want to dull a color, add some of its complement. The more complement you add, the duller it will become. However, if you add too much, the results will look muddy.

USING JAR (GRADATION) DYEING

If you have tried gradation dyeing in jars and have achieved splotchy, uneven results, here are a few tips.

After using boiling water to dissolve the dye in a Pyrex cup, use only hot tap water to distribute the dye solution to the rest of the jars. Don't make the water around the jars hotter than the water in the jars (hot tap water).

Vigorously agitate and stir the wool in the jars as often as you think of it, especially in the first half hour. The idea is to keep the water and the wool in each jar the same temperature throughout. If you don't stir for a few minutes, the temperature will be higher at the bottoms of the jars because they are closer to the heat source.

As you stir, raise the burner heat slowly until the water around the jars simmers. Don't try to get it to a rolling boil. If you raise the heat a bit every time you stir until it reaches about medium low, and then if you hold it there, you will get good results.

Follow my suggestions about putting salt in the water with the dye and wool and then adding vinegar later in the process. A little salt acts as a retardant when working with acid dyes. Do not add more salt if you are having trouble with splotchy results; if anything, add less. Follow the jar dye instructions for the recommended amounts of salt and vinegar.

In each jar, make sure that the wool is covered by water. After the wool is stirred in and completely submerged, add water to within 1" of the top of each jar. Only the part of the wool that is submerged will take up dye, so if it's not completely covered, it will end up splotchy. Poke it down under the water each time you stir.

Keep in mind that water is the mystery ingredient in our dye baths. It may be safe to drink, but it definitely varies in its suitability for dyeing. Try different things until you find what works for you. Be willing to share what you learn on your own, and others will be willing to share with you.

Two Open-Pan Dyeing Methods

Sunset Sheep, *7 1/2" x 5 3/4", #3 and 5-cut wool on burlap. Designed and hooked by Maryanne Lincoln, Wrentham, Massachusett, 1996. Maryanne describes how to dye the wool for this scene's sky and grass.*

SOMETIMES I DEVELOP A NEW DYE FORMULA WITH NO PARTICULAR USE FOR IT IN MIND. OTHER TIMES, AS I HAVE DONE HERE, I PLAN COLORS FOR A PROJECT AND THEN DEVELOP FORMULAS AND DYEING METHODS TO OBTAIN WHAT I NEED.

For my *Sunset Sheep* piece I dyed two wools with different open-pan methods. They were both dyed with PRO Chem Wash Fast acid dyes. The sky was dyed in layers of overlapping color with a dip-dye method. The grass was done by putting the wool into the dye bath all at once so that it acquired the same depth of color all over, but in a slightly mottled manner.

PREPARING THE DYE SOLUTIONS

To dye the sky you will need a 9" x 24" piece of white or off white wool. For the grass you will need a 9" x 24" piece of yellow wool (I used Dorr #83). Soak the wool in hot tap water with a little detergent or Synthrapol added.

Here are the dye solutions for the sky and grass (mix them ahead of time and add as directed):

- 1/128 tsp #119 yellow in 1/2 cup boiling water
- 1/128 tsp #338 red in 1/2 cup boiling water
- 1/128 tsp #490 blue in 1/2 cup boiling water
- 1/64 tsp #672 black in 1/2 cup boiling water
- 1/64 tsp #728 green in 1/2 cup boiling water

Measure each dry dye into a separate container. To help the dye dissolve completely, first make a paste with the dry dye and 1 teaspoon of tepid water and then add the 1/2 cup of boiling water. Stir briskly until the dye is completely dissolved. You will end up with five separate dye solutions. Don't mix them together. Each color will be used separately in careful sequence.

Prepare a dye bath of water and white vinegar. I fill a medium-sized, white enamel saucepan about 1/3 full of water and add 3 tablespoons of white vinegar. Use heavy, loose-fitting rubber gloves and tongs when you dip dye. I dip with my gloves on and then use tongs to poke the wool down and stir it after it is dipped.

HOOKED SUNSET SHEEP

This project offers me the opportunity to tell you how I actually used the dyed materials. I created different textures in this little picture by manipulating the cut and density of the wool in each area.

The sheep is #3-cut, off-white wool hooked in little circles with the loops as close together as possible. I tried to hook a loop in every hole and keep the loops as even as I could.

	X		X		X		X		X		X
X		X		X		X		X		X	

Figure A

X		X		X		X		X		X	
X		X		X		X		X		X	

Figure B

The grass is hooked with #5-cut wool in straight horizontal lines. I hooked a loop in every other hole and skipped every other **Figure A** row of holes. Furthermore, I nested the alternating rows. In other words I hooked the second row with the loops in holes directly above the holes that were skipped in the first row. (The X's in **Figure A** represent the hooked loops.)

The sky is also hooked in horizontal lines. It is #5-cut wool hooked in every other hole and in every other row. This time, I hooked in the holes directly above the ones hooked in the first row (**Figure B**).

The challenge was keeping the strips of wool in order as I cut them lengthwise so that the hooked sky would look like the dyed, uncut wool. There are several ways to accomplish this. In the past, I have arranged the strips in order and placed them on the sticky side of a piece of masking tape so they wouldn't get mixed up. This time, I cut three strips and hooked them right away, and then I cut three more and hooked them. I continued in this manner until I had finished the sky. An advantage to this method is that you don't have a lot of cut wool left over when you are finished with the project.

TO DYE THE SKY

Add 1 or 2 ounces of the yellow solution to the dye bath. Raise the heat to bring the bath to a gentle boil and dip the white wool about 3/4 of the way into the bath. Hold the wool sideways to dip it. The part that goes in the water first should get the most yellow on it, and the yellow should gradually lighten so that the top 2" of material is not colored at all. Keep dipping the wool until the dye bath clears. The water must boil and you must be patient—it takes a few minutes.

Please note that sky colors are usually very light. Add color to the dye bath with that in mind—don't just dump it all in. Add a little at first and then add the rest if it is needed. You might have to use more dye (if you'd like it darker) or more vinegar (if your water is less acidic) than what I have suggested.

After the dye bath is clear, add 1 or 2 ounces of the red solution to it and dip the yellow part of the wool. Leave a little pale yellow at the top but let the red dye flow right over the rest of the yellow. Where the yellow is most intense the red will barely affect it, but near the middle it should color it pale orange. When the water clears, add the rest of the red and dip again, but don't come up over that orange.

When the bath clears, add 1 tablespoon of white vinegar and a drop or two of the blue solution

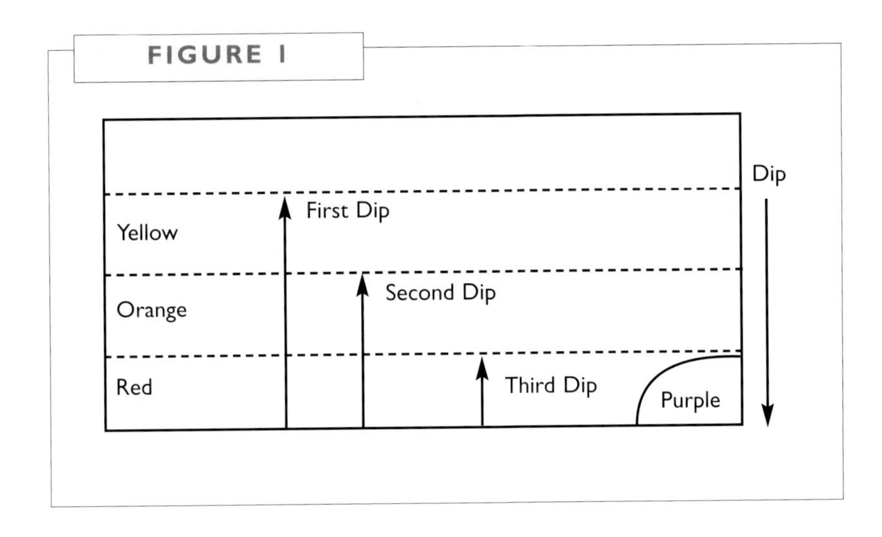

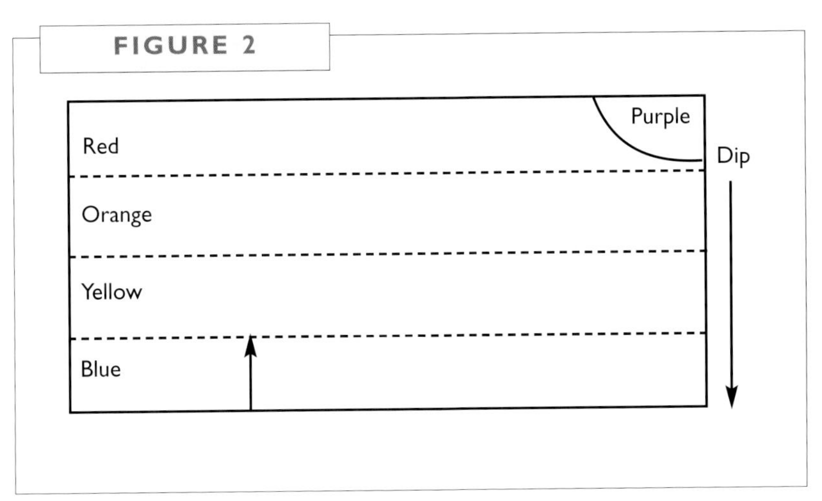

that you have ready. Dip only one small corner of red into the blue for a slightly purple cast on the red. (**Figure 1** shows the four dipping steps.)

Take the wool out after the water clears or start with clean water and 1 tablespoon of white vinegar to which you will add a few drops of the blue solution plus a few drops of the black. Keep a gentle boil going and dip the white edge into this blue dye bath (**Figure 2**). Be careful that you don't let the blue come down over the yellow, and don't add too much blue to start with. Start with just a drop or two and add more until it looks right to you. After the water clears completely, simmer the wool for just a few minutes in water with a few tablespoons of white vinegar to set the colors. Remember that light tints do not require long processing times.

TO DYE THE GRASS

Prepare the dye bath for the grass as you did for the sky Add all of the green dye solution and then put the 9" x 24" yellow wool into the pan. Do not dip it—just push it down into the dye solution so that it is totally submerged. Don't stir it around much as you want it to be slightly mottled, but push it under the solution so all areas will take up some of the green. Bring the solution to a gentle boil and simmer the wool until the water clears. If you think it needs more dye, mix up another 1/64 teaspoon of #728 green, remove the wool, add the dye solution to the bath, and put the wool back into this new bath. Simmer it again until the water clears.

These two dyeing methods can be used with a variety of colors, and not just for backgrounds. The next time you want to achieve subtle gradations in different colors or add character to a solid color, try one of these open-pan methods. They are two easy ways to add interest to your hooked pieces.

Variations on a Theme

Floral chair seat, *17" diameter, #3-cut wool on burlap. Designed by Pearl McGown. Hooked by Maryanne Lincoln, Wrentham, Massachusetts, 1978. Maryanne used 8-value swatches dyed with Cushing dyes to hook this.*

SOMETIMES A DYE FORMULA DOESN'T GIVE YOU THE EXACT COLOR YOU WANT, BUT IF YOU CHANGE THE FORMULA'S INGREDIENTS SLIGHTLY, YOU CAN ARRIVE AT THE DESIRED COLOR. MANY TIMES I EXPERIMENT WITH A BASIC FORMULA—ADDING A LITTLE MORE OF THIS DYE, A LITTLE LESS OF THAT ONE—UNTIL I AM SATISFIED WITH THE RESULTING HUE.

Country Blue is one of my favorite Country Colors formulas. (Country Colors is the name of a series of dye formulas I've devised and sell.) I have used Country Blue in many ways over the years. Sometimes I use the formula just the way it is written, but other times I adjust it a little to make it brighter or duller. I also dye over wool with it for a background or sky instead of using it just for a multiple value swatch. Other times I vary the proportions of the two dyes that make up the formula, or add a little red or yellow to swing the color around the color wheel.

These formulas all started with Country Blue. They call for PRO

Floral mat, *12 1/2" diameter, #3-cut wool on cotton warp. Designed and hooked by Maryanne Lincoln, Wrentham, Massachusetts, 1997. Maryanne used variations of one basic formula to create all the colors used in this mat.*

Chem wash-fast acid dyes, but I discuss achieving similar colors with Cushing dyes at the end of the article.

The basic formula for Country Blue is:

3/32 teaspoon #672 black
1/16 teaspoon #490 blue

When the formula is dyed over six 6" x 24" pieces of off-white wool using the jar dyeing method, the result is a 6-value swatch.

VARYING THE FORMULA

Let me suggest some simple ways to change this basic formula to create interesting variations. To achieve a brighter blue, decrease the black to 1/16 teaspoon. For a slight purple cast, add 1/128 teaspoon #338 red. To make Country Blue a bit green, add 1/64 teaspoon #119 yellow to the formula. To create an old looking blue, decrease the blue dye and dye over Dorr #42 beige wool; for example, 3/32 teaspoon #672 black plus 1/32 teaspoon #490 blue, or 1/8 teaspoon #672 black plus 1/32 teaspoon #490 blue.

The last formula has four parts black to one part blue, and the one before it has three parts black to one part blue. Although there seems to be an overpowering amount of black, that is not a mistake. Because of the strength of the #490 blue, the resulting color is definitely a blue and not a gray.

Another simple way to get these same variations is to use the Country Blue formula as written and dye over pastel wool instead of off-white. Dye over pale blue for a brighter blue and over light gray for a duller blue. Country Blue dyed over light pink yields a slightly purple blue, and over light yellow a greenish blue.

I played with the Country Blue formula and came up with a whole palette of soft colors. The box on page 56 lists the formulas I used to hook the floral mat. If you like the colors but wish they were a bit brighter, decrease the black by 1/32 teaspoon in each formula. The swatch will be the same color, only brighter.

Each of these formulas was dyed over 6"x 24" off-white wool using the jar dyeing method. The "6" after each color name means I dyed 6 values. The exception is Corn; I dyed 8 values to show you the beautiful ivory color that is possible by carefully combining these bright dyes.

HOOKING THE DYED WOOL

I designed the small floral mat and hooked it with #3-cut wool on cotton warp. The very center is one of the values of Corn. The large petals with hearts are hooked alternately with Wisteria and Dusky Lilac. Seafoam forms the leaves, and Winter Bark the veins. For the center, hearts, and outer area I used a blend of Antique Rose and Old Clay Pots, with accent lines of Winter Bark.

Here are samples of the swatches Maryanne dyed for the mat.

USING CUSHING DYES

There are many published formulas for soft, muted colors made with Cushing dyes, including my Country Colors formulas for Victorian Rose, Country Iris, Country Lilac, Magnolia, White Sand, Sage Green, Moss Green, Aquagreen, and Golden Basket. There are also dye books available that are written for Cushing dyes, including *Antique Colours for Primitive Rugs* (W Cushing & Co., 1996) and *TOD Books I, II,* and *III*. Investigate some of them; try some of the formulas. The TOD books were written when the old Cushing union dyes were in use. With the new acid dyes the results will not be the same, so you may have to experiment with the formulas. Add your own touches to the formulas as I suggest above or dye over different colors and textures of wool.

TOD Books I, II, and *III* are still available from rug hooking suppliers and teachers. Many of the colors remind me of the soft colors I developed for this chapter. Of course, there are also many formulas in the books for brighter colors.

The chair seat on page 54 was hooked with 8-value swatches dyed with the following formulas as found in *TOD Books I* and *II*. It is a Pearl McGown chair seat design to which I have added a larger hooked border. The background is hooked with camel colored wool that I purchased at a local mill end store.

- Yellow daisy = Family 33, #108
- Red iris and rose = Family 4, #14
- Blue morning glory = Family 7, #22
- Green tulip and daisy leaves = Family 19, #63
- Yellow-green rose leaves and foliage = Family 15, #50
- Brown shaded border = Family 17, #56

As I've said before, the best way to arrive at colors you are pleased with is to experiment. Don't be afraid to try something new. The more you dye, the more you'll learn, and pretty soon you'll be developing your own formulas.

FORMULAS

These formulas correspond with the wool samples pictured above.

Antique Rose -6

3/32 tsp #672 black
3/32 tsp #233 orange
3/32 tsp #338 red

Dusky Lilac -6

3/32 tsp #672 black
1/32 tsp #490 blue
1/32 tsp #338 red

Seafoam -6

3/32 tsp #672 black
1/32 tsp #490 blue
3/32 tsp #119 yellow

Corn -8

3/128 tsp #672 black
3/128 tsp #233 orange
1/4 tsp #119 yellow
1/256 tsp #490 blue
(estimate—it's half of the 1/128 tsp)

Old Clay Pots/Terra Cotta Brick -6

1/16 tsp #672 black
1/8 tsp #233 orange
1/32 tsp #338 red

Winter Bark -6

3/32 tsp #672 black
1/64 tsp #490 blue
3/32 tsp #233 orange

Wisteria -6

3/32 tsp #672 black
1/64 tsp #490 blue
3/64 tsp #338 red

Adjusting Formulas to Match Colors

The Owl's Nest, *21" x 14", #5-cut wool on burlap. Designed by Jean Armstrong. Hooked by Maryanne Lincoln, Wrentham, Massachusetts, 1998.*

AFTER HOOKING MY FIRST RUG WITH EDNA CALLIS IN THE 1960S, I BEGAN TO DREAM ABOUT DYEING WOOL TO MATCH THE COLORS I SAW IN MY MIND. I DIDN'T HAVE ENOUGH EXPERIENCE AT THE TIME TO START FROM SCRATCH, BUT I HAD SAMPLES OF FORMULAS AND DYE BOOKLETS TO WORK FROM AT HOME. I WOULD THINK ABOUT COLORS WHILE I WAS HOOKING AND THEN LATER TRY OUT MY IDEAS.

At that time, we were struggling with dye colors that were not consistent from package to package. Cushing's Turquoise Blue union dye was a beautiful color, but sometimes it dyed too bright. Edna had to adjust formulas, and as she did, I watched and learned. Eventually I decided to try adjusting formulas to accomplish other things, not just fix problems. That was the beginning of a long adventure with color, which is still exciting after more than 38 years.

START WITH WHAT YOU KNOW

One of the reasons to adjust a formula is to match a color. Examine the color you need to match and compare it to samples or swatches for which you already have the formulas. When you find a close match, try the formula on some small pieces of wool. Adjust the dye amounts as necessary to

"Look closely at the Foxglove swatch on page 59 and you will see that the lighter values are a peachy hue while the darker values are in the red family. In my opinion that is why the color is appealing. It is not color-wheel bright and yet it seems to sparkle because of the analogous colors."

THREE FORMULAS FOR JAR DYEING

The following formulas use the jar dye method to dye 6 or 7-value swatches. The dyes listed in the formulas are Cushing Perfection dyes.

Foxglove

To be dyed in 7 values
over 3" x 24" white wool.
1/8 tsp Old Rose
1/16 tsp Garnet

Mix the dyes together in 1 cup of boiling water. (Place the dry dyes in a 1-cup glass measure. Add a few teaspoons of tepid water and stir to make a paste. Fill the cup with boiling water and stir it briskly until the dyes are completely dissolved.) Distribute the solution by the jar method into 7 jars. Add to each jar the following amounts of dry Maize dye: 1/64 teaspoon in the jar with the lightest solution; 1/64 teaspoon in the next lightest solution; 1/128 teaspoon in each of the rest of the jars. Stir the contents of each jar briskly and continue with jar dyeing to dye the wool.

Pink Scroll

To be dyed in 6 values
over 9" x 12" white wool.
1/8 tsp Old Rose
1/16 tsp Garnet
1/128 tsp Turquoise Blue
1/64 tsp Black

Mix the dyes together in 1 cup of boiling water. Distribute the solution by the jar method into 6 jars. Next add 1/64 teaspoon of dry Maize dye to each jar. Stir the contents of each jar briskly and continue with jar dyeing to dye the wool.

Peacock Green

To be dyed in 6 values
over 9" x 24" natural wool.
1/128 tsp Cherry
1/8 tsp Peacock
1/8 tsp Canary
1/128 tsp Black

Mix the dyes in 1 cup of boiling water. Distribute by the jar method into 6 quart jars. (You must use quart jars to dye these large pieces.) Stir the contents of each jar briskly and continue with jar dyeing to dye the wool.

achieve the target color and dye it again.

I recently used this method to match a wool sample I received in the mail that came with a request that I dye more of that color. The hue was not one from my regular formulas, but it looked familiar. Tucked on my shelf behind some wool, I found a swatch called Foxglove. At first glance I thought it was exactly what was needed, but when I compared it to the sample, I found that my swatch was a bit brighter.

Look closely at the Foxglove swatch on page 59 and you will see that the lighter values are a peachy hue while the darker values are in the red family. In my opinion that is why the color is appealing. It is not color-wheel bright and yet it seems to sparkle because of the analogous colors (neighbors on the color wheel). Now take a close look at Pink Scroll, the color I needed to match. It also has light values in a peachy color and darker values in red, but it is not as bright as Foxglove.

Starting with the Foxglove formula saved me an hour or two of fiddling around. I simply had to figure out how to adjust the dye amounts to get the Pink Scroll swatch. I worked out a version of the adjusted formula,

Maryanne describes how to adjust the formula for Foxglove (center) to create Pink Scroll (top). The formula for Peacock Green (bottom) is also included in the box on page 58.

wrote it in my dye log, and then dyed it.

ADJUSTING THE FORMULA

Look at the formulas in the sidebar and notice my changes. The amounts of Old Rose and Garnet are the same in both swatches, but I needed to add something to dull the color a little. A color can be dulled by adding a bit of its complement or black, or both. Since I wanted to tone down some of the bright peach (which is in the orange family), I needed to add its complement, blue. I added 1/128 teaspoon Turquoise Blue to dull the orange, and I also added 1/64 teaspoon Black to make the color a little smoky. My trained eye knew it needed some of both.

I am giving you the formulas for Foxglove, the original formula, and Pink Scroll, the adjusted formula. Both peach-to-red swatches are dyed over Dorr's white wool. I am also including the formula for Peacock Green because it is a great companion color to either of the red swatches. It is dyed over Dorr's natural wool.

ORIENTAL TABLE MAT

An 8' x 10' kilim in my family room inspired the color plan for the mini Caucasian rug on page 57. Of course, I added my own variations and had fun with my interpretation.

The dyed red wool I had on hand was too bright for what I envisioned, so I tore off a piece and overdyed it with a little green to dull it slightly. In effect, this was the same as adjusting the formula by adding a little of its complement to dull the red. I used the bright red for the outline of the center zigzag and on a few of the motifs in the wide black border. The kilim combines red and orange in a fashion similar to that in my miniature Caucasian; left to my own imagination I probably wouldn't have thought to use them together. The black is off-the-bolt wool, as is the border line of dark blue-green.

"One of the reasons to adjust a formula is to match a color."

Snow White

Left: **Snowman 1**, *6 1/2" x 7 1/2", #4- and 5-cut wool on burlap. Designed and hooked by Maryanne Lincoln, Wrentham, Massachusetts, 2000. Right:* **Snowman 2**, *6 1/2" x 7 1/2", #4- and 5-cut wool on burlap. Designed and hooked by Maryanne Lincoln, Wrentham, Massachusetts, 2000.*

WHEN WE WANT TO EXPRESS THAT SOMETHING IS UNTAINTED, WE OFTEN SAY IT IS AS PURE AS THE DRIVEN SNOW. THIS IS MISLEADING, HOWEVER, BECAUSE SNOW IS NOT PURE WHITE. IF YOU'RE HOOKING A PICTURE THAT CONTAINS SNOW, BE AWARE THAT SNOW TAKES ON MANY HUES DEPENDING ON THE TYPE AND TIME OF DAY, THE COLOR OF OTHER OBJECTS IN THE PICTURE, AND THE MOOD OF THE SCENE. YOU MAY DECIDE ON A SEPIA TONE FOR THE SHADOWS ON SNOW, TREES, BUILDINGS, AND SO ON. OR YOU MAY WANT TO ENLIVEN THE SNOW BY HAVING IT REFLECT SOME SUNSET COLORS FROM THE SKY.

Spend some time looking at other artists' winter scenes for ideas. I have a collection of old Currier and Ives calendar pictures with lots of different snowscapes that I often refer to or show to students for color ideas. I want to show you a simple way to dye wool for snow scenes to create deep shadows, rocks and trees, and lightly mottled snow.

For this dyeing exercise, prepare three pieces of 12" x 24" white wool. Usually I tell you to soak all your wool, but this time soak only one of the pieces in hot tap water and a little Synthrapol or dish detergent. You will put the other two into the dye pot dry, first one and then the other.

FORMULAS

If you're using Cushing acid dyes, mix up a half-strength solution of the Winter Cedar formula from my book *Recipes From the Dye Kitchen* (*Rug Hooking* magazine, 1999). Here is the formula at half strength:

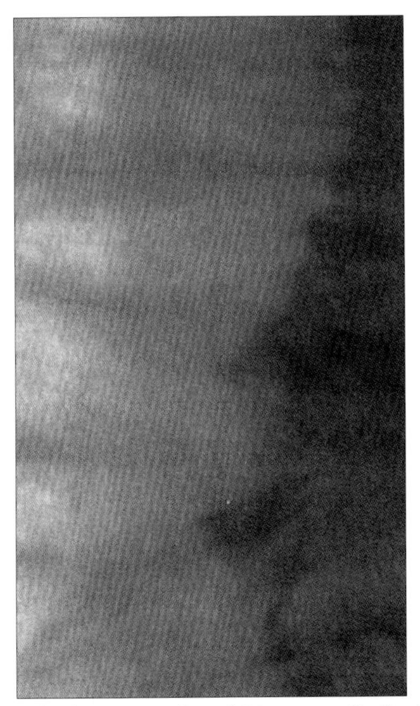

The first piece of wool Maryanne dyed is the darkest and can be used for tree trunks and rocks in a winter scene.

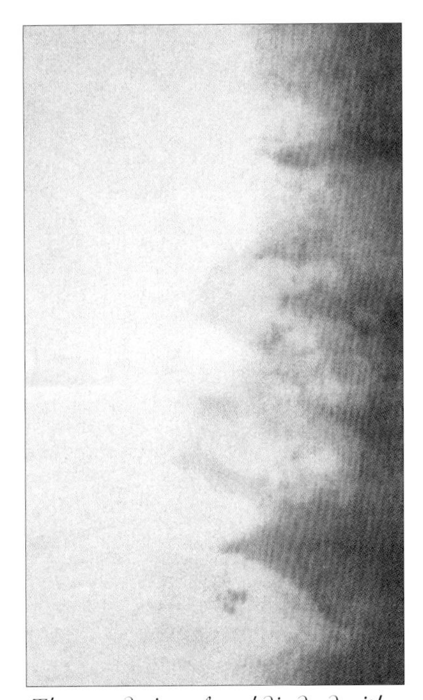

The second piece of wool dip dyed with Maryanne's formula is appropriate for snow with deep shadows.

Scrunching the final piece of wool into the dye pot results in lightly mottled fabric, perfect for snow with light shadows.

1/4 tsp Canary
1/64 tsp Peacock
1/128 tsp Black
1/64 tsp Cherry

Dissolve the dyes in 1 cup of boiling water. (Place the dry dyes in a 1-cup glass measuring cup and add a few teaspoons of tepid water to make a paste. Add boiling water to the 1-cup level and stir the solution briskly until the dye is dissolved.) You will use about 1/4 cup of this formula.

For PRO Chemical & Dye brand acid dyes, use this half-strength mixture of Winter Bark from *Recipes From the Dye Kitchen*:

3/64 tsp #672 black
1/128 tsp #490 blue
3/64 tsp #233 orange

Dissolve the dyes in 1 cup of boiling water as described above. You will use about 1/4 cup of this formula.

If you're wondering why you need to mix a whole cup of formula when you need only 1/4 cup, it's because it is difficult to measure less than 1/128 teaspoon of dye as you would have to do with the PRO Chem blue and the Cushing Black. (When you need half the amount of 1/128 teaspoon, mix 1/128 teaspoon in 1 cup of boiling water and use 1/2 cup of it.)

You will need a large pan to dye these formulas. I use a rectangular pan that measures about 15" x 8" x 3". Put about 1" of hot water and 4 tablespoons of vinegar in the pan and turn the burner to high heat. Add 1/4 cup of the dye solution to the dye bath and, while wearing heavy rubber gloves, carefully hold the soaked 12" x 24" piece of wool sideways and dip just the first couple of inches into the pan. Keep it moving up and down in the hot dye bath, dipping it slightly deeper each time. Since there isn't much depth to the bath, it is easy to control the dyeing. You want to use up more than half of the color in the bath to dye this first piece of wool, which you can use on tree trunks and rocks in a simple winter scene. Place the whole piece in the dye bath while there is still some color left in the bath.

Remove all but the darkest edge you dipped first and stack the wet wool accordion style at one end of the pan. Let it rest, mostly out of the water, while you do the next step.

Now take one of the dry pieces of 12" x 24" white wool and dip it sideways into the remaining bath, gradually lowering it as you dip. This piece will be perfect for hooking deep shadows on snow.

Because the wool is dry, not only will it absorb color from the water, it will also absorb some of the water. Push this second wool piece next to the first piece and stack it with its darkest edge in the dye bath.

With the remaining water a fraction of an inch deep and only slightly colored, quickly take the last piece of wool and cram it down into the remaining shallow dye bath at one end of the pan, working it with your gloved hands so all of it goes in the water at some point. The minimal color will mottle the wool and make it good for hooking lifelike snow, with its light peaks and dull valleys. The dry wool will absorb the rest of the color and most of the remaining water. Make sure there is enough liquid in the pan to steam the wool, then quickly cover the pan loosely with foil and let the water simmer for about 10 minutes. Remove the wool, rinse it, and allow it to dry.

This procedure must be completed rather quickly so there will be enough color in the dye bath for the second and third pieces. It took just a few minutes for me to use this dyeing method on the wool shown on page 61.

As you can see with my hooked snowmen, plain white wool sometimes works fine for snow. However, there are times when you'll want more color, and with this method you can add it easily.

FOR EXPERIENCED DYERS

Sometimes I like to add quite a bit of color to my snow. For instance, I like to mix up weak amounts of red, yellow, blue, orange, and black dyes and then dye by eye to create beautiful snow and ice with shadows and reflections.

Depending on the size of the project and the amount of snow or ice I need, I sometimes start by dissolving $^1/_{64}$ or $^1/_{128}$ teaspoon of each dye in 1 cup of boiling water so I have the five colors mixed separately. Then, using my knowledge of complementary colors, I create some combinations by pouring a little of the individual solutions into another beaker and applying that mixture to soaked wool.

For example, I may mix green by pouring a little yellow into an empty beaker, adding blue to it until I get green, and then putting in a few drops of red to make a grayed green, which I then spoon onto the wool in a shallow pan. Then I may pour some black into another beaker, add a few drops of blue to it until I get a bluish gray, and then apply this dye to the same wool, overlapping some of the green. If my scene is to have a sunset sky or if there is a red house, sleigh, or clothing in the picture, I might add a little of the red liquid to another empty beaker, add a touch of orange solution, a few drops of black, and some extra water to dilute it and then apply this to the wool in the dye pan. For a weak purple that's nice for shadows, start with a little red, add a few drops of blue to make purple, add some black to smoke it up, and then apply the dye to your wool. I keep mixing these weak combinations and applying them to the wool until I get the depth of color and variation I want. Use as much of the solutions as necessary to achieve the look you want. Squish the wool around with your gloved hand as you add each color so you don't end up with bright splotches.

When you achieve the color you want, add vinegar and enough water to create steam, cover the pan loosely with foil, and steam the wool for a few minutes. Allow time for the wool to absorb the color the whole way through.

THE SNOWMEN

My snowmen are part of a series of hooked decorations I make and sell. You could hook a few for quick, easy gifts. They're both the same pattern, but their expressions and hats make them distinctive. I used the reverse stitch to hook the undyed blue background. One snowman picture has a dark blue outline around the outside edge; the other has a brown hound's-tooth outline. Both are lined on the back with the brown hound's-tooth wool. Before attaching the lining to the back of a snowman I machine stitched around the lining, then sewed it to the hooking with small, nearly invisible hand stitches.

I used plain black wool for the hats and scraps of dip-dyed blue and green wool for the scarves. For the star-shaped buttons I used soft rose-colored wool scraps; for the eyes and mouth, scraps of black; and for the carrot nose a scrap of orange. Each snowman is outlined in medium gray-brown. The snow is hooked with plain white wool, also in the reverse stitch.

CHAPTER FOUR

GRADATION DYEING

New Methods and Formulas

Maryanne provides the Cushing formulas for five new colors in this section. She also describes various gradation dyeing methods, which you can use to create the hooked top of this small **card box**.

DO YOU DYE GRADATION SWATCHES WITH A METHOD OTHER THAN MY JAR DYEING METHOD (ALSO KNOWN AS THE POUR METHOD)? AT TIMES MY HEAD GETS STUCK IN A FOG BANK AND IT TAKES ME MONTHS TO REALIZE THAT I HAVEN'T TALKED ABOUT SOMETHING IMPORTANT, LIKE THE DIFFERENT METHODS OF GRADATION DYEING. EVEN THOUGH IT IS MY FAVORITE WAY OF DYEING SWATCHES, MY JAR METHOD IS CERTAINLY NOT THE ONLY WAY TO DYE THEM.

Many long-time rug hookers dye swatches with an open pan method. Others use a jar method, but they measure out spoonfuls of dye solution for the different values instead of pouring and refilling measuring cups. Will the formulas and colors I recommend

From the left, Rusty Orange, Lady Slipper, Mahogany, Winter Cedar, and Foliage.

for use with the pour method work with other methods? The simple answer is yes. Please make note of the following information, however.

DYEING VARIATIONS

The pour method is based on a dye solution made with 1 cup of boiling water, half of which is poured into the first jar. Then the cup is refilled with fresh hot tap water back to the 1-cup level, stirred, and half is poured into the second jar. This operation is repeated until the required number of jars contain dye solution.

When I dye six or more swatches at one time (so there are six or more pieces of wool in each jar), I mix the dye solution in a 2-cup measure and use half of it each time. The important thing is that you use half of the solution for each value no matter how many pieces are in each jar.

The other common jar dye method is done using 1/2 or 1 cup of solution, from which you measure out amounts with spoons according to a chart. How much you measure for each value depends on the procedure and what the formula author tells you. You can use this type of gradation dyeing with my Country Colors formulas or any other gradation formulas I have developed for *Rug Hooking* magazine, this book, and my color course notebook. You will get results similar to what I get with the pour method.

Some of you do all of your dyeing with an open-pan method. Feel free to use it instead of what I use. The results with it will be satisfactory, but slightly different from my samples of jar-dyed swatches, because the wool takes up the dye more quickly in a pan. But different is okay. Just be consistent with what you do and keep a log so you will be able to replicate the color if necessary.

DYE BOOKLETS

Sometimes I dye formulas from one of the many dye booklets available. I usually use the pour method even for swatches created by spoon measuring. I just adapt the formula by adding the dry dyes to 1 cup of boiling water and then following the jar dye method as described above. Occasionally, to fulfill a customer's request, I will follow the author's directions to the letter.

Some of the more popular dye books I have used are *TOD Book I* and *II* by Lydia Hicks, *Color Flow 1* and *2* by Jane Elliott, *Green Mountain Colors* by Anne Ashworth and Jean Armstrong, *Rug Hookers' Dye Manual* by Connie Charleson, and *The Rug-Hooker's Dye Manual* by Clarisse C. Cox.

If you don't have these booklets, but are a member of the Association of Traditional Rug Hooking Artists or the National McGown Guild, you may be able to borrow the books from these guilds. Some of the books are also available for sale through teachers or suppliers.

"Even though it is my favorite way of dyeing swatches, my jar method is certainly not the only way to dye them."

"Will the formulas and colors I recommend for use with the pour method work with other methods? The simple answer is yes."

NEW CUSHING FORMULAS

Now that we've discussed dyeing methods, try your hand at some new formulas of mine, They are Lady Slipper (a pink hue), Winter Cedar (green), Foliage, Mahogany, and Rusty Orange. They are created with Cushing's Canary, Cherry, Peacock, and Black dyes. For each formula, mix the dyes in 1 cup of boiling water. Dye a gradation swatch with the jar method, using a 6" x 24" piece of wool in each jar.

I use white wool when I dye these colors for the first time and for the sample sets that I assemble, because it clearly reveals the color of the dye mixture. You are free to dye over any color you want. If you dye over natural wool the results will be similar. If you dye over other colors, the results will be noticeably different, but you may be pleasantly surprised. For example, for a green that is more of a grass color, dye Foliage over pale yellow wool.

The most important thing about the wool when you are dyeing a gradation swatch is that each value should be dyed over the same total number of square inches to achieve an evenly stepped gradation. A 6" x 24" piece is 144 square inches. If you only have odds and ends of wool to dye over, you may not have a 6" x 24" piece for each jar. Maybe you only have half-yard pieces of wool. Use an 8" x 18" piece instead; it still is 144 square inches. A 12" x 12" piece would also be equivalent.

In other words, use wool in a size that is as close as possible to the total square inches necessary. If you use more wool in each jar, the values will be a little lighter. If you use less wool in each jar, the values will be a little darker. Just be sure to use the same total amount in each jar. Keep track of the amount you dyed in a notebook so you can refer to it at another time.

Foliage

1/2 teaspoon Canary
3/16 teaspoon Peacock
1/32 teaspoon Black
1/32 teaspoon Cherry

Winter Cedar

1/2 teaspoon Canary
1/32 teaspoon Peacock
1/64 teaspoon Black
1/32 teaspoon Cherry

Lady Slipper

1/8 teaspoon Canary
1/128 teaspoon Peacock
1/128 teaspoon Black
3/8 teaspoon Cherry

Mahogany

1/2 teaspoon Canary
1/32 teaspoon Peacock
1/64 teaspoon Black
3/16 teaspoon Cherry

Rusty Orange

1 teaspoon Canary
1/128 teaspoon Peacock
1/8 teaspoon Cherry

THE HOOKED BOX TOP

The small hooked project on page 63 is a playing card box with a hooked top. The design is an oval dollhouse pattern by Pearl McGown that I adapted to fit the box. I hooked it on burlap with leftover #3 strips from two of my Country Color 8-value swatches, Magnolia 1 and 2. The background is undyed off-white wool. Use one of the methods described above to dye the Country Colors, or use your favorite formula and pattern to create a small piece to decorate a similar container. Mine is great for storing T-pins, tacks, and a hook or two.

Charcoal Colors

Charcoal Rose, *8 1/4" x 7 1/2", #3-cut wool on cotton rug warp. Designed and hooked by Maryanne Lincoln, Wrentham, Massachusetts, 1999. Maryanne dyed the wool for this rose with a formula built from a gradation of black.*

HOOKING A REALISTIC ROSE CAN BE A GREAT TEST OF ONE'S DYEING AND HOOKING SKILLS. THE SINGLE ROSE I CREATED IS TYPICAL OF ONE YOU MIGHT FIND ON A LARGE PATTERN. (CAN YOU IMAGINE HOOKING FOUR OR FIVE OF THESE LARGE, MULTI-PETALED FLOWERS ALONG WITH THE LEAVES THAT WOULD ACCOMPANY THEM?) I DESIGNED THIS ROSE AS A CHALLENGE—IT DEFINITELY ISN'T A BEGINNERS PROJECT.

There are petals that wrap around and define the center and petals that flow outward from the base. My careful placement of values and careful hooking assured a successful blossom. I found, however, that the direction of my hooking lines and the fingering of values were difficult to determine at first, but through trial and error I figured it out. Also, because I was using a swatch that had very dull darker values, I had to be cautious about not using too much of the two darkest values.

Using a swatch that goes from a smoky dark version of a color to a very bright version in the light values makes it easier to create a shaded flower than using just a straight dark-to-light gradation swatch. The dark values help create shadows, and the light, bright values bring up the edges and highlighted areas.

Based on this observation, I created a new group of formulas that build from a weak gradation of black. Below are formulas for the four swatches pictured on page 67, plus a few additional formulas for you to try.

FORMULAS FOR PRO CHEM DYES

The formulas for Charcoal Cherry, Shrimp, Seawater, and Rose employ PRO Chemical & Dye wash-fast acid dyes. Each

Clockwise from top left are Charcoal Shrimp, Charcoal Seawater, Charcoal Jade, and Charcoal Cherry.

was dyed over 4" x 24" white wool, except Charcoal Rose, which was dyed over 4 1/2" x 24" white wool. The formulas are written for the jar dyeing method. Refer to page 44 for jar dyeing instructions.

Charcoal Cherry
(6 values)

Place 1/8 teaspoon #672 black in a 1-cup glass measure and add a few teaspoons of tepid water. Stir it to make a paste. Pour in 1 cup of boiling water and stir it briskly until the dye has completely dissolved. Distribute the solution into 6 jars according to the jar dyeing method. Then add 1/32 teaspoon #338 red to each jar. Briskly stir the solution in each jar and continue with the jar dyeing steps.

Charcoal Shrimp
(6 values)

Dissolve 1/32 teaspoon #672 black in 1 cup of boiling water as described above, then distribute the solution into 6 jars according to the jar dyeing method. Next mix 1/16 teaspoon #119 yellow and 1/32 teaspoon #338 red in 1 cup of boiling water and add 3 teaspoons of the solution to each jar. Stir the solution and continue with jar dyeing.

Charcoal Seawater
(6 or 8 values)

Dissolve 1/16 teaspoon #672 black in 1 cup of boiling water as described above and distribute the solution to 6 or 8 jars according to the jar dyeing method. Next mix 3/16 teaspoon #490 blue and 1/16 teaspoon #119 yellow in 1/2 cup of boiling water. Add 2 teaspoons of this solution to each jar. Stir the solution and continue jar dyeing.

Charcoal Rose
(6 values)

The hooked rose on page 66 was done with this swatch variation. Dissolve 1/16 teaspoon #672 black in 1 cup of boiling water as described above and distribute the solution to 6 jars according to the jar dyeing method. Then dissolve 1/32 teaspoon #338 red and 1/64 teaspoon #119 yellow in 1 cup of boiling water and add 2 1/2 tablespoons of this mixture to each jar. Stir the solution and continue jar dyeing to color the swatch.

FORMULAS FOR CUSHING

Dye each of the Cushing formulas below over 4 1/2" x 24" white wool. As with the PRO Chem formulas, these Cushing formulas are used with the jar dyeing method.

Charcoal Rose
(6 values)

Place 1/32 teaspoon Black in a 1-cup glass measure and add a few teaspoons of tepid water. Stir it to make a paste. Pour in 1 cup of boiling water and stir it until the dye has dissolved. Distribute the solution into 6 jars according to the jar dyeing method. Then mix 1/32 teaspoon Cherry and 1/64 teaspoon Canary in 1 cup of boiling water and add 2 1/2 tablespoons of the solution to each jar. Continue jar dyeing.

In this formula, I suggest using 1/32 teaspoon of Black instead of 1/16 teaspoon as I did in the PRO Chem Charcoal Rose formula, because experience tells me that Cushing's Black is stronger than PRO Chem's #672 black. Therefore, it is wise to use less so the red mixture you add will have a chance to show up when added to the black gradation. Another way to offset the stronger black would be to double the strength of the red and yellow mix-

Twisted Scroll, *13" diameter, #3-cut wool on burlap. Designed by Jane McGown Flynn. Hooked by Maryanne Lincoln, Wrentham, Massachusetts, 1986. The scrolls in this chair pad were hooked with wool dyed with Maryanne's Charcoal Jade formula.*

ture. Try it both ways and see which one you like the best.

Other beautiful variations of this charcoal color would be green, yellow-green, red-purple, purple, blue, and possibly a yellow. Use my formulas and then try creating some of your own.

Charcoal Blue (6 values)

Dissolve 1/16 teaspoon Black in 1 cup of boiling water as described above and distribute the solution into 6 jars. Then add 1/32 teaspoon Peacock to each jar. Stir the solution in the jars briskly to dissolve the dye. Continue with the jar dyeing.

Charcoal Jade (8 values)

This is one of my favorite Country Colors, which is also called Smoky Jade. Dissolve 1/8 teaspoon Black in 1 cup of boiling water as described and distribute the solution into 8 jars. Then mix 1/16 teaspoon Hunter AF, 1/128 teaspoon Bronze, and 1/128 teaspoon Turquoise in 1 cup of boiling water and stir this solution into each jar according to the chart (Light-to-Dark) below. Continue jar dyeing to color the swatch.

With an 8-value swatch of Charcoal Jade I hooked an over-and-under twining scroll design by Jane McGown Flynn. The chair seat's background is charcoal. The design was tricky to work out because I had to carefully place the values on the arms of scrolls that go over other arms, and because I had only 8 values to work with. I love the look of the finished scroll and the way your eye travels around and through the design.

ANOTHER VARIATION

Another variation of charcoal swatches is one built from a gradation of brown instead of black. Mix up a favorite brown and distribute it into jars according to the jar dyeing method, then mix up a brighter color to add by the spoonful to each jar (you decide how much). Then add wool and dye the swatch. For example, a green mixture (a combination of blue and yellow) added to a brown gradation makes a beautiful swatch. If done carefully, the darker values are brown and the lighter values are green.

One suggestion is to mix the basic brown gradation at about half strength to allow for the addition of the lighter color. You don't have to do this, but otherwise the brown may overwhelm the added color. Experiment with different combinations and colors—that's the fun of dyeing.

LIGHT-TO-DARK

Lightest	=	2 tablespoons
Next light	=	4 tablespoons
Third light	=	6 tablespoons
Middle light	=	8 tablespoons
Middle dark	=	5 1/2 tablespoons
Third dark	=	5 tablespoons
Next dark	=	4 tablespoons
Darkest	=	4 tablespoons

Transitional Gradation Swatches

Padulas, *14" diameter, #5- and 6-cut wool on burlap. Designed by Jane McGown Flynn. Hooked by Maryanne Lincoln, Wrentham, Massachusetts, 1999. Maryanne says, "It was a challenge to balance the values [in this piece] because I wanted white flowers and they are all on one side of the design. I think it looks best with the large, five-petaled flower at the bottom."*

THE FORMULAS I HAVE CREATED FOR YOU THIS TIME ARE TRANSITIONAL GRADATIONS (EXCEPT FOR THE ONE THAT IS THE BASE GRADATION FOR ALL OF THEM). ONE OF THE WAYS WEBSTER'S NEW COLLEGIATE DICTIONARY DEFINES TRANSITION IS "A MOVEMENT, DEVELOPMENT, OR EVOLUTION FROM ONE STATE, STAGE, OR PLACE TO ANOTHER; CHANGE." THE SAME DICTIONARY DEFINES GRADATION AS "A GRADUAL PASSING FROM ONE TINT OR SHADE TO ANOTHER."

Thus, each swatch created with these formulas (except the base gradation) shows a transition of color flowing from the dark value of one hue to the light value of another. Compare the lightest values of each swatch with the darkest values and you will see the change in hue. There is more than one way to dye a transitional gradation swatch. However, I have created this new group of formulas using just one of the ways. The base gradation, which is the first step in each formula, is what creates a transition from light to dark in a neutral color. The second step of the formula produces a transition in a particular hue.

If you compare **Step 1** in all of the following formulas, you will see that they all contain PRO

Maryanne provides the formulas for the transitional gradations shown here. In the top row, from left to right, they are Rich Gold, Bittersweet, and Red Hot; in the middle row, left to right, Emerald-Green, Jewel-Blue, and Grape; in the bottom row, the base gradation.

Chem dyes #490 blue and #233 orange. Although the amounts of blue and orange are smaller in two of the formulas than they are in the others, the proportion of blue to orange (1:4) is the same in all of them, including the base gradation.

FOR ADVANCED DYERS

Those of you who have done jar dyeing know that you first dissolve the dry dyes in 1 cup of boiling water and then pour half of the solution into the first of your 6 or 8 jars. Essentially, you are using half of the total dry dye for this first, darkest value. Furthermore, you know by experience that you can cut the basic dry dye formula in half to eliminate this darkest value.

When I was planning to dye Emerald-Green and Rich Gold, I decided I did not want the darkest value in my base gradation for those colors, so I started with half the amounts of blue and orange instead of mixing up the total amount. The proportions remain the same, however—1 part blue to 4 parts orange.

FORMULAS

All of the formulas use PRO Chemical & Dye wash-fast acid dyes, and are to be dyed over 6" x 24" natural wool for each value.

Base Gradation

1/32 tsp #490 blue
1/8 tsp #233 orange

Dissolve the dyes in 1 cup of boiling water. (Place the dry dyes in a 1-cup glass measure and add a few teaspoons of tepid water to make a paste. Add boiling water to the 1-cup level and stir the solution briskly until the dyes are completely dissolved.) Dye 6 values with the jar dyeing method. (See page 44 for instructions.)

For **Step 1** in each of the following formulas, dissolve the dyes in 1 cup of boiling water and distribute the solution into 6 jars according to the jar dyeing method. For **Step 2**, add the indicated amounts of dry dyes to each jar, then continue with jar dyeing as described below.

Grape

Step 1
1/32 tsp #490 blue
1/8 tsp #233 orange
Step 2
1/128 tsp #490 blue
1/64 tsp #338 red

Emerald-Green

Step 1
1/64 tsp #490 blue
1/16 tsp #233 orange
Step 2
1/128 tsp #490 blue
1/64 tsp #119 yellow

Jewel-Blue

Step 1
1/32 tsp #490 blue
1/8 tsp #233 orange
Step 2
1/64 tsp #490 blue

Red Hot

Step 1
1/32 tsp #490 blue
1/8 tsp #233 orange
Step 2
1/128 tsp #119 yellow
1/32 tsp #338 red

Bittersweet

Step 1
1/32 tsp #490 blue
1/8 tsp #233 orange
Step 2
1/32 tsp #119 yellow
1/64 tsp #338 red

The following formula is slightly different for **Step 2**.

Rich Gold

Step 1

1/64 tsp #490 blue
1/16 tsp #233 orange

Step 2

1/8 tsp #119 yellow
1/64 tsp #338 red
1/64 tsp #672 black

For **Step 2**, dissolve the dyes in 1 1/3 cups of boiling water and distribute the solution evenly among the 6 jars. (Add 1 teaspoon of solution to each of the jars, then another teaspoon to each of the jars, and so on until all of the solution is distributed among the jars.) Continue jar dyeing following the directions below.

COMMENTS ON JAR DYEING

In the formulas above, I tell you to add dry dyes directly to the jars of solution. Once the dry dyes have been put in the jars, add extra water (boiling water at this point, to be sure the dye dissolves) directly to the jars of solution until the quart jars are about 2/3 full. Add 1 teaspoon of salt to each jar and stir the solution briskly. Then add a 6" x 24" piece of natural wool (that has been soaked in hot tap water and Synthrapol) to each jar. Stir the wool briskly and make sure it is submerged in the dye solution.

As usual for jar dyeing, process the wool for 1 hour, stirring it every 10 to 15 minutes. After about 45 minutes, add 2 tablespoons of white vinegar to each jar and stir the solutions briskly. Process the wool for another 15 minutes. Turn off the heat and stir the solution in each jar. Allow the wool to stand for another 10 or 15 minutes before rinsing and drying it. When you're finished you will have a swatch that goes from the dark of one color to the light of another.

MAKING ADJUSTMENTS

The formulas I've presented can be adjusted to dye 1-yard pieces of wool using the open pan method. (To dye 1/2-yard pieces, you cut the ingredients in half.) I have written out the formulas for values of Bittersweet, but you can make the dye substitutions and apply them to Red Hot, Jewel-Blue, and Grape. Emerald-Green and Rich Gold cannot be dyed following this chart because their formula strengths must be adjusted.

Bittersweet (1 yard)

Darkest Value

7/32 tsp #490 blue
7/8 tsp #233 orange
7/16 tsp #119 yellow
7/32 tsp #338 red

Next Darkest

7/64 tsp #490 blue
7/16 tsp #233 orange
7/16 tsp #119 yellow
7/32 tsp #338 red

Middle Value

7/128 tsp #490 blue
7/32 tsp #233 orange
7/16 tsp #119 yellow
7/32 tsp #338 red

Next Lightest

3.5/128 tsp #490 blue*
7/64 tsp #233 orange
7/16 tsp #119 yellow
7/32 tsp #338 red

Lightest Value

1.75/128 tsp #490 blue**
7/128 tsp #233 orange
7/16 tsp #119 yellow
7/32 tsp #338 red

* For 3.5/128 teaspoon, dissolve 4/128 or 1/32 teaspoon in 1 cup of boiling water and use 7/8 cup in the formula.

** For 1.75/128 teaspoon, dissolve 2/128 or 1/64 teaspoon in 1 cup of boiling water and use 7/8 cup in the formula.

If you would like to get similar results with Cushing dyes instead of PRO Chem dyes, substitute Peacock and Orange for blue and orange. Cushing's Orange is stronger and slightly redder than PRO Chem's orange, so we must adjust the base gradation and all the other formulas (Step 1) to reflect this. Use the same amount of Peacock, but only half the amount of Orange. The proportion now becomes 1:2 instead of 1:4 (1/32 teaspoon of Peacock and 1/16 teaspoon of Orange).

THINKING AHEAD

After I completed all this dyeing, I looked at the dull-to-bright swatches and knew I could come up with formulas for straight gradations from the values in them. Usually I like to use gradations of subtle colors, not bright ones. I could create quite a number of gradations once I came up with a formula for each of the values of these transitional swatches. For instance, I would like to take the third value from the darkest of Rich Gold and dye a straight gradation based on that color. It would be a beautiful, soft, antique gold.

From Transitional to Straight Gradations

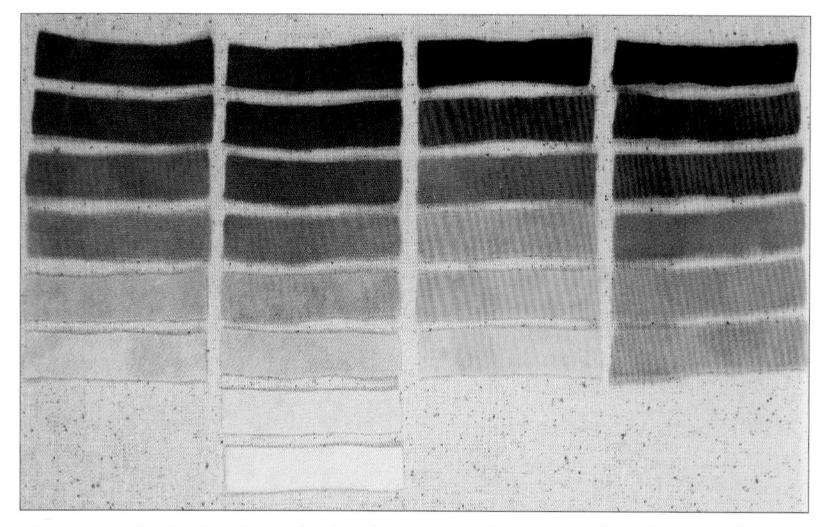

Maryanne has devised formulas for three new gradation swatches (left to right): Red-Orange Brown, Warm Gray-Brown, and Soft Blue-Green (all dyed over 6" x 24" white wool). On the right is Soft Blue-Green dyed double strength over 9" x 24" gray-beige wool.

IN THE LAST SECTION, I DEVELOPED A GROUP OF TRANSITIONAL GRADATION SWATCHES, WHICH GO FROM THE DARK VALUES OF A NEUTRAL BASE COLOR TO THE LIGHT VALUES OF ANOTHER HUE. BITTERSWEET, ONE OF THOSE TRANSITIONAL SWATCHES, APPEALED TO ME MORE THAN THE OTHERS. I ESPECIALLY LIKED ONE OF ITS MIDDLE VALUES AND THOUGHT I WOULD LIKE TO DYE A STRAIGHT GRADATION THAT WOULD HAVE THAT MIDDLE SHADE AS ONE OF ITS VALUES, SO I'VE TAKEN THAT MIDDLE VALUE AND USED IT TO DEVELOP TWO BROWNS.

When I base a new color on another hue, I look at a sample of the original color and consider the different values in it. Then I imagine how I might add to the formula or take away from it to create an interesting variation. After calculating the proportions of the dyes that were needed based on the Bittersweet value, I came up with the two new colors.

FORMULAS

The following formulas use PRO Chemical & Dye brand wash-fast acid dyes. For each formula, first dissolve the dyes in 1 cup of boiling water. (Place the dry dyes in a 1-cup glass measure and add a few teaspoons of tepid water to make a paste. Fill the measuring cup to the 1-cup level with boiling water and stir it briskly until the dyes are completely dissolved.) Use the jar dyeing method on page 44 to dye six values over 6" x 24" white or natural wool.

Warm Gray-Brown

1/32 tsp #490 blue
1/32 tsp #233 orange
1/8 tsp #119 yellow
7/128 tsp #338 red
1/128 tsp #672 black

Red-Orange Brown

1/64 tsp #490 blue
1/16 tsp #233 orange
1/16 tsp #119 yellow
1/32 tsp #338 red
1/128 tsp #672 black

By eliminating the red dye and altering the amounts of blue and yellow, another formula, a soft blue-green, emerged to complement the two browns. I dyed this green first over natural wool and then over Dorr's #42 beige for a variation.

Soft Blue-Green

3/64 tsp #490 blue
1/16 tsp #233 orange
1/32 tsp #119 yellow
1/64 tsp #672 black

USING NEW FORMULAS

Chat Noir, designed by Jane McGown Flynn, is a small rug I have always wanted to hook with a fine cut (page 74). Even a small

"Will the formulas and colors I recommend for use with the pour method work with other methods? The simple answer is yes."

rug takes quite a long time to hook with #3-cut strips, especially if you can't work on it every day. It developed beautifully, though.

The outer background is black. Inside the ribbon border is a soft, brownish, light green. I used the 6-value swatches described above to hook flowers, leaves, and the winding, over-and-under border. The white flowers are hooked with all six values of Warm Gray-Brown, plus white for the petal edges. The flower centers are hooked with a soft orange-yellow outline and stripes, filled in with a lighter soft yellow for a textured look. For the leaves and stems I used the Soft Blue-Green over both white and beige, and for the ribbon-like border I used Red-Orange Brown. Now I just need to put the hook to it and get it finished.

ANOTHER FORMULA

As I worked on this rug I realized that a solution to a problem was staring me in the face. I had told a friend that I didn't have a formula for copper, to which she replied incredulously, "What do you mean, you don't have a formula for copper?" As I sat looking at *Chat Noir*, in which I was using wool dyed with the Red-Orange Brown, it dawned on me that I could easily take this formula a step further and create a beautiful formula for copper.

Let's think this through together. The copper needs to be

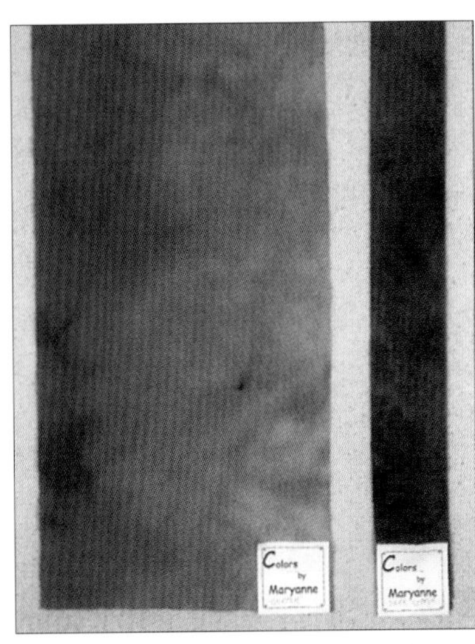

Maryanne describes her formula for her new Copper Color Sheet (left) and a darker, similar hue.

brighter and slightly clearer in color than the Red-Orange Brown. To make a formula brighter, just take away some of the color that is dulling it. In this case it was blue because blue dulls orange, so I cut down on the blue—and also on the black, because black makes the color a little smoky. I left the quantities of orange, yellow, and red the same. A slightly used copper penny became my visual aid as I set about dyeing some samples.

The rug hooker who wanted copper-colored wool needed more than one little strip. Therefore, I made a strong enough formula to be sure that I could dye a decent quantity of wool with it. However, it was a gradual process to achieve the desired color.

When you're uncertain about the amount of dye solution to add to a dye pot, start out by adding small amounts until you get what you want. It is always easy to add a little more, but if you add it all at once, the color could end up too dark and you might have to start the whole dye project again. Once you work out how much solution to use, you can easily repeat the process.

I dip-dyed eight 12" x 24" Color Sheets using natural wool and the following formula and procedure.

Copper

$^3/_{64}$ tsp #490 blue
$^1/_4$ tsp #233 orange
$^1/_4$ tsp #119 yellow
$^1/_8$ tsp #338 red
$^1/_{64}$ tsp #672 black

Dissolve the dyes in 2 cups of boiling water and set it aside. Soak the eight pieces of 12" x 24" wool in very hot tap water with Synthrapol. Place a large rectangular pan, about 4" to 5" deep, on the stove with 2 $^1/_2$" to 3" of hot water and $^1/_2$ cup of white vinegar in it. Turn the heat on high and add $^1/_2$ cup of the dye solution to the pan of water.

Wearing heavy, lined rubber gloves, gather the eight pieces of wool together in both hands, grasping them at the top so you'll be dipping them lengthwise into the dye bath. Dip the free ends of the strips in the dye bath. Dip the strips all the way into the bath several times and then place the pieces in the dye bath to absorb the rest of the dye. Make sure the wool is submerged so you don't get any white or light areas on the wool.

When the water clears, remove the wool and add another 1/2 cup of solution to the bath. Dip all eight pieces together once again and keep dipping them until the water almost clears. The strips should now be darker on one end than on the other.

Remove the wool and add another 1/2 cup of solution, along with 1/2 cup of vinegar. This time hold the strips together along their width so you'll be dipping them sideways into the bath. Continue dipping the wool until the water clears, then lay the strips in the dye bath. Cover the pan loosely with foil and steam the wool for around 10 minutes. Remove the wool, rinse it in warm water, and allow it to dry.

Add the remaining 1/2 cup of dye solution to the dye bath along with 1/2 cup of vinegar. Place two 9" x 12" pieces of natural wool in the bath and simmer them until the water clears (there's no need to dip the strips). This will give you darker compatible strips to use for accents and outlines.

I was pleased with this new Copper, which will make great weather vanes. Remember, it and the other three colors presented here all evolved from a single value of a transitional swatch. With a little experimentation, there's no end to the variations you can produce.

Chat Noir

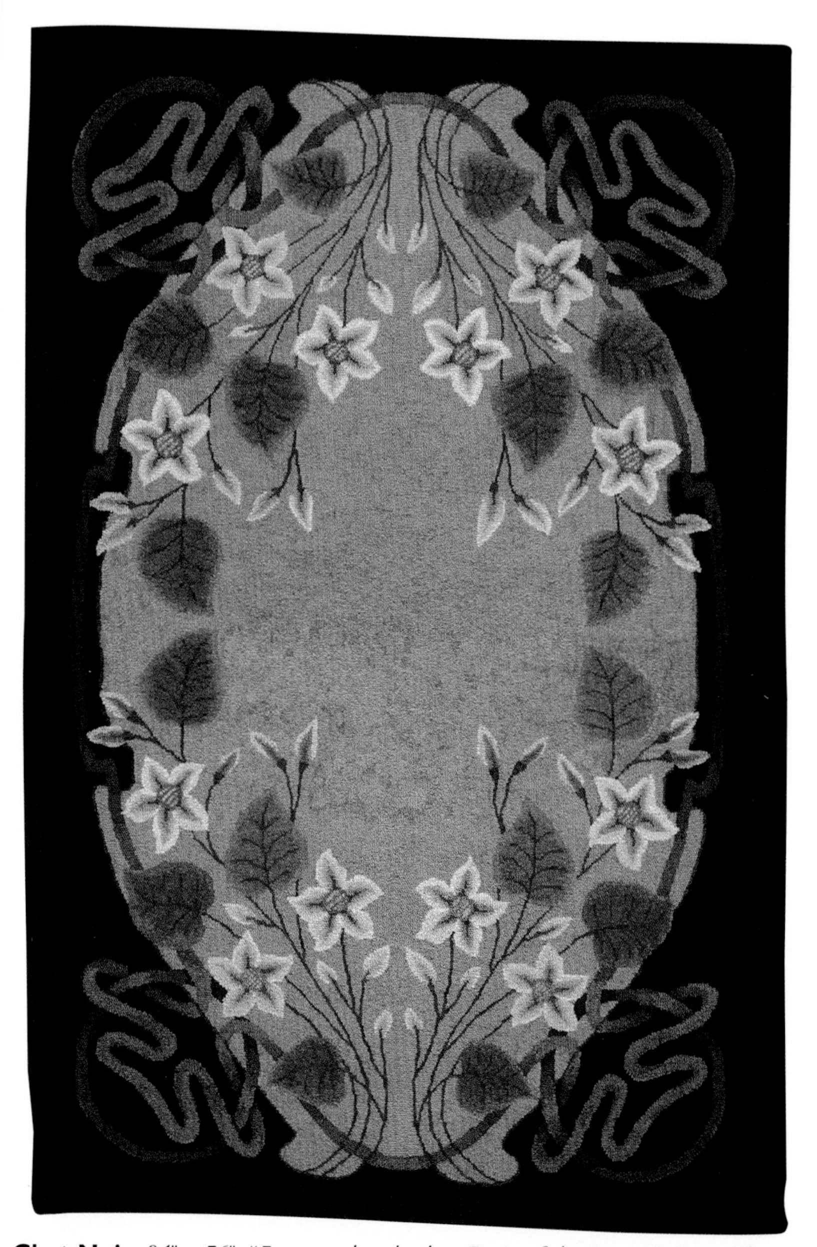

Chat Noir, *24" x 36", #3-cut wool on burlap. Designed by Jane McGown Flynn. Hooked by Maryanne Lincoln, Wrentham, Massachusetts, 2001.*

SOMETIMES WE SEE A RUG THAT WE WANT TO HOOK, BUT WE NEED TO WAIT TO START IT UNTIL WE FIND THE RIGHT COLORS FOR IT. *CHAT NOIR* WAS SUCH A RUG FOR ME. I HAVE WANTED TO HOOK THIS JANE MCGOWN FLYNN RUG EVER SINCE SHE DESIGNED IT, YET IT TOOK ME UNTIL 2000 TO DO SO WHEN I DEVELOPED SOME NEW DYE FORMULAS. THIS PIECE CAME TO MIND AS THE PERFECT RUG TO SHOW OFF MY NEW COLORS.

> *"The edges of a detail (whether a flower petal, leaf, or border) have to be at least three values lighter or darker than the background to create contrast."*

These formulas may look familiar to you, as they, along with photographs of swatch samples, were featured before. I mentioned then that I had developed transitional gradation swatches, which go from the dark values of a neutral base color to the light values of another hue. Bittersweet, one of those transitional swatches, appealed to me more than the others. I especially liked one of its middle values and thought I would like to dye a straight gradation that would have that middle shade as one of its values. I used that middle value to develop the two browns I present here: Warm Gray-Brown and Red-Orange Brown.

MY *CHAT NOIR*

The outer background of my rug is black (not antique black), used right off the bolt without dyeing. All the rest of the wool in the rug has been dyed. The background inside the ribbon like border is a soft, medium-light brown, and if you have a trained color eye you might see that it has a very slight greenish tint.

Usually it is wise to pick the background color of your rug first before choosing the swatches for the details, but in this case it was the swatch colors that inspired me to hook the rug. I knew that I wanted black on the outside background and light on the inside. I tried different light values of the swatches until I came up with one that looked good. I mixed up the formula for Warm Gray-Brown and used a small amount to dye the two yards of background that I would need. While the wool was in the dye pot I adjusted the color so it became slightly green. I did this by adding a drop or two of blue and yellow to the simmering bath. (See the box on page 76 to learn more about adding small quantities of dye to a dye bath.)

Along with the six values of Warm Gray-Brown, I used an outline of plain white wool to hook the flower petals. The white was necessary because I needed to create a contrast so the flower edges wouldn't get lost in the background. That is always a concern when using a medium or medium-light background.

The edges of a detail (whether a flower petal, leaf, or border) have to be at least three values lighter or darker than the background to create contrast. Sometimes it is fun to let some of the edges of a detail blend into the background while others are sharply contrasted. You can do this by manipulating values. I varied the leaves in *Chat Noir* by not hooking every one alike. Since I used only four values to hook each leaf, I varied them by using the four darkest values for some leaves and the four middle values for others.

The flower centers were hooked with two values of a soft gold, which I happened to find in my store of odds and ends of different colors. The darker of the two was used to outline the center, and the centers were filled with alternating stripes of the golds. You can achieve a similar effect by using a gold texture, dyed or as is.

FORMULAS

I used jar dyeing to create the swatches for the details in my rug using PRO Chem wash-fast acid dyes. For each formula, first dissolve the dye in 1 cup of boiling water. (Place the dry dyes in a 1-cup glass measure and add a few teaspoons of tepid water to make a paste. Fill the measuring cup to the 1-cup level with boiling water and stir the solution briskly until the dyes are completely dissolved.)

Warm Gray-Brown

Dye 6 values over 6" x 24" pieces of white wool.

1/32 tsp #490 blue
1/32 tsp #233 orange
1/8 tsp #119 yellow
7/128 tsp #338 red
1/128 tsp #672 black

Red-Orange Brown

Dye 6 values over 6" x 24" pieces of natural wool. The color is almost the same as if it were dyed over white, except in the lightest values.

1/64 tsp #490 blue
1/16 tsp #233 orange
1/16 tsp #119 yellow
1/32 tsp #338 red
1/128 tsp #672 black

> *"The border was a challenge to hook because it is an important element in the overall rug plan. The winding, over-and-under, ribbon-like border is hooked with the four darkest values of Red-Orange Brown."*

ADDING A DROP OF DYE

I am able to add a drop or two of a basic color to a dye pot because I regularly keep on hand five colors of liquid dye. With them I can dye fruits, leaves, backgrounds, or whatever else I want by just reaching into the cabinet for the squeeze bottles they are in.

The five colors are: PRO Chem #338 red, #490 blue, #119 yellow, #233 orange, and #672 black. I mix 1/2 teaspoon of dry dye in 1 cup of boiling water, and then I store the liquid dye in 16-ounce squeeze bottles available from PRO Chem.

When mixing dry dye, put the dye into a glass-measuring cup and add about a teaspoon or two of tepid water. After stirring the dye around in the water, add boiling water to the paste up to the 1-cup level. Stir the liquid with a long-handled spoon until the dye is thoroughly dissolved.

The border was a challenge to hook because it is an important element in the overall rug plan. The winding, over-and-under, ribbon-like border is hooked with the four darkest values of Red-Orange Brown. As far as color goes, this border allows the rug maker to add a variation of color and value to bring out the center details and to separate the inner and outer backgrounds.

There are several ways that I could have hooked the ribbon. For example, I could have outlined it and used all one value for it, but I liked the challenge of the corner circles. To make the bands look like they pass over and under each other, I made them darker where they go under and light where they go over. I restricted the values to just the darkest four values because of the medium-light background. If I had used any of the lighter values, the edges of the bands might have gotten lost in the background.

By changing the emphasis of the dye mixture from weak blue (as it is in the two brown formulas) to strong blue, and eliminating the red, another formula—a soft blue-green—emerged to use with the two browns.

Soft Blue-Green

Dye 6 values over 6" x 24" pieces of natural wool. The color is almost the same as if it were dyed over white, except in the lightest values. I also dyed this recipe over Dorr Mill's #42 beige wool for some of the leaves.

3/64 tsp #490 blue
1/64 tsp #233 orange
1/32 tsp #119 yellow
1/64 tsp #672 black

Since *Chat Noir* is hooked with a #3-cut of wool, I knew it would take more than a couple of months to hook it. I worked on it until it was half completed and then I had to set it aside while I finished other projects. A problem arose with the background when I picked the project back up again to complete it. Because the lighter background was dyed, it was not evenly colored. The background wool I started to use to complete the rug was a little darker in spots than the piece I had used to hook the first half of the rug. When I noticed this was happening I worked the two pieces of wool together for a pleasing effect. If I had thought about it ahead of time I would have cut background from both pieces of wool when I started the rug, instead of using up one whole piece before starting to use the other.

CHAPTER FIVE

BACKGROUNDS

Dark Backgrounds

MANY RUG HOOKERS INQUIRE ABOUT HAND-DYEING DARK BACKGROUNDS, SO I DECIDED TO DEDICATE AN ENTIRE CHAPTER TO THE SUBJECT. BACKGROUNDS IN GENERAL MERIT SERIOUS DISCUSSION BECAUSE THOSE COLORS SHOULD BE CHOSEN FIRST WHEN COLOR-PLANNING A RUG. I ACCEPTED THAT DOCTRINE IN 1964 WHEN I STARTED HOOKING, AND IT IS STILL GOOD ADVICE TODAY. WHENEVER POSSIBLE, CHOOSE BACKGROUND COLORS FIRST SO YOU CAN COLOR-PLAN THE DESIGN ELEMENTS TO CONTRAST AGAINST THE BACKGROUND.

However, no rules are hard and-fast. The world will not come to an end if you don't finalize the background colors first. Sometimes it's not clear which background color might look best until some of the design elements are in place. Or, you may have several colors that look equally appropriate, but you just can't decide on one. If nothing else, determine a value for the background color: light, medium or dark.

For example, on the *Pansy & Peach Mat I,* I considered several choices for background colors. My first choice was light ivory splashed with hints of dull purple, green and light red. Instead, I decided to make the background dark because the flowers, fruit and other design elements would "pop" off it well.

After considering several dark colors, I chose basic black. For one thing, I have plenty of it on hand, so I didn't have to dye anything. More importantly, black would make the crispest contrast for the design elements. (For printing purposes, black also photographs best.) I could just as easily have chosen any number of complementary dark backgrounds or antique brown as discussed below.

BLACK OVERDYEING DARK COLORS

Any dark color of plain or textured 100-percent wool can be overdyed with black for dark backgrounds. The final color will be very dark—predominately black with hints of the original color and texture peeking through. To achieve that mottled effect, use a dye pot that is barely large enough to completely immerse the wool in the dye

Vegetable Seed Packets: Beets, Peas and Carrots, *11 1/2" x 15 1/2" each, all #6-cut wool on linen. Designed by Florence Petruchik and Maryanne Lincoln. Hooked by Maryanne Lincoln, Wrentham, Massachusetts, 1994. Flo and Maryanne created these wall hangings (the other two are on the next page) as demonstration pieces for dyeing seminars that Maryanne conducts around the country. Maryanne hand-dyed the antique-brown backgrounds by overdyeing medium-dark orange-brown wool with blue dye, adding black dye toward the end of the process. In this section, she provides formulas and instructions for creating a variety of unique dark backgrounds.*

solution. Crowding the wool in the pot will force the solution to overdye different portions of the wool to varying degrees of darkness. (Remember that wet wool looks darker than dry wool.)

To start, use 1 teaspoon of black dye per yard (Cushing Black or Pro Chem #672 black). Add more dye as needed in small amounts. When overdyeing a very dark color,
1 teaspoon of black dye is probably enough. For medium or medium-dark values, you probably need more dye.

When the wool looks just dark enough and the water still contains some dye, remove the wool from the dye solution; put it in a pan of plain-water with 1/4 cup of white vinegar. Simmer until the wool absorbs all the black dye that runs out into the fresh water. Don't rush the process of overdyeing dark backgrounds; be generous with vinegar and cooking time. When the dye is completely reabsorbed, turn off the heat and allow the solution to cool before rinsing well.

In addition to white vinegar in the original dye bath (about 1/4 cup per yard), add a few drops of a wetting agent. (I use Synthrapol.) Salt is not necessary. Use medium heat, and reduce to a simmer when the solution gets very hot. If it starts to boil, turn it down to stop the rolling boil. Add more vinegar if the wool doesn't absorb the dye at

Vegetable Seed Packets: Carrots and Peas.

higher temperatures. The solution will gradually clear. After it is clear, simmer a while longer. Rinse in room-temperature water until no dye rinses out of the wool.

If some of the original color comes out of the wool as the black is absorbed, just make sure enough black is absorbed to achieve the desired color. It is usually pointless to try to get the original color back into the wool. Rinse very well until no color—original or black—comes out of the overdyed wool.

COMPLEMENTARY DYES

Create an interesting dark background by overdyeing any dark wool with its complementary color. Use a color wheel to determine the complement. For purposes of overdyeing dark colors, don't worry about being too specific when determining the complement. Any of the 12 basic color classifications on the color wheel will do.

Brightly colored wool can also be used for dark backgrounds when overdyed with a complementary color, sometimes also including black dye to darken. Complementary colors turn "poison" colors—very bright colors—into treasures. Bright turquoise green becomes blackish green when overdyed with red and black. Electric blue overdyed with orange becomes dark blue. Conversely, Day-Glo™ orange becomes dull rust when overdyed with blue.

ANTIQUE FORMULAS

Antique colors have the appearance of colors faded from years of use and sunlight. When wool is dyed with an antique formula, only random spots are actually the darkest value of the color. Overall, the wool is mottled with varying dark values.

ANTIQUE BROWN

The backgrounds of the *Vegetable Seed Packets* are antique brown. Using the principle of overdyeing with a complementary color, I started with a medium-dark orange-brown and overdyed it with blue and black. I actually overdyed the wool twice: first with blue, then with black. I used Pro Chem #490 blue and #672 black; try Cushing Sky Blue and Black.

You can also make antique brown from camel-colored wool. Overdyeing with blue and black yields green; overdye again with red (the complement of green) to dull it down. Better yet, mix the red and blue together to make a purple solution, and use it to overdye the camel for a browner version of antique brown. As always, add a little dye at a time to slowly achieve the desired color.

ANTIQUE BLACK

A popular background color, antique black means different colors to different colorists. I associate the color with an unevenly dyed green-black. Other rug hookers think of it as black overdyed with gray and beige to "age" it.

Starting with medium values of gray wool, simply overdye with black until it's as dark as you like. Start with a black-green wool (like Dorr #44), overdye with red (the complement of green) to darken the wool and to add a hint of red. When overdyeing black wool, you will need to use a strong dye solution to make any effect. Start with 1 teaspoon per yard and add small amounts. Regardless of the color wool you start with, if your antique black gets dark but not dull, simply add a bit of the color's complement to dull it down.

Dyeing Mottled Backgrounds

ALTHOUGH I STUDIED WITH A TEACHER FOR THE FIRST FIVE YEARS OF MY HOOKING CAREER, I HAVE ALWAYS DONE MY OWN DYEING FOR RUGS AND OTHER HOOKING PROJECTS. MY FIRST TWO RUGS HAD PLAIN, FLAT COLORS FOR THEIR BACKGROUNDS, HOOKED WITH WOOL I BOUGHT BY THE POUND AT A NEARBY WOOLEN MILL. AS A BEGINNER, I HAD MY HANDS FULL JUST TRYING TO LEARN HOW TO SHADE FLOWERS AND HOW TO DYE SPECIAL COLORS FOR THEM. HOWEVER, AS I GAINED EXPERIENCE WITH COLOR PLANNING AND DYEING, I BEGAN EXPERIMENTING WITH DIFFERENT WAYS TO DYE BACKGROUND WOOL.

Each dyeing technique holds a slightly different challenge when it comes time to hook the background into the rug. For example, a dip-dyed background that I dyed for a Chinese oriental required me to be conscious of the order in which the strips were hooked. Because one end was darker than the other, each strip had to be carefully hooked into the rug in a certain order to achieve the look I wanted.

DYEING A MOTTLED BACKGROUND

A less complicated way for inexperienced dyers to create an interesting rug is with the following procedure for dyeing a mottled background. Choose the color and amount of dye to use based on the color you want and the wool you start with. (For instance, if you want to dye antique black and the only color of wool you have is beige, it will take a lot more dye to get to antique black than if you start with dark green wool.) Use a color wheel to remind you of complements, which darken and dull each other.

To dye wool for a mottled background, soak 1/2 yard of wool off the bolt, or about 1/2 pound of recycled wool, in hot water with Synthrapol (a commercial wetting agent) added. Prepare a dye bath that allows you to push the wool under the surface of the water, but does not have a lot of room for the wool to move around. (To figure the amount of water you'll need, put the wet wool in your dye pot and add enough water so that the wool is not completely covered, yet can be poked under the surface of the water.) Remove the wool from the pot and proceed.

Cherries, *8 1/2" x 9 1/4", #5-cut wool on linen. Designed and hooked by Maryanne Lincoln, Wrentham, Massachusetts, 1996. Maryanne describes how to dye the mottled background.*

Add the wool, 1/8 cup of white vinegar, and the prepared dye solution to the dye pot, according to the formula you have chosen. Turn the heat up so the water simmers. Poke the wool under the water occasionally, but don't stir it constantly. This will allow the dye to splotch on the wool. Once the water has simmered and cleared, remove the wool and check the color. If you like it, put it back in the pot and simmer it a few minutes longer.

If you want to add more of the same color or another color, add the dye before returning the wool to the dye bath. Poke the wool around a little and let it take up the dye. Keep track of what you do so you can dye more wool later and have it come out looking the same way. Repeat the procedure until you have enough wool for your background.

DYEING THE BACKGROUND FOR *CHERRIES*

Let me show you an example of the dyeing I've just told you about. Take a look at the photograph above. I have hooked this cluster of cherries against a light, mottled orange-brown. I used one of my Color Sheets for the cherries. (Color Sheets are 12" x 24" dip-dyed swatches.) The wool for the stems, leaves, and border was dyed with a casserole method. This type of background, because of the way it is dyed and hooked, contains interesting color variations and is relaxing to hook. I hooked it in curved, rather than straight, lines. The background was dyed over cream-colored wool, first with a weak orange solution and then a blue-black solution.

To recreate this mottled background, prepare two batches of dye solution. In the first, dissolve 1/64 teaspoon of PRO Chem #233 orange dye in 1 cup of boiling water. In the second, dissolve 1/128 teaspoon #490 blue, plus 1/64 teaspoon #672 black, in 1 cup of boiling water. (When dissolving dyes, first add a teaspoon or two of tepid water to the dry dye to make a paste. Then add the boiling water and stir briskly to dissolve the dye.)

Add 5 teaspoons of the orange solution, plus 1 teaspoon of the blue-black solution, to a dye bath prepared as described above. Add 1/8 cup of white vinegar and then stuff a 1/2-yard piece of wool into the pan all at once. Poke it under here and there as needed so that all the wool has been submerged at some point during the process. Make sure the heat is turned up so the water simmers.

When the water clears, examine the wool. If you want more

color, repeat the first step until the color pleases you. Each dyeing technique holds a slightly different challenge when it comes time to hook the background to the rug. Color should look a little bright, because the second step will dull it.

Remove the wool, add 3 teaspoons of the blue-black mixture to the dye pot, and plunge the wool in again. Be sure to poke it down as it simmers. The water will clear quickly as the pot will be very hot at this point. This blue-black mixture will make the orange look brown and smoky in places. Repeat this step until you like the results. Let the water simmer for a few minutes after it clears to set the color.

Keep track of what you do and continue dyeing 1/2-yard pieces until you have enough wool for your background. Here are two different ways to calculate how much wool you'll need:

- Allow for 1/2 pound of wool per square foot. If your rug measures 2' x 3', or 6 square feet, you should have about 3 pounds of wool.
- Lay 4 or 5 layers of wool over the area of the pattern that is to be hooked. Then dye that amount of wool.

More is better when you are dyeing. It is a real nuisance to have to dye more background later when you may not have the dye or wool that you used originally. So plan accordingly and always dye a little more than you think you'll need.

Adapting Swatch Formulas for Backgrounds

Untitled, *7" x 7", #3-cut wool on burlap. Designed by Pearl K. McGown. Hooked by Maryanne Lincoln, Wrentham, Massachusetts, 1987. Maryanne describes how to dye background wool using the three darkest values of a 6-value swatch.*

IT IS BEST TO USE EITHER A BRIGHT OR DARK BACKGROUND FOR A RUG IF DETAILS ARE HOOKED IN NEUTRAL OR SUBTLE SHADES. TO HELP YOU ACCENTUATE MUTED MOTIFS, I'LL DISCUSS HOW TO DYE THE THREE DARKEST VALUES OF THREE SWATCH FORMULAS.

The formulas for Bright Red Rose, Blueberry, and Seafoam that I am working with this time have already appeared as jar dye formulas for 6-value swatches. The red and blue appeared when I developed basic hues around the color wheel, and the green one on page 10.

The chart on page 83 indicates how much of each formula to use to dye all six values. (Use the chart figures for either PRO Chem or Cushing dyes.) The amounts are accurate—but only to a point. The width of the wool, its color, and the care with which

Maryanne explains how to increase or decrease formulas to dye six values of Blueberry, Seafoam, and Bright Red Rose. From the left, the values are darkest, next dark, middle dark, middle light, next light, and lightest.

you measure the dyes all have an effect on the outcome.

I use Dorr wool, which is approximately 56" wide with the selvages. Wider wool may result in a lighter color because there are more square inches per yard to take up the dye. My formulas are dyed over Dorr's white and natural wool so you can see the true color of the dye mixture. If you dye over other colors, the results may not be the same. For example, Blueberry dyed over a light blue will result in much the same blue, but dyed over beige or apricot it will be duller. Bright Red Rose dyed over pink will be very similar to my results, but dyed over beige, celery, or mint, it will be duller.

You will save yourself some aggravation if you dye a generous amount of background wool before you start hooking or, at the very least, make good notes and set aside a sample of the dyed wool in case you need to match it later. Sometimes you have to dye more background when a rug is almost finished. You may decide the rug would look better with a few lines of the background color around the outside of the design, or you may run out of background wool and need to dye more to complete the project.

HOW TO DYE THE DARKEST VALUES

Each of these three formulas uses some or all of these PRO Chemical & Dye wash-fast acid dyes: #338 red, #119 yellow, #490 blue, and #672 black. The dry dyes for each value are mixed together in boiling water to form a solution. The formulas for the three darkest values of each color are as follows.

Bright Red Rose

- Middle dark = 3/8 teaspoon #338 red + 1/8 teaspoon #119 yellow + 1/128 teaspoon #490 blue
- Next dark = 3/4 teaspoon #338 red + 1/4 teaspoon #119 yellow + 1/64 teaspoon #490 blue
- Darkest = 1 1/2 teaspoons #338 red + 1/2 teaspoon #119 yellow + 1/32 teaspoon #490 blue

Blueberry

- Middle dark = 1/128 teaspoon #338 red + 1/64 teaspoon + 1/2 teaspoon #672 black
- Next dark = 3/16 teaspoon #119 yellow + 1/16 teaspoon #490 blue + 3/8 teaspoon #672 black
- Darkest = 3/8 teaspoon #119 yellow + 1/8 teaspoon #490 blue + 38 teaspoon #672 black

To dye each value consult the chart at right to see how much dye you'll need. Then mix the

VALUE CHART

Value of Swatch	*1/2-Yard Background*	*1-Yard Background*
Darkest	4 x the formula	8 x the formula
Next dark	2 x the formula	4 x the formula
Middle dark	1 x the formula	2 x the formula
Middle light	1/2 x the formula	1 x the formula
Next light	1/4 x the formula	1/2 x the formula
Lightest	1/8 x the formula	1/4 x the formula

dyes all together in 1 or 2 cups of boiling water. (Place the dry dyes in a 1 or 2-cup measure and add a few teaspoons of water to make a paste. Next, add enough boiling water to fill the cup and stir until the dye is completely dissolved.) Add some of the solution to a pan of water (deep enough to cover the wool) over medium heat, along with a few drops of Synthrapol (a wetting agent) and 1/4 cup of vinegar. Put the wool in and simmer it until the water clears, stirring the wool as it takes up the dye. Lift the wool out, add more of the dye solution, stir the dye bath, and put the wool back in. Stir it as it simmers. When the water clears, lift the wool out and add more dye solution. Repeat the process until all the solution has been used or the wool becomes the color you want.

Keep in mind that wet wool lightens in color as it dries. For an accurate match when dyeing more than one piece of a color, compare the wet wool to a wet sample. If you use all the solution and the color is still not dark enough, mix up more and continue to dye until you achieve the desired color.

The formulas here are based on dyeing 1/2 -yard pieces of wool. If you need 2 yards of wool for a background, you can dye four 1/2 -yard pieces in separate batches, using the chart amounts shown above as a guide, or you can use a large pan, quadruple the dye amounts, and dye all of the wool at once.

ADDITIONAL TIPS FOR EXPERIENCED DYERS

When you want to dye the three lightest values for a background, it can be awkward to measure 1/2, 1/4, and 1/8 of the dry dye amounts. There are two ways to deal with the challenge. First, you can mix the formula in 1 cup of water and then use only 1/2, 1/4, or 1/8 of the whole solution to dye what you need as indicated in the chart. Keep the remainder of the solution for future use.

Second, you can dye more wool than the formula indicates. Instead of using half of the solution to dye just one 1/2-yard piece of wool, dye two pieces and use all of the solution. For the next lightest value, dye two 1/2-yard pieces using half of the solution, or dye four pieces using all of the solution. To dye the lightest value, use 1/4 of the solution to dye two 1/2-yard pieces or 1/2 of the solution to dye four 1/2 -yard pieces. In other words, either divide the solution rather than the dye amounts or increase the amount of wool you dye.

The next time you need wool for a background, look to swatch formulas for ideas. By following the chart I've included, you can dye just the three darkest or lightest values of a formula for an interesting and subtly variegated background.

"More is better when you are dyeing. It is a real nuisance to have to dye more background later when you may not have the dye or wool that you used originally."

Dyeing Woodsy Backgrounds

Wentworth Antique, *56" x 32", #6-cut wool on burlap. Designed by Ruth Hall. Hooked by Maryanne Lincoln, Wrentham, Massachusetts, 1996.*

In the 1970s I took a few hooking lessons with Sally Newhall, who helped me plan a fairly large Pearl McGown rug called *Woodsy*. The design had a wide border of wildflowers and leaves around the perimeter of the rug, and a large, plain field in the middle. I especially loved the design because it brought back pleasant memories of playing in the woods and pastures around my childhood home in Ipswich, Massachusetts. I remember walking through the woods in the springtime in one certain area where all these flowers bloomed. My brother and I watched for them and enjoyed them each year.

Sally helped me plan colors for the jack-in-the-pulpits, trillium, lady's slippers, and the various large leaves. She then suggested I dye lots of different wools together in an enamel baby tub for the open background area, I followed her suggestion and it worked out very well.

After finishing *Woodsy* I had lots of background wool left over and used it to complete *Wentworth Antique*, above. I had helped a student start this rug, but she later found she could no longer hook and gave it back to me unfinished. When I received it, more than half the flowers and leaves were hooked and the background was started with an ivory color. The colors of the motifs looked great, but I decided to use a dark, mottled background instead of the ivory. It took only a few months to finish the rug. It now hangs on the wall in my family room.

USING COMPLEMENTS TO DULL COLORS

When I accepted Sally's suggestions on how to dye a woodland background, I didn't understand why she had me use Cushing's Dark Brown and Dark Green dyes over the assorted colors. As I did the dyeing and then hooked the fabrics into the rug, however, I saw how the wool had taken

> "*What's important is that the dyes you are adding are absorbed into the wool and that none of the fabrics bleed color after you simmer them.*"

on the colors of the ground in the woods where the wildflowers grew. Of course, on medium-colored wools more of the dye colors appeared, while on the darker wools, the dyes simply added interesting splotches of muted color.

Dark Brown and Dark Green are complements (Dark Brown is actually a dull red-brown), so they dull each other. Dark Brown dyed over green wools appears darker and duller, not brown. Likewise, Dark Green over brown wools appears darker and duller, rather than green.

Other combinations of Cushing dyes that work similarly are Dark Brown and Green, Dark Brown and Myrtle Green, Seal Brown and Reseda Green, and Seal Brown and Bright Green. Also, a combination of brown dyes works if you have mostly green wools to dye over and you want to tone down the green. Or you can use a combination of Dark Green, Bright, Green, and Bronze to dye over mostly browns and grays to play up the green combinations. You may discover your own combinations as well.

BACKGROUND DYEING IN AN ENAMEL TUB

To overdye an assortment of wools for a dark background, collect mounds of wool in a variety of medium to medium-dark colors, such as grays, browns, burgundies, and greens, as well as checks, tweeds, and other textures. Soak them in an enamel tub in warm water with a wetting agent added, and then dye them together in the same tub. I use Synthrapol from PRO Chemical & Dye as a wetting agent. After the wool is thoroughly wet, leave the Synthrapol in the dye bath and add the dyes.

While wearing heavy rubber gloves, sprinkle a whole package of Dark Brown dye over the wool in the bath and push the wool down with tongs, a large spoon, or your gloved hand. Add the dye slowly, sprinkling it all over the water surface as you would sprinkle cinnamon sugar on buttered toast. When the package is empty, use both gloved hands to push the wool around and turn it over, working the dye into the wool. Pour 1/2 cup of white vinegar over the wool and work it in as you did the dye. Cover the pan loosely with foil and simmer it over medium heat until the water becomes clear.

It will take about 30 minutes of simmering for the water to clear. Don't allow it to boil. If the color is too blotchy or if the original color of the wool doesn't change, sprinkle a package of Dark Green over the wool and work it in as you did the Dark Brown. (You will have to use tongs this time, because the wool and water will now be hot.) Simmer it until the water clears again.

If it's still not dark enough, or if you don't like the color of some pieces, remove the pieces you like and sprinkle another partial or whole package of Dark Green or Dark Brown over the wool that remains in the tub. You probably won't need more vinegar, but if it's taking too long for the water to clear, add more. Continue simmering the wool until the water clears. Remove and rinse all the wool, spin it in the washing machine to remove as much water as possible, and hang it to dry.

Some of the wools you dye over may bleed their colors into your dye bath. No matter what you do, the wool will not absorb the color back into itself, and therefore the water may not clear completely. Just discard this water when you're finished. What's important is that the dyes you are adding are absorbed into the wool and that none of the fabrics bleed color after you simmer them. If some continue to bleed, I would advise you to not hook with them. If your finished rug ever gets wet, the color may bleed onto other parts of the rug.

The pattern for *Wentworth Antique* is available from Joan Moshimer's Rug Hooker Studio, PO Box 351, Kennebunkport, ME 04046, (800) 626-7847.

Dyeing Wool Selvages and Pink Backgrounds

Maryanne's New England Tulip, *30" x 19 1/2", #5-cut wool on burlap. Adapted from a pattern by DiFranza Designs. Hooked by Maryanne Lincoln, Wrentham, Massachusetts, 1998. Maryanne used dyed wool selvages to hook parts of this rug.*

THE PROJECT I CHOSE TO HOOK FOR THIS SECTION IS AN ADAPTATION OF A DIFRANZA DESIGNS PATTERN CALLED *NEW ENGLAND TULIP*. I LIKE TO TAKE SOMEONE ELSE'S DESIGN, ADD PERSONAL TOUCHES TO IT, AND THEN PLAY WITH COLOR.

When I started to hook the center of this rug, I decided to modify the big tulip's stem and leaves. The printed pattern had naked stems for the tulip and the two groups of three leaves. I added the tiny leaves to please my eye, and then I just let my imagination flow freely as I hooked the center detail. The border is a simple lamb's tongue pattern that I turned into tiny muted rainbows, each with a tulip flowering under it.

HOOKING THE BACKGROUND

The pink background is mostly hooked with dyed selvages cut on a #5 cutting wheel. I was quite certain when I started to fill in the background that I wouldn't have enough wool using just the selvages, so I dyed some odds and ends of white and natural wool with a similar pinkish brown color. With the selvages, I hooked the background in wiggly lines, which broke up the whole area and left tiny irregular spaces to be filled later with a mixture of pink selvages and the odds and ends that I had dyed. That way, the new dyed pieces were scattered throughout the background and it didn't matter if the color didn't exactly match the selvages. It worked out just as I planned.

You can see the wiggly lines in the background in the photo above. Before I filled in around

> *"I often hook the background of my rugs with similar wiggly lines and then later, at my leisure, go back and fill in the tiny open areas."*

the wiggly lines, they attracted many comments and questions as I worked on the border of rainbows while attending the Caraway Rug School in Asheboro, North Carolina. One woman said the background looked like lace, and she was sure I was going to leave it like that; she was terribly disappointed when I told her I was going to fill it in.

I often hook the background of my rugs with similar wiggly lines and then later, at my leisure, go back and fill in the tiny open areas. Hooking a background can sometimes be tedious, and this method makes a game of it. In this rug I did it because I wanted the background to be mottled in a certain way. The spaces allowed for new dyed materials, which were a slightly different color, to be worked into the rug and not look like an afterthought.

DYED SELVAGES

Since I have an extensive collection of dyed selvages, I was able to hook most of the rest of the rug with them. When I didn't have a dyed selvage in the right color, I just reached into my boxes of regular dyed wool pieces and found what I needed. In other words, the rug was hooked with a combination of selvages and regular wool.

How did I happen to have all those dyed selvages on hand? Sometimes when I am dip dyeing my swatches called Color Sheets, there is a weak solution left in the dye bath after I finish with a

DYEING BY EYE

for Experienced Dyers

To dye a brownish pink color by eye, follow this procedure with PRO Chemical & Dye wash-fast acid dyes. Mix up separate solutions with these dyes: 1/32 teaspoon #119 yellow, 1/32 teaspoon #338 red, 1/32 teaspoon #490 blue, and 1/32 teaspoon #672 black. For each color, measure the dry dye into a 1-cup glass measure. Add a teaspoon or two of tepid water and stir it to form a paste. Then add boiling water to the 1-cup level and stir it briskly to dissolve the dye. When all four solutions have been mixed, get a pan large enough to dye a 1/2-yard piece of wool. Fill the pan with very hot water, add 1/4 cup of white vinegar, and place it over medium heat,

The following amounts are approximate. Trust your eyes to guide you. Pour about 1/4 cup of the red solution into a separate cup. Add about 1/8 cup of the yellow solution to that red. Pick up the cup and slosh the colors together, then carefully add a few drops of the blue, and finally, a few drops of the black. This should result in a brownish pink. If it is too bright, add a few more drops of the blue and black solutions. If it gets too muddy, add a little more of the red and yellow. When it looks about right, pour it into the hot dye bath and add the wool that has been soaked in hot water and a wetting agent. Stir it a little, cover the pot loosely with foil and then simmer it until the water clears. Turn off the heat and let the wool cool for 15 to 20 minutes, Remove the wool, rinse it in warm water, and hang it to dry.

"Sometimes when I am dip dyeing my swatches called Color Sheets, there is a weak solution left in the dye bath after I finish with a color. I don't like to stop, empty the pan, wash it, and start over with fresh water, so I throw a handful of selvages (in whatever colors I have) into the hot dye bath and turn up the heat for a minute or two until the water clears."

color. I don't like to stop, empty the pan, wash it, and start over with fresh water, so I throw a handful of selvages (in whatever colors I have) into the hot dye bath and turn up the heat for a minute or two until the water clears. The color is almost always soft and pretty after the first bath, but sometimes I throw the same handful into several baths before finally rinsing and drying them. This is definitely not a scientific way of dyeing wool, but it is a nice way to turn throwaway wool edges into beautiful, intriguing scraps for use in future projects. At the same time, it clears the dye bath before I start the next batch of dip dyes.

DYEING PINK BACKGROUNDS

I would describe the background color in this rug as a light brownish pink. Dye something similar to it by using my Country Color formula for Pink Blush or the older version of the formula that I called Country Color Flesh. If you have one of these formulas, or any other formula that you like for dyeing swatches, just mix it up as if you were going to dye swatches, then spoon some into a clear dye bath with 1/4 cup white vinegar added and dye 1/2 yard of wool at a time. If you want the dyed piece to be light in color, add a little dye at a time. Remove the wool after it takes up the dye, add more dye, and then return the wool to the dye bath. Continue doing this, a little at a time, until the wool is the right color. Remember that when it's wet, wool looks darker than it does when it's dry.

Another way to get a similar color is to combine two brown Cushing dyes. Mix 1/32 teaspoon Mahogany with 1/128 teaspoon Medium or Seal Brown in 1 cup of boiling water. (Place the dry dyes in a glass 1-cup measure and add a few teaspoons of tepid water. Stir it to make a paste. Add boiling water to make 1 cup and stir it briskly until the dyes are completely dissolved.) Add about 1/4 cup of the solution to hot water in a pan large enough to dye 1/2 yard of wool. Add 1/4 cup of white vinegar and white or natural wool that you have soaked in hot water with a wetting agent. Stir the wool a little when you first put it in. Cover the pan loosely with foil. Bring the heat up to boiling, but not a rolling boil. Hold it at that temperature for a few minutes until the water clears. When the water clears, turn off the heat and allow the wool to cool for 16 to 20 minutes, then rinse it in warm water and let it dry.

For the wide outer border I used the same color, but in a darker shade. To dye it, use the Cushing formula above, but add 1/2 cup of dye solution to the dye bath to dye 1/2 yard of wool.

I always recommend soaking wool in hot water and a wetting agent prior to dyeing it. Commercial wetting agents are available from several suppliers.

Wetter Than Wet can be purchased from Ramona Maddox, 7108 Panavista Lane, Chattanooga, TN 37421, (423) 894-1858, or from Harry M. Fraser Co., 433 Duggins Road, Stoneville, NC 27048, (910) 573-9830.

Synthrapol is available from PRO Chemical & Dye, Inc., P.O. Box 14, Somerset, MA 02726, (508) 676-3838, (800) 2-BUY-DYE (orders only).

CHAPTER SIX

THE GREAT OUTDOORS

Fruitful Dyeing

Pear Flashcard, *9" x 10 1/2", #3- and 6-cut wool on burlap. Designed and hooked by Maryanne Lincoln, Wrentham, Massachusetts, 1996.*

HOOKED FRUIT IS FUN TO DYE AND A CHALLENGE TO HOOK, NO MATTER WHAT CUT OF WOOL YOU USE. FORTUNATELY, THERE IS NO SHORTAGE OF VISUAL AIDS AVAILABLE TO HELP YOU HOOK REALISTIC APPLES, PEACHES, OR WHATEVER. A PLENTIFUL VARIETY OF FRUIT CAN BE FOUND AT THE SUPERMARKET ALL YEAR LONG, AND MANY GARDEN, NATURE, AND ART BOOKS CONTAINING EXCELLENT PICTURES ARE IN THE LIBRARY.

When I hook fruits, especially unfamiliar ones such as a pomegranate or an unusual type of apple, I reach for several books I own that have fruit and vegetable illustrations. I study how the stem goes into the fruit and the coloration of the leaves. Sometimes I sketch the fruit with colored pencils. This helps me see where I need to add shadows and highlights and how to overlap different hues to get the finished color of the fruit. When I've finished my research, I get out my wools and dyes.

The fruits in *Pear Flashcard* and *Pear with Blueberries* are hooked with realistic coloring, but don't limit yourself to absolute accuracy. Fruit-patterned wall hangings often lend themselves to monochromatic color interpretations. I have seen panels of fruit done in soft rose tones, blue tones, and brown tones.

PEAR FLASHCARD

Here's how I hooked and dyed the two pears. The background of *Pear Flashcard* is hooked with #6-cut white wool in a reverse stitch. The reverse stitch is hooked from the back, and the loops are pulled flat against the front of the backing. Alternating the placement of the loops in adjacent rows creates the look of a brick wall. The leaf is hooked with a 6-value gradation swatch of Gray Green, one of my Country Colors.

To dye the pear as I did, use Cushing Perfection dyes over Dorr Mill's #83 yellow wool. First

Pear with Blueberries, *9 1/4" x 5 3/4", #3-cut wool on burlap. Designed and hooked by Maryanne Lincoln, Wrentham, Massachusetts, 1996.*

soak a 12" x 24" piece of wool in hot water with a drop or two of Synthrapol (a wetting agent) added. Pour enough hot tap water into a 2-quart white saucepan so it is 1/3 full; add 1/8 cup of white vinegar. Place the pan on the stove and turn the heat on so the water simmers.

Add 1/128 teaspoon of Mummy Brown to the dye bath and stir. With rubber gloves or tongs hold one end of the wet wool and dip the entire strip up and down in the dye bath until the water is almost clear (as in **Figure 1a**). When the water has only a trace of color to it, remove the wool and add another 1/128 teaspoon of Mummy Brown. Then dip the lower two thirds of the strip (b) up and down in the dye bath until the water clears.

FIGURE 1

Take out the wool and add 1/64 teaspoon of Golden Brown to the dye bath. Dip the lower two thirds of the wool (c) until the water clears.

Take the wool out of the bath and add 1/32 teaspoon of Medium Brown, Dip only the lower half of the wool (d) up and down until the water clears.

Remove the wool, add 1/64 teaspoon of Black, and dip the lower third of the wool (e) in the dye bath until the water clears, Simmer the whole piece in the cleared water for a few minutes. Remove the wool, rinse it, and allow it to dry.

PEAR WITH BLUEBERRIES

The background of *Pear with Blueberries* is hooked with #3-cut dark brown wool, used as-is. I hooked the leaves with one of my Country Colors. The pear is dyed with PRO Chem wash-fast acid dyes over Dorr's #42 beige wool. (For a brighter pear, use #83 yellow wool.) Normally I use the basic dye colors red, blue, yellow, and black, but this time I used #233 orange along with #490 blue and #672 black. When I want to mix browns, as I did for this pear, I like the results I get by using orange with a little bit of blue, its complement, added to it.

To recreate this brown pear, soak a 9" x 15" piece of wool in hot tap water with Synthrapol added. Use a 2-quart white enamel saucepan 1/3 full of hot tap water with 1/8 cup of white vinegar added. Place the pan on the stove and turn the heat on so the water simmers.

Add 1/64 teaspoon of #233 orange to the dye bath and dip the wool up and down in this sequence: First dip the bottom third of the strip down and up, then the bottom two thirds down and up, and finally the whole strip down and up (**Figure 2**). Repeat this sequence until the water clears.

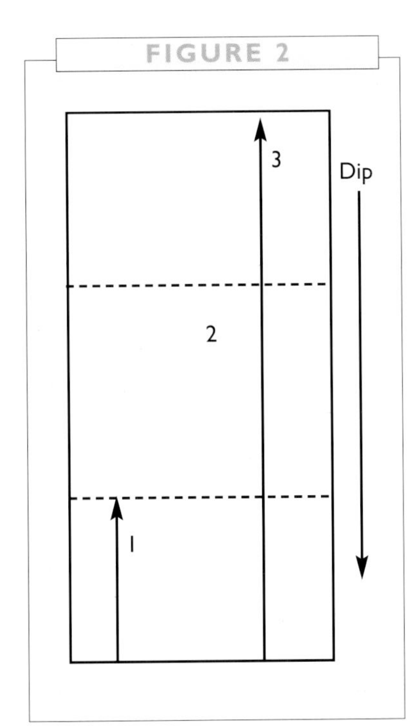

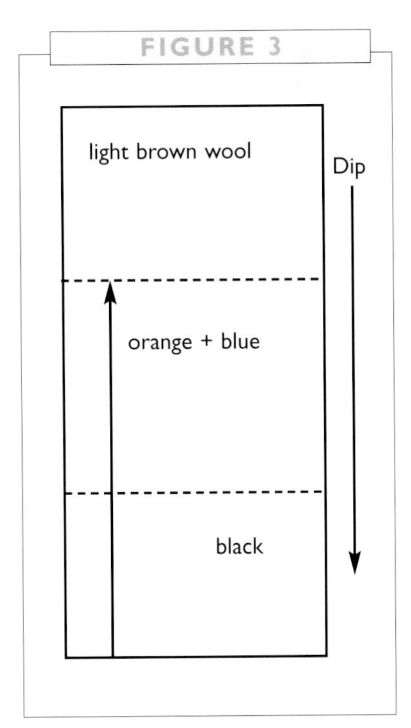

Dissolve 1/128 teaspoon of #490 blue in 1/2 cup of boiling water and add 3 teaspoons of the solution to the dye bath. Dip the wool as you did in the previous step. Keep adding blue by the teaspoonful until the dipped wool looks brown to light brown. Don't overdo it.

Add 1/128 teaspoon of #233 orange and 6 teaspoons of the blue solution to the dye bath and dip the lower two thirds of light brown wool until the water clears. Add 1/64 teaspoon of #672 black and dip just the lower third of the wool (**Figure 3**), When the water clears, simmer the whole piece for a few minutes. Rinse it and allow it to dry

DYEING THE BLUEBERRIES

Dye the blueberries over pale blue wool. If you're using Cushing Perfection dyes, use a 2-quart white saucepan 1/3 full of hot tap water with 2 tablespoons of white vinegar added. Add 1/64 teaspoon of Sky Blue to the dye bath. Dip a 9" x 12" piece of wet wool into the dye bath, following the dipping sequence shown in **Figure 2**. After the water clears, add 1/128 teaspoon of Black and dip just the lower third of the strip. If it is not blue enough, repeat both steps.

If you're using PRO Chem wash-fast acid dyes, prepare a dye bath as above and add 1/64 teaspoon of #490 blue to it. Dip the entire piece of wool in the dye bath until the water clears. Then add 1/64 teaspoon of #672 black and dip just the lower third of the wool. If it's not blue enough, repeat the first step. If it's too bright, repeat the second step. Simmer the wool in the clear bath for a few minutes. Rinse it and allow it to dry.

DYE SPECIFICATIONS

You may wonder why I specify wash-fast dyes when I write about PRO Chem dyes. PRO Chem has many types of dyes for dyeing different fabrics, so it's important to be specific. Likewise, I refer to Cushing Perfection dyes as opposed to their acid dyes. Write or call the companies at the addresses below for a list of all their dyes.

PRO Chemical & Dye Inc.
PO Box 14, Somerset, MA 02726
(508) 676-3838

W Cushing & Company
21 North Street, PO Box 351
Kennebunkport, ME 04046-0351
(800) 626-7847

A Garden of Color

Tulip Garden, *18" x 11 1/2", #5-cut wool on burlap. Designed and hooked by Maryanne Lincoln, Wrentham, Massachusetts, 1997. Maryanne describes how to dye wool for the leaves and stems of this colorful flower garden. Also shown are the Color Sheets Maryanne used for the tulips for this project.*

UNLIKE THE MUTED COLORS IN MY HOOKED *TULIP GARDEN*, REAL TULIPS AND THEIR FOLIAGE COME IN BRIGHT REDS, YELLOWS, PINKS, AND GREENS. HOWEVER, I NEVER FEEL RESTRICTED BY GARDEN COLORS WHEN I HOOK FLOWERS AND LEAVES. REALISTIC COLORING IS AN OPTION, NOT A NECESSITY.

Nevertheless, the first thing I do when planning a pattern with flowers and leaves is look at visual aids to figure out how to shape petals and stems, and to see some of the natural colors of the flowers. Tulips are familiar to most of us, but I still spent time looking through gardening books, catalogs, and art books before designing this piece.

THE COLOR PLAN

The colors I chose for my tulips swing from red through orange to yellow on the color wheel. I wanted my tulips in those hues to complement those in the room where this piece will hang.

I designed this pattern to use the 12" x 24" dip-dyed swatches I created called Color Sheets. First I drew the design on paper and used colored pencils to work out a color plan that pleased me. I often use colored pencils in this way, especially when I have concerns about achieving a pleasing color balance.

Once the colored drawing is done, however, I do not feel locked into following it exactly. It

DIP DYEING WITH ACID DYES

Because different color dyes can activate at slightly different temperatures, there is always the chance that the color will separate if you add all the dye to the dye bath at once and try to dip the wool strips in one step. If this happens, add the dye in small amounts. Dip the strips until the water clears and then add more dye and dip again. Keep adding small amounts of dye and dipping until you get the color you want.

Always start with a dye bath of water and vinegar that is very hot (simmering, not boiling) and keep it hot until you achieve the color you desire.

is merely a guide. I referred to it as I started hooking each tulip to remind myself of the placement of each color, and also used it to help sort out all of the leaf lines from the background areas.

Most of my Color Sheets are dyed with PRO Chem wash-fast acid dyes, but a few are dyed with Cushing Perfection dyes. I have never had a problem dip dyeing with PRO Chem dyes, but some of you have told me that you do. Please read the box above for some tips on dip dyeing with acid dyes. Although simple dips—like what I used for the tulip leaves—have only two steps, most of my Color Sheet formulas take three or four steps to get the right color.

The antique black background of *Tulip Garden* is Dorr's #44 black wool spotted with PRO Chem #338 red dye. I used 1/8 teaspoon of dye for each half yard of wool dyed. A variety of closely related pinks and yellows and dull, light orange tones were combined to create the tulips. I used my regular stock of Color Sheets in Sunflower, Yellow Rose, Sunrise Sunset, Victorian Moss, Peppermint Pink, Peaches, Terra Cotta, and Pink Blush Smoked to hook the springtime blossoms. All are relatively soft in color and look nice together.

DYEING THE LEAVES

I chose a color for the leaves that would complement the tulip colors. All of the foliage is done with one green dip dye, which goes from the dull, grayed, deep tones of a soft green to the lighter, brighter green of the tips and highlights. This greenery forms a backdrop for the tulips. I first hooked all of the tulips and stems and then the leaves and background.

To dye the wool for your own tulip leaves, soak two 12" x 24" pieces of natural or off-white wool in hot tap water with a few drops of Synthrapol added. Heat to a simmer about 2 1/2" of water in a large rectangular pan (6" deep or more) with 1/8 cup of white vinegar added. Add 1/16 teaspoon of #728N green PRO Chem wash-fast acid dye and 1/64 teaspoon of' #233 orange to the dye bath.

Keep the dye bath simmering and dip the two pieces of wool in the following manner. (Wear loose, heavy-duty, lined rubber gloves for this work.) Dip one end of the strips into the dye bath at one end of the pan and gently lay the pieces on their sides lengthwise in the pan. Then lift the strips and dip the other ends in the dye bath at one end of the pan and lay the other side of the strips in the pan lengthwise. Repeat this procedure until you have dip-dyed pieces going from light green at one end to darker green on the other end.

This procedure is used rather than the traditional dip-dyeing method to accommodate the large strips. Because you will be placing the strips in the bath without spreading them out, the dye will be uneven and mottled when you finish, but one end of the strips will definitely be darker than the other end. Between the two extremes of light and dark are layers of color all along the strip.

When the water clears, remove the strips and put them in a small pan or basin while you prepare the second step of the formula. Add 1/16 teaspoon #672 black to the dye bath and stir it a little. Dip the darker ends of the two green strips into the dye solution. Do not lay the strips in the solution yet. When there is still color in the dye bath but you can begin to see through it, quickly put the strips into the bath—first on one side and then the other. The water will clear rapidly. Inspect the strips. If you are satisfied with the results, let the strips simmer for a few minutes so the dye can penetrate to the core of the wool. Rinse the wool thoroughly.

With this variegated green and the muted pinks, yellows, and oranges of Color Sheets or your own favorite formulas, you can hook a garden of tulips to enjoy year round.

Sunflowers in Winter

Sunflowers in Winter, *14 1/2" x 19 1/2", #5-cut wool on linen. Designed and hooked by Maryanne Lincoln, Wrentham, Massachusetts, 1997. Maryanne describes how to dip-dye wool for the sunflower's petals and greenery.*

MANY OF YOU HAVE EXPRESSED INTEREST IN LEARNING TO DYE THE 12" X 24" DIP DYES I CALL COLOR SHEETS. THIS SECTION WILL EXPLAIN HOW TO USE THE TECHNIQUE TO DYE WOOL FOR THE PETALS AND LEAVES OF A SUNFLOWER.

Those who live in northern climes know it's impossible to see bright yellow sunflowers in the garden during the harsh cold of winter, but it is possible to hook them into rugs and wall hangings. If your sunflower will hang on the wall, try hooking the background with the reverse stitch as I have done in the piece shown above. It requires less wool and hooks up quickly. The reverse stitch is hooked from the back, and the loops are pulled flat against the front of the backing. Alternating the placement of the loops in adjacent rows creates the look of a brick wall. This stitch is not recommended for floor rugs because it is easily snagged and pulled out.

DYEING COLOR SHEETS

To dye the Sunflower Color Sheet, you will need a deep rectangular pan about 12" x 15" and 5" to 6" deep. Deep refrigerator pans are perfect. I use a rectangular stainless steel pan I found in a restaurant supply store.

You will also need heavy duty, loose-fitting rubber gloves to handle the wool as you dip and lay it into the hot dye solution. Heavy gloves are not an option for this type of dyeing—they are a necessity. Steam and boiling water are the most dangerous parts of dyeing. I buy Bluette brand gloves at my local hardware store; regular latex gloves are not heavy enough. Make sure the gloves are lined and are a size bigger than your normal choice for rubber gloves so you can slip your hands into and out of them quickly and easily.

The formula for the sunflower's petals requires five PRO Chemical & Dye wash fast acid dyes: #338 red, #490 blue, #119 yellow, #672 black, and #728N green. To dye the wool as I did, you will need 9 pieces of Dorr's #100 natural wool, each measur-

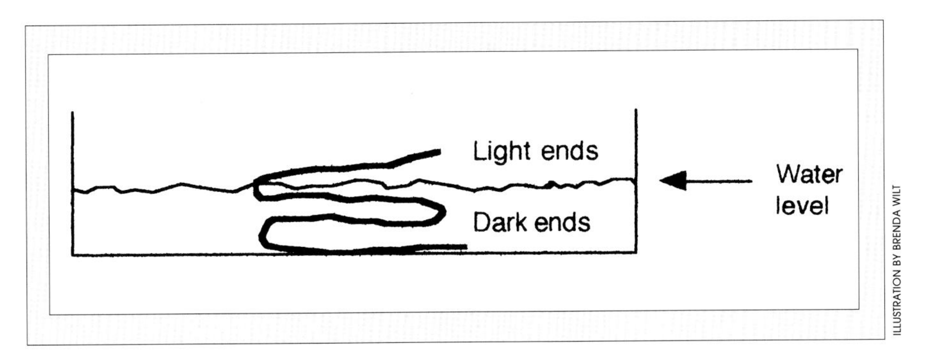

ing 12" x 24". If you want to dye only 3 pieces, mix the dyes as directed in 1 cup of boiling water, but use only 1/3 of the dye solution for each step.

Soak the wool in hot tap water and Synthrapol. Fill the rectangular pan with hot water to a depth of 2 1/2" to 3". Add 1/4 cup of white vinegar to the pan and place it over high heat.

Dissolve 3/16 teaspoon of #119 yellow, 1/128 teaspoon #338 red, and 1/128 teaspoon #672 black in 1 cup of boiling water. (Measure the dry dyes into a 1-cup measure. Add 1 or 2 teaspoons of tepid water and stir it to make a paste. Add boiling water to the 1-cup level and stir until the dye is completely dissolved.) This solution will be used for the first two dips.

Add half of the dye solution to the dye bath. Stir it a little. Wearing your gloves, gather all nine wool pieces together, hold the wool at the top with both hands, and dip the ends into the dye bath. Dip the ends a few times and then lay the pieces in the bath. Lift the pieces and lay them on their other sides. This will result in yellow from dark to light the entire length of the strips.

When the water clears, remove the strips and place them in a clean pan next to the one you're working in. Add the rest of the dye solution to the dye bath, gather the strips, and dip them again. This time dip only the lower 2/3 of the pieces (the darker ends) so the upper ends will keep their pretty yellow color. When the water starts to clear, stack the strips accordion style with the light ends on top and out of the water (see illustration). Cover the pan loosely with aluminum foil. The water should be right at a boil but not rolling—keep it hot. Let the pieces steam while you mix the next solution.

Dissolve 1/32 teaspoon #338 red, 1/16 teaspoon #119 yellow, 1/128 teaspoon #490 blue, and 1/128 teaspoon #672 black in 1 cup of boiling water. Remove the strips from the dye bath and place them in the resting pan. Add the new dye solution to the dye bath, stir it, and only dip the strips 1/2 to 2/3 of their length. When the water starts to clear, stack the strips accordion style with the light ends at the top and out of the dye bath. Cover the pan loosely with foil and let it steam as you did before while you mix the next solution.

Dissolve 1/128 teaspoon #490 blue in 1 cup of boiling water. Remove the strips to the resting pan, add the blue to the dye bath, and dip only the darkest 1/3 of the strips until the water clears. Stack the pieces with the light ends out of the water. Cover loosely, reduce the heat to low, and steam for five minutes. Rinse the wool thoroughly and hang it to dry.

THE LEAVES AND STEM

There are fewer steps to dye the green for the leaves and stem. The following directions are for dyeing six pieces of 12" x 24" natural wool. To dye three pieces, use only 1/2 of the dye solution in each step.

Dissolve in 1 cup of boiling water 3/16 teaspoon #119 yellow, 1/4 teaspoon #728 N green, 3/64 teaspoon #338 red, and 1/128 teaspoon #672 black. Add the solution to the dye bath and dip the strips all the way to the top, then lay them in the dye bath so the full length can take up the color. Cover the pan loosely and steam for a few minutes while you mix the next solution.

Create a dye solution identical to the one you just made. After removing the wool, add the solution to the dye bath and dip the bottom half of the strips so one end gets darker. Stack the strips accordion style with the lightest ends on top and out of the dye solution. Cover loosely and steam about five minutes, or until the water is perfectly clear. Rinse the wool thoroughly and hang it to dry.

The dark center of my sunflower is a green and gray check overdyed with red, dull red, and a bit of black. The background is bright blue overdyed in a mottled fashion with 1/16 teaspoon #672 black. Hooking in the reverse stitch really sets off the sunflower.

Leafy Greens

IF YOU HOOK WITH #3-CUT STRIPS, DO YOUR OWN DYEING, AND LIKE TO USE LOTS OF VALUES AND SHADES OF A COLOR, WHAT I HAVE DONE WITH THE PRINCESS PINE GREEN SWATCH WILL APPEAL TO YOU. IF YOU HOOK WITH #3 STRIPS BUT DON'T DO YOUR OWN DYEING, THIS MAY MOTIVATE YOU TO GET OUT THE DYE POTS AND TRY IT.

Using the jar dyeing method on page 44, I have dyed Princess Pine three times: First I dyed the formula over natural wool; second, over yellow wool; and third, over natural with an equal amount of yellow dye added to each value.

The three versions of the color are very similar, with the greatest noticeable differences in the lightest three values of each. However, the one I dyed with extra yellow dye added to each value is definitely brighter than the other two throughout the entire swatch.

I want to encourage you to use formulas you already have to create variations that will add interest to your hooked pieces. The variations need not be complicated to be interesting. Apply what I have done with this green to other formulas to add more variety to the colors in your projects.

EXPERIMENT WITH COMBINATIONS

Try other combinations with this same formula to create more interesting variations. Dye Princess Pine over Dorr's #42 gray-beige to make a soft gray-green swatch. Or dye it over medium-light turquoise wool for another lively leaf variation. Experiment with my Khaki Country Color over medium-light turquoise wool, as well as mint-green or yellow.

When you are trying to decide what colors to overdye with for interesting combinations, remember what happens when you put complements together: Complementary colors dull each other when mixed together. For example, if you were to dye Princess Pine over pink wool, the color would be very muddy, because red and green are complementary colors. If the pink were strong enough, you might even end up with a dull red-brown.

On the other hand, analagous colors (which fall beside each other on the color wheel) add interest when used together. I chose to dye green over yellow wool and add yellow dye to the green formula because yellow is analogous to green. Yellow added to the green formula creates yellow-green, especially in the light values, and adds a feeling of sunshine to the hue. If you were to add turquoise dye to the formula or dye this green over turquoise

Leaves Bellpull, *6" x 36", #3-cut wool on burlap. Designed by Pearl K. McGown. Hooked by Maryanne Lincoln, Wrentham, Massachusetts, 1998. Maryanne explains how to dye the greens for the leaves in this piece.*

Dyed samples of Maryanne's formulas include (left to right) Princess Pine dyed over natural wool with yellow added, Princess Pine dyed over natural wool, Princess Pine dyed over yellow wool, and Khaki, a Country Color swatch.

wool, you would be adding an analogous color on the blue side of green and also adding sparkle.

LEAVES OF GREEN

Leaves are one of my favorite things to hook. They are not just boring things that have to be hooked to go with the pretty flowers in our rugs. Leaves are beautiful in their own right. They come in all shapes, sizes, and shades of green. Some, of course, are more yellow than other leaves, or browner or bluer. Some are even quite gray. Others are bright and shiny as if they were covered with oil. Furthermore, most leaves are different on the back than they are on the front, and some, like rose leaves, have reddish veins.

The *Leaves Bellpull* has five different leaf shapes arranged in an interesting combination with colorful berries. I used variations of Princess Pine to hook the strawberry, blueberry, and raspberry leaves. The five grape leaves were hooked with two variations of a Khaki formula. For the berry leaves, I dyed Princess Pine over Dorr's #100 natural wool and over Dorr's #83, a soft yellow. This gave me two variations of the same color. These two versions can be used in the same leaf or in two different leaves.

I also created another variation of Princess Pine by using the formula, as written, over natural wool, but before adding the wool to the dyeing jars, I added 1/128 teaspoon of #119 yellow dye to each jar. (Don't forget to stir the dye solution vigorously before adding the wool.) This swatch is much brighter than the Princess Pine dyed over yellow wool. I used it in the greenest looking grape leaf.

I dyed two variations of Khaki Green for the remaining leaves. The first was Khaki Drab dyed over apricot wool. See it used in the bottom and middle grape leaves. The top grape leaf is done in Khaki, one of my Country

MARYANNE'S LEAFY GREENS

Princess Pine

(To be jar dyed in 6 values over 9" x 12" wool with PRO Chemical & Dye wash-fast acid dyes)

1/16 tsp #672 black
3/64 tsp #490 blue
9/32 tsp #119 yellow
3/128 tsp #338 red

The following 3 formulas are to be jar dyed in 6 values over 9" x 12" wool with Cushing brand dyes.

Foliage

1/32 tsp Black
3/16 tsp Peacock
1/2 tsp Canary
1/32 tsp Cherry

Khaki Drab

1/4 tsp Khaki Drab

Khaki (Country Color)

1/16 tsp Black
1/8 tsp Medium Brown
1/128 tsp Plum

For this last formula, mix together the three dyes in 1 cup of boiling water and dispense to jars according to the jar method. Then add 1/64 teaspoon Maize to each jar before adding the wool.

> *"When I hook fruits, especially unfamiliar ones such as a pomegranate or an unusual type of apple, I reach for several books I own that have fruit and vegetable illustrations."*

Colors, dyed over natural wool. The background for the bellpull is Dorr's natural wool, undyed.

For those of you who use Cushing dyes; I am including a green gradation formula for you to experiment with. Dye it over natural wool and then try some of the variations I've suggested. This is a beautiful formula for leaves, and I am sure you will be pleased with the many interesting alternatives you can devise.

You can do the same sort of variations by starting with just one of the Cushing greens. For example, Reseda Green, Olive Green, Bright Green, and Bronze Green are beautiful leaf colors themselves. Try dyeing Reseda over pale turquoise wool or adding 1/128 teaspoon Turquoise to each jar before adding the wool. I guarantee you will be pleased with the results.

COLOR THEORY THOUGHTS

One of the greens, Khaki Drab, was dyed over apricot and deserves special comment because apricot is a light version of orange. Think back to our color theory discussions and you will remember that orange is a combination of red and yellow. Red is complementary to green and will dull it.

Yellow, however, is analogous to green and will liven it up and change it to a slightly yellowed green. Therefore, when you dye Khaki Drab (which by itself is a grayed green) over apricot you have two things going on: Both red and yellow are being added because of the color of the wool. The dyed color will be slightly duller and also slightly more yellow.

Three Greens

FOR JANE MCGOWN FLYNN'S *LITTLE MILLBURY*, MY COLOR PLAN INCLUDED THREE DIFFERENT GREENS: A MEDIUM GRAY-GREEN FOR THE SCROLLS, DYED OVER A WHITE-AND-GRAY HOUND'S-TOOTH WOOL; A LIGHT AQUA-GREEN FOR THE BACKGROUND, DYED OVER NATURAL WOOL; AND A GRAY-GREEN DIP DYE FOR THE ROSE LEAVES, DYED OVER NATURAL WOOL.

Little Millbury, *43 1/2" x 24" #5-cut wool on burlap. Designed by Jane McGown Flynn. Hooked by Maryanne Lincoln, Wrentham, Massachusetts, 1999.*

As I was planning my colors, I decided to hook the scrolls with the outline-and-fill method and shade the flowers and leaves. To brighten the medium-value gray-green scrolls I chose a quiet version of their complement to outline them—a medium-light dip-dyed swatch called Victorian Moss. One end of the strip is slightly pink and the other end ranges from dull green to brownish green. The color variation added interest to the otherwise plain scrolls.

Victorian Moss is one of my Color Sheets, which I developed for use in wide-cut rugs. Each dip-dyed swatch measures 12" x 24". Flo Petruchik helped me create the first Color Sheets, and I have since produced many variations of the original colors as well as quite a few new ones. I hooked the rose in *Little Millbury* with a new Color Sheet called Peach Blush #1. The light to middle values of my Sunflower Color Sheet worked well for the yellow padulas, and the middle-dark to dark values formed some of the padulas' brownish leaves.

One of the padulas in my rug is a brownish pink. At first I hooked all four padulas with yellow, but that made the color plan boring. When I changed one of them to pick up the rose color, everything fell into place. If my initial color plan doesn't please me, I try to figure out what will improve it and then start changing things, one small thing at a time, until I am satisfied with the result.

SCROLLS

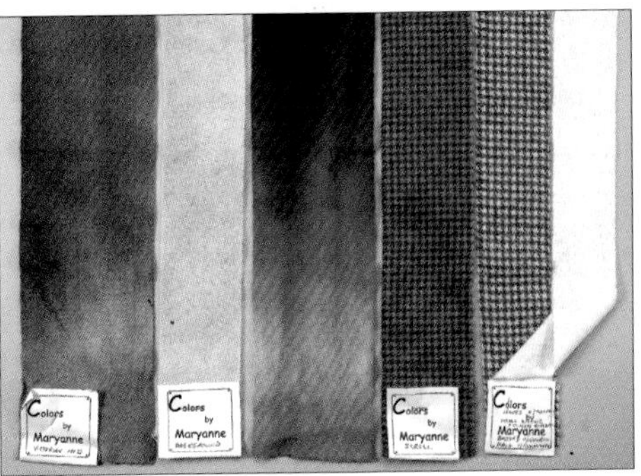

The wool Maryanne used to hook **Little Millbury** *includes Victorian Moss (left) for the scroll outline, and three greens (center) for the background, rose leaves, and scrolls. At the far right are the hound's tooth and natural wool before they were dyed. Formulas for the three greens appear in the accompanying*

I hooked the scrolls with one yard of gray-and-white hound's-tooth wool dyed a medium-gray-green.

Cushing Formula

1/4 tsp Silver Gray Green

Dissolve the dye in 1 cup of boiling water. Put the dye solution and 1/4 cup of white vinegar into a pan with enough hot water to cover 1 yard of wool. Place the soaked wool in the dye bath and stir it until the wool is completely submerged. Simmer the wool over medium heat until the water clears (at least 10 minutes). After the wool cools, rinse it well and hang it to dry.

PRO Chem Formula

3/32 tsp #672 black

1/32 tsp #490 blue

3/32 tsp #119 yellow

Dissolve the dyes in 1 cup of boiling water. Add 1/2 cup of the solution and 1/4 cup of white vinegar to a pan with enough hot water to cover 1 yard of wool. Add the soaked wool to the dye bath and stir it until it is submerged. Simmer the wool over medium heat until the water clears (at least 10 minutes). If the wool is not dark enough to please you, add the rest of the dye solution and continue dyeing. After the wool cools, rinse it well and hang it to dry.

If you prefer a shaded scroll, use 1/2 the formula to dye the 1-yard piece of wool. Soak the wool as usual. Add the wool to a large pot or refrigerator pan with about 4" of very hot tap water and 1/4 cup of white vinegar. Simmer the wool over medium heat and stir it around to make sure all of it has a chance to absorb the dye. Then lift the wool out of the dye bath and add the rest of the solution, along with another 1/4 cup of vinegar.

Put on a pair of heavy, lined rubber gloves so you don't burn yourself handling hot wool. Gather the wool at one end and dip the other end into the dye bath. Dip the wool up and down a few times, gradually lowering the wool each time you dip it until you have dipped 3/4 of its length. Keep dipping the wool until the dye bath almost clears. Then lower the entire length of wool into the bath, cover the pan loosely with foil, and let the wool simmer for 5 to 10 minutes. If you want the wool to have more color, mix up the solution again and repeat the dipping. Continue with this procedure until you get the depth of color you want.

DYE FORMULAS

Here are Cushing formulas and PRO Chemical & Dye formulas for the background, scrolls, and rose leaves of *Little Millbury*. Use the formulas for whichever brand of dyes you prefer.

PALE GREEN BACKGROUND

The background required a total of 2 yards of natural wool; I dyed 2/3 yard of it at a time. Out of all that material, I had only two 3" x 24" strips left after hooking the background. If you get nervous about running out of background wool, dye an extra 1/3 yard.

Cushing Formula

1/32 tsp Aquagreen

1/128 tsp Black

This formula will dye 2/3 yard of wool. Soak the wool in hot tap water and a wetting agent. Dissolve the dyes in 1 cup of boiling water. (Measure the dry dyes into a 1-cup glass measure and add a few teaspoons of tepid water to make a paste. Add boiling water to the 1-cup level and stir it briskly until the dye is dissolved.) Add the dye solution to a pan with 1/4 cup of white vinegar and enough hot water to cover the wool. Place the soaked wool in the dye bath and stir it until it is submerged. Simmer the wool over medium heat until the water clears (about 10 minutes for this light color; darker colors will take longer). Allow the wool to cool, rinse it well, and hang it to dry. Repeat this procedure twice more with 2/3-yard wool pieces to dye a total of 2 yards.

PRO Chem Formula

3/16 tsp #672 black

1/16 tsp #490 blue

3/16 tsp #119 yellow

This formula will dye 2 yards of wool so use 1/3 of the solution to dye one 2/3-yard piece. Dissolve the dyes in 1 cup of boiling water as described above. Add 1/3 cup of the dye solution and 1/4 cup of white vinegar to a pan with enough hot water to cover the wool. Add the soaked wool to the dye bath and stir it until it is submerged. Simmer the wool over medium heat until the water clears (at least 10 minutes). After the wool cools, rinse it well and hang it to dry. Repeat this procedure twice more with 2/3-yard pieces of wool.

ROSE LEAVES

The rose leaves were hooked with a special dip dye. I used 9" x 24" strips and dip dyed 6 at one time.

Cushing Formula

There are three steps to this formula.

1/8 tsp Silver Gray Green

Dissolve the dye in 1 cup of boiling water, and then add the solution and 1/4 cup of white vinegar to a simmering dye bath. Wearing heavy rubber gloves, gather the six strips at one end and dip them into the dye bath together. Gradually dip the strips lower into the bath until the entire strips are in. When the water clears, remove the wool.

1/4 tsp Silver Gray Green

Next, dissolve 1/4 teaspoon of the dye in 1 cup of boiling water and add it to the dye bath. Dip the strips as in the first step, this time stopping when you've dipped them to 2/3 of their length.

1/32 tsp Black

Finally, dissolve 1/32 teaspoon Black in 1 cup of boiling water and add the solution to the dye bath. Dip the strips as you did before, but dip only the bottom 1/3. When the water is almost clear, lay the strips in the pan, cover the pan loosely with foil, and let the wool simmer for 10 minutes. After the wool cools, rinse it well and hang it to dry.

PRO Chem Formula

There are three steps to this formula.

3/32 tsp #672 black

1/32 tsp #490 blue

3/32 tsp #119 yellow

Dissolve the dyes in 1 cup of boiling water. Add the solution to a dye bath that includes 1/4 cup of white vinegar. Dip six strips together as described above, gradually dipping the strips lower into the bath with each dip until you finally put the entire strips in. When the water clears, remove the wool.

3/32 tsp #672 black

1/32 tsp #490 blue

3/32 tsp #119 yellow

Next, mix up the same solution and add it to the dye bath. Dip the strips as you did before, but this time stopping when you've dipped the strips to 2/3 of their length.

1/32 tsp #672 black

1/64 tsp #490 blue

Finally, dissolve 1/32 teaspoon of #672 black, plus 1/64 teaspoon of #490 blue in 1 cup of boiling water and add it to the dye bath. This time, dip just the bottom 1/3 of the strips until the water nearly clears. Lay the wool in the pan, cover it loosely with foil, and let it simmer for 10 minutes. Allow the wool to cool, then rinse it well and allow it to dry.

Dip Dye Colorful Flowers

Above: Maryanne used Victorian Moss for some of the small flowers in **Little Millbury**.

Below: Peach Blush #2 (left), Peach Blush #1, and Sunflower.

Little Millbury, *detail, 24" x 43 1/2", #5-cut wool on burlap. Designed by Jane McGown Flynn. Hooked by Maryanne Lincoln, Wrentham, Massachusetts, 1999.*

HERE ARE THE FORMULAS FOR THE FLOWERS IN *LITTLE MILLBURY*: PEACH BLUSH FOR THE BIG CENTER ROSE, AND VICTORIAN MOSS AND SUNFLOWER FOR THE FOUR SMALL FLOWERS. VICTORIAN MOSS WAS ALSO USED FOR THE OUTLINE AROUND THE SCROLLS (PAGE 98).

"Unless the dye instrictins tell you otherwise, before dyeing your wool always soak it in very hot tap water with PRO Chem's Synthrapol or a similar wetting agent."

These colors are scrunchy dip dyes that I call Color Sheets. Each is a 12" x 24" dyed sheet of wool. The formulas were developed to dye large amounts of wool, so I always dye several pieces together. At the end of this section I will offer suggestions for dyeing smaller amounts.

PREPARING TO DYE

You will need a pair of loose-fitting, heavy, lined rubber gloves and a large, deep rectangular pan to do this type of dyeing. A rectangular pan, not a round pot, is necessary to get the color variations you want when dyeing these Color Sheets. My favorite pan is a 6" deep refrigerator pan (a crisper drawer from the days when they made them out of white porcelain). Sometimes you can find these pans at yard sales and flea markets. Otherwise, use a 6" deep stainless steel pan from a restaurant supply store. The pan I have is large enough (12" x 24") to almost cover two burners on the stovetop, but I use it over the big burner on my dye kitchen electric range.

Unless the dye instructions tell you otherwise, before dyeing your wool always soak it in very hot tap water with PRO Chem's Synthrapol or a similar wetting agent. The amount needed depends on your water; I add a few drops. Start with about 1/2 teaspoon of Synthrapol. If the wool doesn't saturate easily, add another 1/2 teaspoon (it takes more to wet natural wool). Go easy because it is very concentrated. Do not rinse it out before proceeding to the dyeing—it helps the water and dye penetrate the wool fibers. On the other hand, don't add gobs of it or you will end up with suds. If that happens, just rinse the wool a little before dyeing it.

THE DYEING PROCEDURE

First I will explain the general dip dyeing procedure. Specific instructions for each color accompany the formulas in the next section.

To prepare the dye bath, add 2 1/2" to 3" of water to the rectangular pan along with 1/4 cup of white vinegar. This procedure does not require salt. Turn the heat on high under the pan so the bath can start heating while you prepare the dye mixtures.

By the time you have mixed the first solution the water in the dye pot will be getting hot. Add the dye solution to the pan as directed for the formula and stir it a little. Put on your gloves and gather up all the wet wool sheets and dip just their ends into the dye solution. You don't have to wait until the water is real hot to begin dipping. Continue dipping the wool, with each dip going deeper into the dye solution. Dip the ends in the pan in one corner and lay the whole bunch lengthwise (without letting go of the strips) toward the diagonally opposite corner. Dip the strips back and forth from corner to corner as the water clears. Open the strips a little to make sure there are no white areas trapped inside where you have been gripping the wool; you don't necessarily want them evenly dyed, however. When the water clears remove the bundle of strips to a resting pan—any sort of pan you can have close to the dye pot.

When all the steps for your formula have been completed and the water is just about clear (the heat has been on high all the while), reduce the heat to low, put the strips in the dye bath, cover the pan loosely with foil, and simmer the wool for a few more minutes. Once the water clears, simmer the wool 5 minutes longer. Allow the wool to cool, rinse it well, and hang it to dry.

FORMULAS

The following formulas require PRO Chem wash-fast acid dyes. In each instance dissolve the dyes in 1 cup of boiling water using the following procedure: Place the dry dyes in a 1-cup glass measuring cup and add a few teaspoons of tepid water to form a paste. Add boiling water to the 1-cup level and stir it briskly to dissolve the dyes.

Sunflower

Dye 9 pieces of 12" x 24" natural wool.

Step 1

3/16 tsp #119 yellow
1/128 tsp #338 red
1/128 tsp #672 black

Pour 1/2 cup of the dye solution into the dye pot and dip all the strips as described above until they are dyed from light to dark. After the water clears add the rest of the solution and repeat the dipping. When the water clears remove the wool.

Step 2

1/16 tsp #119 yellow
1/32 tsp #338 red
1/128 tsp #490 blue
1/128 tsp #672 black

Add the full cup of the solution to the dye pot and dip the strips together 2/3 of their length until the water clears.

Step 3

1/128 tsp #490 blue

Add the cup of solution to the dye bath and dip the strips the bottom 1/3 of their length until the water clears.

Victorian Moss

Dye 9 pieces of 12" x 24" natural wool.

Step 1

3/64 tsp #338 red

Pour the full cup of the dye solution into the dye bath. Dip all the strips together until they range from light to dark pink. Remove the wool after the water clears.

Step 2

3/128 tsp #119 yellow
1/64 tsp #338 red
1/128 tsp #490 blue
1/128 tsp #672 black

Put the 1 cup of dye solution into the dye bath. Dip the strips together 1/2 to 2/3 of their length until the water clears.

Step 3

1/128 tsp #119 yellow

Pour the cup of solution into the dye bath. Dip just the bottom 1/3 of the strips until the water clears.

Peach Blush #1

Dye 6 pieces of 12" x 24" natural wool.

Step 1

1/16 tsp #119 yellow
1/32 tsp #338 red

Add the cup of solution to the dye bath. Dip the strips together, and then lay them in the dye bath. When about half of the dye is absorbed, remove the wool and continue dipping just one end of the strips until the water begins to clear.

Step 2

1/32 tsp #338 red

While there's still a little yellow in the water, add the red dye solution and continue dipping the strips until the water clears.

Step 3

1/64 tsp #490 blue
1/64 tsp #672 black

Add 1 1/2 cup of the solution to the dye bath and dip the strips together 2/3 of their length. When the water clears add the remaining solution and dip the strips to darken 1/3 of their length.

Peach Blush #2

Dye 7 pieces of 12" x 24" natural wool.

Step 1

1/16 tsp #119 yellow
1/16 tsp #338 red

Pour the cup of solution into the dye bath. Dip the strips together until the water clears a little, and then lay the strips in the dye bath. Allow the wool to simmer until the water clears.

Step 2

1/32 tsp #672 black

Add this cup of solution to the dye bath and dip one end of the strips until the water clears.

Step 3

1/32 tsp #338 red

Put 1 cup of this dye solution into the dye bath and dip the peach ends of the strips (not the dark ends) until the water clears.

VARIATIONS

Although the formulas above call for PRO Chem wash-fast acid dyes, you can get comparable colors with Cushing dyes. In each formula substitute Cushing's Canary, Cherry, Peacock, and half the amounts of Black for similar results.

To dye fewer sheets at a time, keep a few things in mind. Many of the formulas contain tiny measurements of dye that can't be divided easily. To reduce 1/128 teaspoon to dye 1/2 or 1/4 the number of strips, mix the dyes as directed in 1 cup of boiling water and use 1/2 or 1/4 of the solution. The leftover solution can be used for other things. Likewise, to dye 1/3 the number of sheets, mix up the 1 cup of solution and use 1/3 of it in each step.

If you dye fewer strips you can also use a smaller pan. Experiment and develop your own variations. If all you have is a round pot, use it. Your results may not look just like mine, but I'll bet the swatches will be beautiful.

Dyed & Sculptured Berries

Strawberry Hand Mirror, *5" diameter, #3-cut wool on burlap. Designed and hooked by Maryanne Lincoln, Wrentham, Massachusetts, 1980s. PRO Chem dyes were used for the wool in this strawberry.*

IN THE SECTION ON BEAR BROWNS (PAGE 120), I SAY THAT SCULPTURED HOOKING (WHERE LOOPS ARE TRIMMED TO ADD DEPTH TO AN OTHERWISE FLAT SCENE) IS OFTEN INTIMIDATING FOR BEGINNING RUG HOOKERS AND SUGGEST THAT BEGINNERS TRY SCULPTURING A SMALL GROUP OF BERRIES TO GET AN IDEA OF HOW TO DO IT. SO HERE I'LL GIVE YOU SOME FORMULAS FOR BLUEBERRIES AND STRAWBERRIES, ALONG WITH DIRECTIONS FOR SCULPTURING ONE OF THE LATTER.

To practice sculpturing, draw a small group of blueberries or strawberries that, when hooked, can decorate the top of a small rectangular box. Or hook and frame a commercial pattern, as I have done with two Pearl McGown designs. Both the strawberries and the blueberries came printed on one large piece of burlap and were intended to be hooked as coverings for brick doorstops. Rather than turn them into doorstops, I cut them apart and framed them individually.

You could also hook a single strawberry and flower, as I did for the back of a wooden hand mirror. The one you see here is not sculptured, but I have hooked others that are. Compare the plain strawberry on the mirror to the sculptured strawberries in the small rectangular picture.

As with the sculptured bear on page 121, the strawberries and blueberries are easily hooked with dip-dyed swatches. Berries are small, however, so instead of yard-long pieces of wool you'll need 12" strips for blueberries and 18" or 24" strips for strawberries. Even those lengths seem large for small berries, but you must allow for the higher loops that are required for sculpturing, which are then clipped to shape.

It is always difficult to judge exactly how much of the dark,

Strawberries, *8" x 4 1/2", #3-cut wool on burlap. Designed by Pearl K. McGown. Hooked by Maryanne Lincoln, Wrentham, Massachusetts, 1980s. Maryanne used Cushing dyes to produce these strawberries.*

medium, and light values to have on the strips, especially when sculpturing. It is an educated guess, and each project is a little different. However, there are some things to keep in mind when dyeing wool for sculpturing. First, dye more wool for a sculptured piece than you would for a regularly hooked one. Second, dye longer strips than you do for regular hooking to avoid a great deal of stopping and starting, as higher loops use more wool. (To dye a multi-value swatch—with jar dyeing, for example—make the strips 24" long.) Third, take a good look at the dyed wool before cutting it so you'll know how to hook the strips after they're cut. Finally, keep in mind that you'll use a little of the dark values of your berry's color for deep shadows or outlines and a little of the light for highlights, but you'll use the middle values the most. If dyed correctly, the middle values will be the color of the berry. (This is true for both sculpturing and regular shading.)

If you hook the berries with dip dyes, you will also need a dark outline color, such as dark red for strawberries and navy blue or black for blueberries. Either dye it or find it in your scrap bag. This dark part is not sculptured, so you'll need just enough to outline the berries. The leaves that accompany the berries may or may not be sculptured.

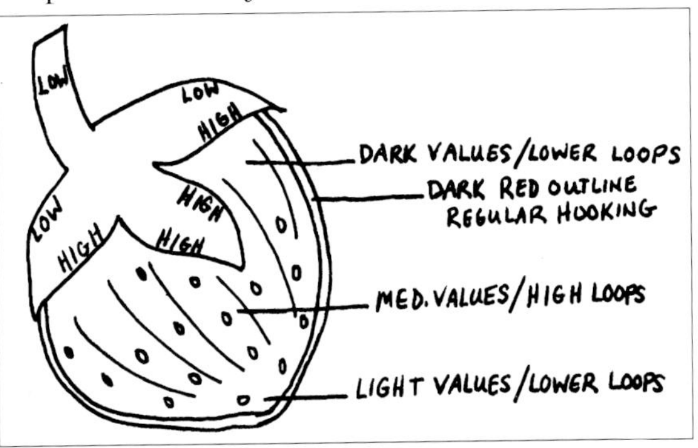

FORMULAS AND DYEING PROCEDURES

The berries I've hooked are representative of both the PRO Chem and Cushing formulas.

Strawberries

PRO Chem

9/16 tsp #338 red
3/16 tsp #119 yellow
1/128 tsp #490 blue

Cushing

1/4 tsp Cherry
1/8 tsp Canary
1/128 tsp Peacock

Blueberries

PRO Chem

1/32 tsp #338 red
1/32 tsp #119 yellow
1/8 tsp #490 blue

Cushing

1/32 tsp Cherry
3/64 tsp Canary
1/4 tsp Peacock

Mix the formula you wish to

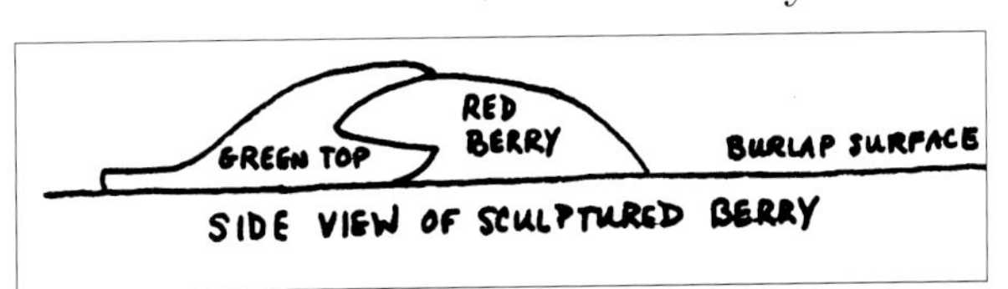

Blueberries, *8" x 4 1/2", #3-cut wool on burlap. Designed by Pearl K. McGown. Hooked by Maryanne Lincoln, Wrentham, Massachusetts, 1980s. Wool dyed with Cushing dyes form these luscious berries.*

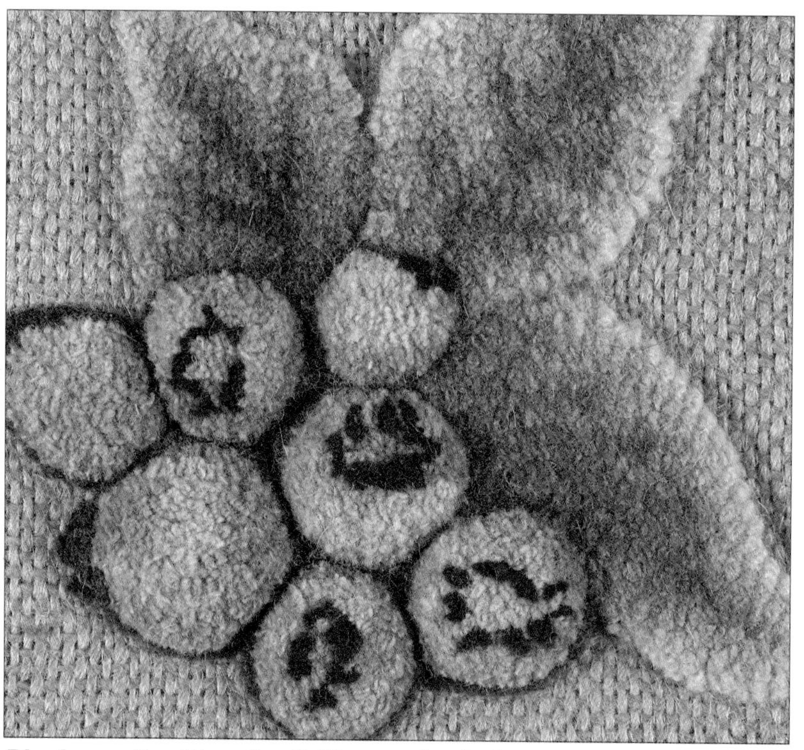

Blueberry Box Top, *4" x 4", #3-cut wool on burlap. Designed and hooked by Maryanne Lincoln, Wrentham, Massachusetts, 1990. Cushing dyes were used for this group of berries.*

use in 1 cup of boiling water. (Put the dry dyes in a 1-cup glass measure and add a few teaspoons of tepid water to make a paste. Fill the measuring cup to the 1-cup level with boiling water and stir it briskly until the dyes dissolve completely.) Use the jar method to distribute the dye solution into 6 jars and dye 6" x 24" white, yellow, or natural wool in each jar. (See page 44.) Or use the open pan method to dip dye the wool. (Refer to page 51.) For dip dyeing, start with a few teaspoons of formula and add more as necessary. Dye one 6" x 18" or one 3" x 24" piece of wool for each strawberry. For blueberries, one 6" x 18" piece will hook several berries, depending on their size.

LEAF FORMULAS

Dye the leaves for the berries with the jar method.

Strawberry Leaves *(6 values)*

PRO Chem

1/32 tsp #338 red
7/16 tsp #119 yellow
3/32 tsp #490 blue

Cushing

1/32 tsp Crimson
1/32 tsp Buttercup Yellow
1/2 tsp Bright Green

Blueberry Leaves *(6 values)*

PRO Chem

1/64 tsp #338 red
1/8 tsp #119 yellow
1/16 tsp #490 blue
1/64 tsp #672 black

Cushing

1 tsp Silver Gray Green

Mix each formula in 1 cup of boiling water and dye a gradation of values with the jar method. Dye over white, natural, celery, pale yellow, or pale blue wool. Use a 9" x 12" or equivalent size piece of wool in each jar.

When I suggest how much wool to dye with each formula, I have taken into consideration the amount of wool you'll need for the project as well as how dark the darkest value should be. I leave it up to you to apply common sense about the quantity. It is the total square inches that count. (For example, pieces measuring 9" x 12", 3" x 36", 6" x 18", and

Maryanne provides PRO Chem formulas to dye these swatches.

4" x 27" all equal 108 square inches.)

If you use pieces of wool that are a little larger or smaller than what I suggest, the world will not come to an end. If you use smaller pieces, each value may be slightly darker than if you had dyed the suggested size. If the pieces are larger than I suggested, each value will be slightly lighter. The important thing is that you use the same total square inches of material in each jar and keep track of what you use so you can repeat the color later.

HOW TO SCULPTURE A STRAWBERRY

Once you have dyed the wool, you can sculpture your strawberry. A green top drooping over the upper part of the red berry must be hooked first, and if you intend to sculpture the berry, you must also sculpture this green top. Hook the green top a tiny bit higher than the berry itself. Look closely at the framed strawberries and you will see what I mean. You'll also see I sculptured one of the leaves in the picture.

To sculpture the strawberry, use dark red wool and regular hooking to outline just the part of the berry that rests against the background. Next hook the green top, pulling each loop high and filling every hole in the backing so the loops will stand tightly together when clipped. Then hook the berry, starting at the top where it meets the green cap, carefully filling in each hole and pulling the loops high. Use darker reds at the top of the berry and gradually work down toward the tip with medium and then lighter values (see the diagram). You can either hook the loops a little lower at the edges near the dark red outline or hook all the loops high and trim them to shape with your scissors. I like to conserve wool and therefore hook shorter loops (although they are still higher than in normal hooking) in those areas that I know will later be trimmed to be lower areas. However, be careful not to have low spots in the middle of the berry because it won't trim up correctly. After hooking the red wool, add seeds by squeezing in a loop or two of the green wool in random spots on the berry.

When you've finished hooking the strawberry, use sharp scissors to trim it to shape. Follow the diagram of the side view of the strawberry to see which areas should be high and which should be low. To sculpture a group of berries, decide which one is in front and hook and trim it to be the highest, then make the next one behind it a little lower, and so on.

Antique Rose & Variations

Antique Rose, *8 3/4" x 8 1/4", #3-cut wool on rug warp. Designed and hooked by Maryanne Lincoln, Wrentham, Massachusetts, 2000.*

PREVIOUSLY, I HAVE TAKEN YOU AROUND THE COLOR WHEEL AND INTRODUCED YOU TO SOME BASIC COLOR MIXTURES. INITIALLY I COVERED ONE COLOR AT A TIME FROM A SIMPLE SIX-POINT COLOR WHEEL, INCLUDING INFORMATION AND FORMULAS FOR BOTH CUSHING AND PRO CHEM DYES.

If you are new to dyeing you may find it helpful to refer to those sections about the first basic colors: red, orange, yellow, green, blue, and purple. Don't just look for the formulas; take the time to read the information and think about each one. Then read subsequent chapters where I have developed variations on a basic color, as I have done here with red.

This time I have dyed Antique Rose and three variations of it. The basic formula, which appears in my book *Recipes From the Dye Kitchen* (*Rug Hooking* magazine, 1999), has equal parts of PRO Chem wash-fast acid dyes #338 red, #233 orange, and #672 black.

I could have used a blue-green mixture (#490 blue and #119 yellow) Antique Rose instead of black to dull the color, but the results would have been different. I add black to a formula to get smoky-looking colors and interesting soft variations that are different from what I would get by just adding the complement.

When you add black to a formula it takes some of the life out of the color—it turns the lights off in the hue. You might say it makes the color look dirty, but its effect is different from what happens when you mix just the pure primaries. There is a downside to this practice, though: It is harder to differentiate the close values of a swatch dyed with black than it is to see the difference between values in a swatch dyed without black. This is particularly true with colors like Antique Rose because of the percentage of black in each of the values (1/3 of the dry dye mixture is black).

Other colors with black added that can be found in my *Recipes* book are Wisteria, Seafoam, Dusky Lilac, and Winter Bark. They all have 3/32 teaspoon of #672 black in their formulas just like Antique Rose. For this chapter I have developed variations of Antique Rose, but you could apply these same alterations to the other colors.

THE FORMULAS

First I dyed Variation #1 of the Antique Rose formula by decreasing the amount of black. Then I decided to do Variation #2 using even less black. Finally I decided it would be fun to see the color with no black at all, so I dyed Variation #3. Here are the formulas:

Maryanne provides formulas for these three variations of Antique Rose.

Antique Rose

3/32 tsp #338 red
3/32 tsp #233 orange
3/32 tsp #672 black

Place the dry dyes in a 1-cup glass measure and add a few teaspoons to tepid water to make a paste. Fill the cup to the 1-cup level with boiling water and stir it briskly until the dyes are completely dissolved. Use the jar dyeing method (see page 44) to dye eight values over white wool.

The hooked rose on page 108 shows what Antique Rose looks like when dyed. The cat's hat, on page 110, has one value of Antique Rose in it.

Variation #1

3/32 tsp #338 red
3/32 tsp #233 orange
1/32 tsp #672 black

Follow the directions above to dye a swatch with this variation. I used all 8 values of this color to hook the dull stripes in *Imagination*'s kitty.

Variation #2

3/32 tsp #338 red
3/32 tsp #233 orange
1/64 tsp #672 black

I haven't hooked with this one yet, but it would work well for many different flowers.

Variation #3

3/32 tsp #338 red
3/32 tsp #233 orange

The bright stripes on the kitty were hooked with this variation of Antique Rose. I used all 8 values.

When I dyed these colors I used 108 square inches of wool in each jar. Sometimes I use 9" x 12" wool pieces, but this time I used 6" x 18" pieces in each jar (both sizes total 108 square inches) because I happened to have 1/2 yard (18") of wool left over from the end of bolt. Instead of cutting 12" off of it and dividing that into 9" pieces, I left it 18" long and cut it into 6"-wide pieces. The important thing is that I put the same amount of wool in each of the 8 jars so that the graduation of color would be smooth without big jumps between the values.

If one of my formulas calls for a 3" x 24" wool piece in each jar and you want to dye a piece that measures 3" x 12", 3" x 18", 9" x 12", 6" x 18", or some other size, you have several options. (Just remember to compare square inches, not dimensions.)

- Dye just what I suggest because you don't feel confident adjusting the formula, and then use only what you need of the wool.
- Adjust the dry dye formula to allow for the different amount of wool—adding more dry dye for larger pieces of wool, or using less dry dye for smaller pieces of wool.
- Call, write, or e-mail me for help (see the end of this book for my address).

When I dyed these variations I dyed a full range of values over white so I would have the wool in hand to decide how I wanted to use the color. Sometimes I dye more of a couple of the values

Imagination, *9 1/2" x 7 1/2", #3-cut wool on burlap. Designed by Colleen Laughran and Maryanne Lincoln. Hooked by Maryanne Lincoln, Wrentham, Massachusetts, 2000. Maryanne and her granddaughter drew the cat, and Colleen added the stripes and hat.*

that I want for a particular project, or I dye some of the values over different colors or textures. By having a sample of the eight values it helps me visualize what I want to do next.

FOR ADVANCED DYERS

Important to the understanding and mixing of color is the knowledge that it is not necessary to add black to a color to dull it. However, something special happens when you add black to colors that have a large proportion of red in them.

For instance, if you have a trained color eye and compare Antique Rose and its three variations, you will notice that as the black in the formula increases, the resulting color not only looks smoky and duller, but also slightly purplish. There is no purple in the black that we add—it is just something that happens when you add black to a red.

If you ordinarily work with Cushing dyes, you can create a similar color to Antique Rose by combining equal parts of Cherry, Orange, and Black Cushing dyes. The color will be different from Antique Rose because the relative strengths of the comparable Cushing dyes of Cherry, Canary, Orange, Peacock, and Black are not the same as PRO Chem #338 red, #119 yellow, #233 orange, #490 blue, and #672 black dyes. My experience with Cushing's Black dye is that it is stronger than PRO Chem's black and may overpower the red and orange in a formula. Therefore, you may want to start by dyeing a Cushing color using less Black. Use my formulas as a starting point, then experiment to develop your own variations.

"Important to the understanding and mixing of color is the knowledge that it is not necessary to add black to a color to dull it."

Dip Dyeing for a Giant Pansy

Giant Pansy, *13"x 14", #5-cut wool on burlap. Designed by Flo Petruchik. Hooked by Maryanne Lincoln, Wrentham, Massachusetts, 2001.*

ONE DAY I DECIDED TO DIP DYE A YARD-LONG PIECE OF NATURAL WOOL FOR USE IN A LARGE, FLAT FLOWER. MY FAVORITE FLOWER OF THIS TYPE IS A PANSY, SO I CREATED TWO PANSY COLORS THAT I WILL SHARE WITH YOU.

As always, when planning to dip dye a new color, it is advisable to have a general idea of what you want before soaking your wool. Try to visualize what color the highlight or lightest part of the color will be, because that is the first color that will be dip dyed. The predominant color of the hooking will be next, followed by the shadow color (the darkest third of the dip dyed wool).

If you have hooked with gradation swatches, you know that you usually use the middle values of the swatch the most. However, it is nice to have available some light hues for highlights and some darker values for shadows and accents. Therefore, in the case of our dip dye, we should end up with a larger amount of the middle values of the color and smaller amounts of highlight and shadow.

In preparation for this dip dyeing I tore the wool in half at the fold so that it was 1 yard in length but only half the width of the bolt. Next I soaked the wool in a basin with hot tap water and 1 teaspoon of Synthrapol wetting agent. After smooshing the wool into the hot soapy water, I left it to soak while I prepared a dye bath and got out my notebook.

RED-PURPLE PANSY

This dip dye process involves three steps. I used PRO Chem dyes for each step.

STEP 1

1/8 tsp #338 red

Prepare the dye bath in a large

Maryanne dip dyed this swatch for her giant pansy.

open pan. I prefer a 3"-deep rectangular pan, but a large, round, enamel soup pot is fine. Add 3" to 4" of hot water plus 1/4 cup of white vinegar to the pot and turn the heat on high. Dissolve the dye in 1 cup of boiling water and add the solution to the bath. Stir the bath.

While wearing heavy dyeing gloves, gather the large piece of wool at one end and dip the other end into the pot of dye. After dipping it up and down a few times, put the whole piece of wool down into the dye bath and let it simmer until the water is almost clear. If the dye bath begins to roll and boil, turn the heat down to about medium or a little less so that it will simmer. Poke and stir the wool occasionally to make sure most of it is under the surface of the dye bath.

Keep in mind that wool will not absorb any dye from the water unless it is submerged, and that is why we don't want the dye bath to boil. In boiling water wool has a tendency to balloon and bubble up above the surface of the dye bath. Therefore, it is important to carefully watch the pot, adjust the temperature of the burner, and stir the wool if needed. As soon as the water begins to clear, lift the wool out and set it aside in a clean pot while you add more dye to the bath.

Step 2

1/16 tsp #490 blue

Mix this dye in 1 cup of boiling water and add the solution to the dye bath. Gather up the wool again and carefully dip just the bottom 1/2 of the wool that is bright pinkish red. Move the wool up and down in and out of the dye bath in a rhythmic way, always conscious of how the color is being affected by the addition of the blue dye. Be careful not to dip the whole piece down into the blue until after the water begins to clear and the blue is almost gone out of the dye bath. At that point, keep a grip on the wool as you dip it all the way under the surface of the dye bath a few times. Use your judgment about how you want it to look. When the dye bath water clears, lift out the wool and set it aside in a clean pot while you add the next batch of dye.

Step 3

1/32 tsp #490 blue
1/32 tsp #672 black

Mix these dyes together in 1 cup of boiling water and add it to the dye bath. Also add another 1/4 cup of vinegar to the bath, because by now some of what was added before will have evaporated. Gather the wool once more in your gloved hands and dip just the bottom 1/3 of it. Keep dipping until the dye bath looks like dirty dishwater and then put the whole piece into the bath and simmer it for a few minutes with the pot loosely covered.

Remove the wool from the dye pot and wring it out a little. Look at it. If you think it needs more color, repeat any or all of the steps. Wool looks lighter when it dries, so don't quit dyeing before it is dark enough. It takes experience as well as patience to be able to judge perfectly. Many times I was in a hurry and didn't take time to look at my wool closely while it was still wet. I've then had to rewet the wool and continue dyeing to get the desired color.

After simmering the wool gently for a few more minutes once the water clears, turn off the heat. Remove the dyed wool, rinse it gently in room-temperature water, then wring, squeeze, or spin dry the water out of it. After you dry the wool, look at it while it is still in one big piece.

YELLOW-ORANGE PANSY

Here's another way to dye for a pansy. These steps transform a natural piece of wool into a yellow-orange piece that dulls to brown at one end.

Step 1

1/8 tsp #119 yellow
1/64 tsp #233 orange

For this recipe use the other half of the yard-long piece of natural wool that you tore for the red-purple pansy. Follow the directions in the previous recipe for preparing your dye bath with hot water and white vinegar, then follow the previous Step 1 directions, but use these dyes. When the water clears, remove the wool as you did before.

A NEW COUNTRY COLOR

In 2001 I adjusted one of my Country Color formulas, Country Lilac, to make it a little brighter and more like the original version of it. When I first created these formulas, the All-Fiber dyes were still available from Cushing, and the major element of the Country Lilac formula was Woodrose dye. If you still have Woodrose and are able to dye this formula as it was originally written, you can continue using it. However, if you have a copy my Country Colors Booklet of Formulas and the Country Lilac formula has Old Rose in it and not Woodrose, I suggest you make a note that I've added blue dye to the recipe.

If you aren't already familiar with Country Lilac, it is a beautiful soft lilac. Don't limit yourself to dyeing it over white or natural wool—try it over light blue or light pink. The formula, using Cushing dyes, is at right. For jar dyeing, pour 6 values and add a piece of 9" x 12" white wool to each jar.

Country Lilac

1/32 tsp Old Rose
1/64 tsp Blue
1/64 tsp Navy
1/128 tsp Plum
1/128 tsp Khaki Drab
1/128 tsp Seal Brown

Step 2

1/32 tsp #233 orange
1/128 tsp #490 blue

After dissolving the dyes in 1 cup of boiling water and pouring it into the dye bath, dip only 1/3 to 2/3 of the length of the wool, starting at one end and gradually dipping it lower and lower into the bath until color comes up the strip. Remove the wool after the water clears.

Step 3

1/128 tsp #490 blue
1/128 tsp #672 black
1/128 tsp #338 red

Add these dyes to 1 cup of boiling water and pour the solution into the bath. Dip just the bottom 1/4 to 1/3 of the wool into the dye bath. When water is just barely colored, dip the entire strip into the simmering bath a few times. Once the water is clear, place the entire strip in it, cover the pan loosely, and simmer the wool for a few minutes to complete the process.

HOOKING A GIANT PANSY

Once the wool is dyed and it is time to hook your flower, take a few minutes to look at the design and plan where you will begin hooking. Consider where the lightest color should be placed; in other words, think about where petals rest on top of each other and where their edges will be. Also think of where the darkest areas should be. If your dip dye doesn't have enough dark hues, use some plain black wool for the whisker areas of the pansy.

I began by hooking the large petal of my pansy, because its edges are on top of the two side petals. Next I hooked the two side petals to complete the petals that are basically colored alike. If you were to try to hook all three at the same time it would be harder to keep the edges defined where they overlap.

Then I hooked the two dark back petals, one at a time. As with the other petals, I made sure the edges of these petals were separated and yet looked alike. Notice that since these two back petals are generally darker than the other three, their edges don't have to be as light to create the needed contrast.

"Try to visualize what color the highlight or lightest part of the color will be, because that is the first color that will be dip dyed."

Pretty In Pink

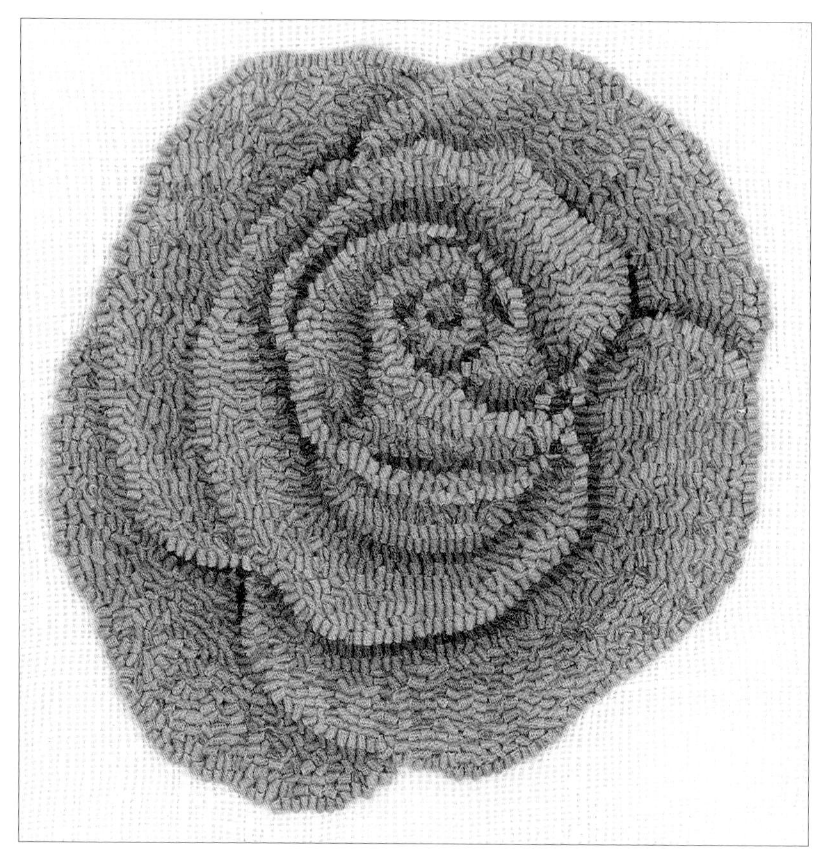

Rose, *9 1/2" x 9 1/2", #5-cut wool on linen. Designed and hooked by Maryanne Lincoln, Wrentham, Massachusetts, 2002.*

ROSES ARE ONE OF MY ALL-TIME FAVORITE FLOWERS TO HOOK, NO MATTER WHAT CUT THE STRIPS ARE. I DESIGNED THIS PARTICULAR ROSE PATTERN FOR A CLASS I TAUGHT ON HOOKING A WIDE-CUT ROSE. THE FLOWER ITSELF IS APPROXIMATELY 8" X 8", AND IT IS PRINTED ON A LOOSELY WOVEN SOFT LINEN BACKING. THE BACKING COULD HAVE ACCOMMODATED EVEN A WIDER STRIP, BUT I CHOSE #5-CUT STRIPS BECAUSE OF THE HOOK I LIKE TO USE AND THE DETAIL I WANTED TO ACHIEVE.

To get intricate shading, I usually hook flowers with #3-cut strips. The small loops created by a #3 cut make it easier to create more realistic flowers. But I still enjoy hooking roses and other flowers with wide strips from time to time; and by using four or five values of a stepped gradation swatch, I have been able to shade them very nicely, even in wider cuts.

For readers who may not be familiar with the different widths of cuts, note that #6-cut strips are twice as wide as #3 cuts. Therefore, when you hook with a #6, the loops are wider, bulkier, and take up more room. As you hook them, you'll find it necessary to skip holes in the backing so as not to crowd your work. On the other hand, if you use #3-cut strips, it is possible to put twice as many loops (and twice as much shading) in the same area on your rug because the loops are not as wide and bulky. This typically enables you to put a loop in almost every hole.

Aside from creating a rose design, I also created a new color. It is a swatch that has a basic gradation of two PRO Chem dyes: #672 black and #490 blue

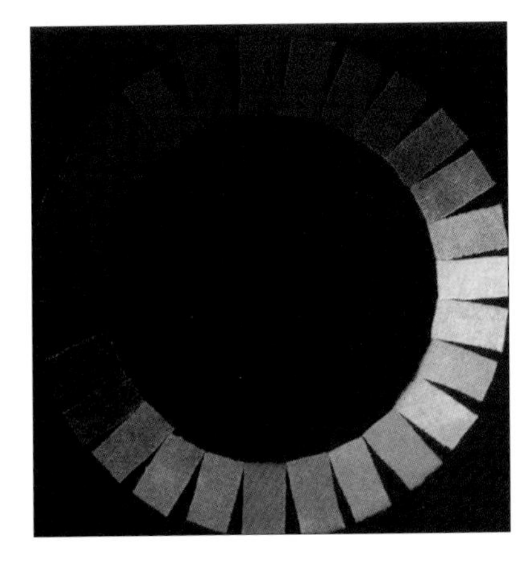

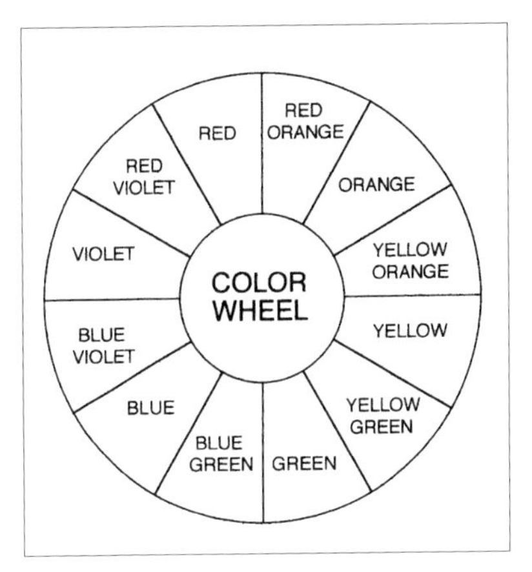

(see **Step 1** on this page). After the gradation is distributed in the jars, I added the same amount of a red-orange mixture (see **Step 2**) to each of the five values before adding salt and the wool to each jar.

In the darker values of the color, the blue/black combination predominates, but as the gradation lightens in each succeeding value, the red-orange of **Step 2** becomes apparent. Finally in the lightest values, the red-orange dominates. This style of swatch gradation is referred to as a transitional swatch because it flows from one color in the dark values to a different color in light values. A transitional swatch is nice to hook a rose with because the darker values in the gradation give us shadow colors. The lighter values give us the true color of the rose plus highlights.

Vermont Pink Rose #1

For this recipe I used 12" x 24" pieces of white wool in each value with the following PRO Chem wash-fast acid dyes.

Step 1

1/4 tsp #672 black
1/64 tsp #490 blue

BASIC COLOR LESSONS FOR BEGINNING DYERS

Creating new formulas by just mixing the basic colors is very intriguing to me. I love the subtle shadings and interactions of colors. Usually, I visualize the colors and how they might look mixed together, and then I write down a formula to start with. Then, I'll just put on the pots and dye it.

Sometimes after I begin the dyeing process, I get a different idea and will make adjustments in the color. As long as I keep track of what I am doing, I can make adjustments to the written formula so that the color can be duplicated later.

Whether I create a new swatch color with PRO Chem wash-fast acid dyes or Cushing dyes, I use the basic colors of dye: red, yellow, blue, and black. Sometimes I use orange because the color works better when I don't want to see any separation of the red and yellow, such as in a brown.

Mixing colors this way demands that one has a working knowledge of the color wheel. It helps to study it to see the relative positions of all the colors around it. You will need to know the basic rules—such as that red and blue will make purple. Once you understand this, the variations will make sense. For example, if you use more red than blue, it will be a red-purple, and if you use more blue than red, you will create a blue-purple. To create green, it is necessary to mix blue and yellow. If the blue is stronger, the green will be a blue-green. If the yellow is stronger, you'll get a yellow-green. To create orange, one must mix red and yellow together. If the yellow is stronger, you'll get a yellow-orange. If the red is stronger, the resulting color will be a red-orange.

Mixing colors from the basic few also means that you must have an understanding of complementary colors and how they interact as well. For example, if you add orange to a formula with blue, the mix will be duller than either of the colors because blue and orange are complementary. This basic rule applies to other complementary colors as well (purple and yellow, red and green).

An example: If you are trying to mix a dull green, there has to be some red added to the formula. Red is the complement of green and will dull it. Add the red until you get the color as dull as you want it. If the green doesn't seem blue enough, you have to add more blue. Conversely, if the green isn't yellow enough, you have to add more yellow.

For a smoky look, add black. Black will dull the color, but it is not the same as adding the complement. When you add black, it is like turning the lights out.

> "To get intricate shading, I usually hook flowers with #3-cut strips. The small loops created by a #3 cut make it easier to create more realistic flowers."

Dissolve these dyes in 1 cup boiling water and pour five values using the jar method. Before adding the salt and wool, add the following color.

Step 2

1/32 tsp #338 red
1/32 tsp #233 orange

Mix these two dyes in 2 cups boiling water. Add this new solution to each of the five jars mentioned in **Step 1** until it is all distributed evenly. (I started by adding 1 tablespoon to the lightest, then the next lightest, etc., and I kept adding to all the values 1 tablespoon at a time until the solution was gone.)

Now add the salt and a 12" x 24" piece of wool to each jar of the solution. Continue with the procedure as per my jar dyeing method.

Vermont Pink Rose #2

For this formula, I used Cushing dyes and a 12" x 24" piece of white wool.

Step 1

1/8 tsp black
1/64 tsp blue

Dissolve dyes in 1 cup of boiling water, and pour five values using the jar method. Before adding the salt and wool, add the following color.

Step 2

1/32 tsp cherry
1/64 tsp orange

Mix these two dyes in 2 cups boiling water. Add this new solution to each of the five jars mentioned in **Step 1** until it is all distributed evenly. (I started by adding 1 tablespoon to the lightest, then the next lightest, etc., and I kept adding to all the values 1 tablespoon at a time until the solution was gone.)

Now add the salt and a 12" x 24" piece of wool to each jar of the solution. Continue with the procedure as per my jar dyeing method.

If you want the orange to have more effect on the color and not look as pink, you can try a couple of things. You can either increase the orange or decrease the blue. Blue and orange are complementary colors and tend to dull and cancel each other out to some degree, which adds softness to the color.

CREATE A NEW COLOR

After you read the sidebar on page 115, I would like to challenge you to create a new formula with me. If you have never done it before, let's start with the first part of my formula, the PRO Chem blue and black. Copy that part of the formula in your notebook.

Step 1

1/4 tsp #672 black
1/64 tsp #490 blue

Now, try to visualize a red-purple for **Step 2**. Use my rose formula on page 115 to guide you. In that formula, I used 1/32 teaspoon of red and 1/32 orange. Try substituting blue for orange to get purple, but only use 1/64 teaspoon. You will use a small amount of blue because you want a red-purple, not just purple. You want the red in the combination to be stronger than the blue, so you'll want to add a touch more red to the formula than blue. A familiarity with the color wheel will help you visualize this.

Step 2

1/32 tsp #338 red
1/64 tsp #490 blue

Follow the same procedure as mentioned in the above recipes to dye this new color. This formula would make a perfect combination for a dark flower, such as a pansy.

CHAPTER SEVEN

CREATURES GREAT AND SMALL

New Formulas for the Birds

Maryanne's Ponies, *46"x 20", #5-cut wool on burlap. Adapted from a Patsy Beaker design and hooked by Maryanne Lincoln, Wrentham, Massachusetts, 1997.*

WHEN I DEVELOP A NEW FORMULA, I HAVE A GENERAL IDEA OF WHAT DYES TO USE, AND THEN I REFINE THEIR AMOUNTS AND ADD OTHERS TO GET THE COLOR I WANT. SOMETIMES, THOUGH, I START WITH A FORMULA THAT IS CLOSE TO WHAT I WANT, THEN ADJUST IT TO MAKE IT BRIGHTER, DULLER, DARKER, OR LIGHTER, OR I SWING IT ONE WAY OR THE OTHER AROUND THE COLOR WHEEL. THE COLORS USED IN THE RUG SHOWN ABOVE SERVE AS GOOD EXAMPLES OF THIS ADJUSTING AND EXPERIMENTING.

Adjusting an existing formula is how I developed the red for the cardinal in my rug. To create the red-orange and brown for the robin, I started with basic dye colors, then modified their amounts and added others until I was pleased with the result. Sometimes, in spite of my recalibrations, a formula doesn't give me the hue I want, but results in a useful color nonetheless. Rosewood wasn't right for the robin's breast, but would be great for flesh tones, so I've included the formula for you. Four of the formulas here use PRO Chemical & Dye wash-fast acid dyes; one uses Cushing Perfection.

THE GOLDFINCH

For the goldfinches in my rug, I used the formula for Cushing Perfection dyes as follows.

Buttercup

3/4 teaspoon Canary
1/128 teaspoon Cherry
1/128 teaspoon Peacock

Mix the dyes in 1 cup of boiling water. Use a small amount of the solution at a time in a dye bath that includes 1/8 cup white vinegar, and dip or scrunch into it half of a 12" x 24" piece of bright yellow wool. Continue adding dye solution and dipping the wool until you get the color you want for the bird. Store leftover dye solution in a container with a tight lid and use it later to dye something else. If you see that the dried wool's color is not as strong as you would like, dye it again. Keep in mind, however, that you are dyeing wool for a yellow bird,

"Sometimes, I start with a formula that is close to what I want, then adjust it to make it brighter, duller, darker, or lighter, or swing it one way or the other around the color wheel."

Maryanne's Ponies *detail. Maryanne gives her formulas for the robin, goldfinch, and cardinal in this rug.*

so don't dip the wool too deep into the dye bath, for you need a lot of the yellow but only a small amount of the medium and dull hue for interest and shading.

THE CARDINAL

Cardinals are bright red, but not the primary red (PRO Chem #338) that I work with. I looked through the formulas I already had to see if there was one I could simply adjust to get the red I wanted. The formula for Bright Red Rose had possibilities. It called for $^{3}/_{8}$ teaspoon #338 red, $^{1}/_{8}$ teaspoon #119 yellow, and $^{1}/_{128}$ teaspoon #490 blue. It was close to what I wanted for the cardinal, but still required some changes.

Experience told me I needed a healthy portion of red to start and then a generous amount of yellow to swing the red around the color wheel a bit. Too much yellow would turn it to orange, so I proceeded carefully. Since I wanted a strong red, I started with $^{1}/_{2}$ teaspoon of the red and added $^{1}/_{8}$ teaspoon of the yellow. Then I added three other colors to get the hue just right.

Cardinal

$^{1}/_{2}$ tsp #338 red
$^{1}/_{8}$ tsp #119 yellow
$^{1}/_{16}$ tsp #233 orange
$^{1}/_{128}$ tsp #490 blue
$^{1}/_{128}$ tsp #672 black

Mix the dyes in 1 cup of boiling water and use the jar dyeing method to dye the four darkest values. (See page 44 for jar dyeing instructions.) Use a 6" x 24" piece of wool in each jar. The sample at right shows six values, but to hook the cardinal you will need only the four darkest ones, plus a piece of plain black.

THE ROBIN

Although the storybooks refer to robin red breast, the breasts of real robins are actually orange. Therefore, to develop the formula for the robin's breast I started with a large amount of orange ($^{1}/_{4}$ teaspoon), then added red because I wanted a red-orange. Once I achieved the orange mixture I added blue and black to tone down its brightness. (Blue is the complement of orange and thus dulls it. Black makes a color smoky and dulls it in a different way.)

Robin's Breast

$^{1}/_{32}$ tsp #338 red
$^{1}/_{4}$ tsp #233 orange
$^{3}/_{128}$ tsp #490 blue
$^{1}/_{32}$ tsp #672 black

Mix the dyes in 1 cup of boiling water. Use the jar dyeing method to dye six values over 6" x 24" pieces of wool in each jar. You will not need all the values for the breast, but I suggest you dye all six values for use elsewhere. (I also used this color in the border of my rug, so I was glad to have the extra values.)

For the robin's back, wings, and head, I developed a dull brown formula that would be great for other birds, too.

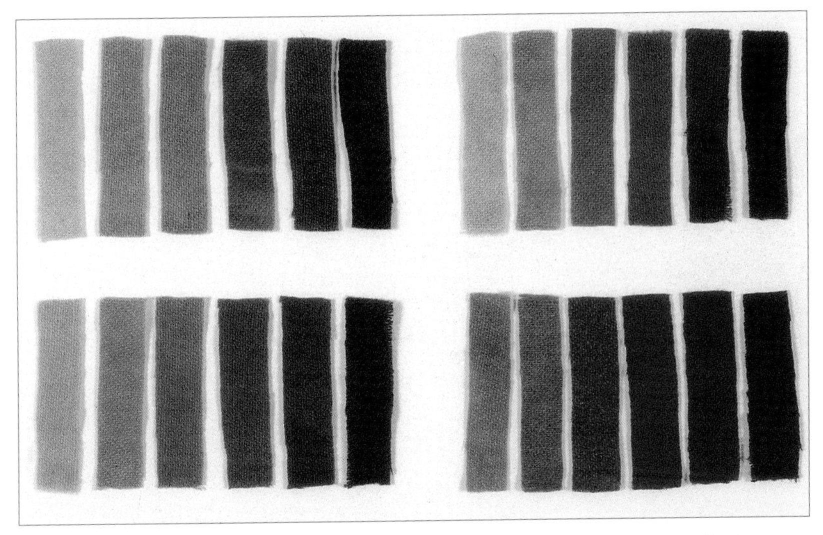

Maryanne's new formulas include (clockwise from upper left) Robin, Robin's Breast, Cardinal, and Rosewood.

Robin

1/64 tsp #338 red
1/8 tsp #233 orange
1/64 tsp #490 blue
1/32 tsp #672 black

Mix the dyes in 1 cup of boiling water and use the jar dye method to dye six values over 6" x 24" pieces of wool in each jar.

FLESH TONES

Rosewood is a bonus formula. It was my first attempt at getting the mixture for the robin's breast. The result was too red, but the values go dark enough for nice contrasts if you need to shade a detailed face or arms and legs.

"Rosewood is a bonus formula. It was my first attempt at getting the mixture for the robin's breast. The result was too red, but the values go dark enough for nice contrasts if you need to shade a detailed face or arms and legs."

Rosewood

1/16 tsp #338 red
1/32 tsp#119 yellow
1/8 tsp #233 orange
1/64 tsp #490 blue
1/64 tsp #672 black

Mix the dyes in 1 cup of boiling water. Use the jar dye method to dye six values over 6" x 24" pieces of wool in each jar.

THE RUG

My rug is an adaptation of *Ann's Ponies*, a Patsy Beaker design. I omitted one of the birds and redrew the others to make them more realistic. I also added flowers at the bottom, and I included a border because the rug will be a wall decoration in my daughter Kathy's house.

I used #5- and 6-cut wool on a coarse weave burlap. The background is hooked in squiggles with bright green wool that I had squished into a bath of red and then black. The white horse is hooked with wool I had on hand that was dyed with Cushing's Silver Gray. If I were to dye it today, I would use PRO Chem #672 black. The other horse is hooked with a brown-orange leftover from another project. To get something similar, I might dye Robin's Breast over gray-beige or light tan.

When I began to think about the birds in the rug, I asked for ideas from my granddaughters Colleen and Naomi. Colleen wanted a cardinal and Naomi asked for a goldfinch. Both of these colorful birds visit the feeders at their house, but we all agreed that the robin is our all-time favorite bird of spring and summer.

Bear Browns

Honey Bear, *9" x 12", #3-cut wool on burlap. Designed by Maryanne Lincoln and Pearl McGown. Hooked by Sue Smith, North Attleboro, Massachusetts, 1999. Sue hooked this outline-and-fill version from a kit provided by Maryanne.*

I'M A TEDDY BEAR COLLECTOR. BEARS DECORATE MY HOME AND PROVIDE LOTS OF ENTERTAINMENT FOR MY GRANDDAUGHTERS. MY BEARS ARE NOT FANCY OR EXPENSIVE, BUT I WOULDN'T WANT TO PART WITH ANY OF THEM. EACH ONE BRINGS BACK MEMORIES OF PLACES I HAVE VISITED.

It's no surprise then that I have hooked some bears—actually, quite a few of them. I created *Teddy*, a pictorial of a sculptured bear in an orange shirt, in 1972. When I suggested to Pearl McGown that she add it to her pattern list, she accepted my offer. She increased the pattern's size, added a honey pot and bird, and renamed it *Honey Bear*. I agreed to teach the pattern as part of a sculpturing lesson at the next teacher's workshop, and have taught it many times over the years.

A BEVY OF BEARS

To prepare for the teaching assignment I hooked two versions of *Honey Bear*, which gave me three bears to line up on my mantel. You would think I would have tired of bears by that time. However. I was inspired to hook another, shaded version of *Honey Bear* using 6-value swatches for the bear, shirt, and pot. And as an easy project for beginners, I hooked yet another rendition that was outlined with black and filled with a solid color.

Many of my students have hooked the outline-and-fill version with my kit, which contains the pattern, cut wool, and an instruction sheet. In fact, Sue Smith, one of my students who just recently found time to return to her hooking frame, completed the one shown at left.

Most people are attracted to the sculptured bear, but it usually is too challenging for beginners. If you want to hook it and have never tried sculpturing, I suggest you hook a small group of sculptured berries to learn how to do it. (See page 104 for how to do sculptured hooking.)

BROWNS FOR BEARS

Bears come in all sorts of colors, but I love the brown ones: light tan, oatmeal, seal-brown, golden, and just plain brown. Use your favorite brown. Dye over yellow or apricot wool for a golden undertone. Cushing's Golden Brown

Left: **Teddy**, *8" x 10", #3-cut wool on burlap. Designed by Maryanne, Lincoln, Wrentham, Massachusetts, 1972. This is Maryanne's original bear pictorial, which Pearl McGown adapted to design* Honey Bear. *Right:* **Honey Bear**, *9" x 12", #3-cut wool on burlap. Designed by Maryanne Lincoln and Pearl McGown. Hooked by Maryanne Lincoln, Wrentham, Massachusetts, 1973. This is Maryanne's sculpted rendition of* Honey Bear.

dyed over light yellow wool makes a nice bear color. For those of you who have my Country Color samples, consider the following colors that are suitable for bears: Golden Basket, Seasoned Basket, New Basket, White Sand, and Sand. (The formulas for these browns appear on page 122)

HOW TO DIP DYE BROWNS

1. Place over medium heat a 4-quart enamel pot containing 3" of water and 1/4 cup of white vinegar.
2. Soak the wool in very hot tap water with a few drops of Synthrapol (a wetting agent from PRO Chem) added. Add a few drops of Synthrapol to the dye bath as well.
3. Put a small, flat pan in a convenient place to serve as a resting spot for the wool when you need to add more dye solution to the dye both, or when you need to rest your arms from dipping the long strips.
4. Add 1/3 cup of the prepared dye solution to the enamel pot and begin to dip the strip. Dip just an inch or two at first to see what affect the dye will have on the wool. Each time you lower the strip into the bath, dip a little farther up the strip until you have dipped the entire strip.
5. Proceed slowly. You want to end up with one end of the strip light in value, the middle area medium, and the other end of the strip dark. Keep in mind that when you hook you usually need a small amount for shadows, a small amount for highlights, and a much larger amount of medium-light, medium, and medium-dark values.
6. After the water clears, remove the wool, add another 1/3 cup of dye solution, and continue dipping as you did in step 4.
7. Repeat step 6 with the remaining solution if the wool has not yet reached the desired color. If the color is still not strong enough, prepare another batch of formula and use it to continue dipping the wool.
8. When the wool reaches the color you desire and the water is almost clear, put the entire strip into the pot and simmer the wool for 5 to 10 minutes to set the color.
9. Allow the wool to cool. Rinse it and hang it to dry, (When you rinse the wool, the water should run clear after a minute or two. If it does not, return the wool to the bath, add more vinegar, and simmer it an additional 5 minutes.)

"Because sculpturing requires you to pull the loops high and then clip them to shape, you must dye yard-long pieces of wool for the needed additional length."

Honey Bear, *9" x 12", #3-cut wool on burlap. Designed by Maryanne Lincoln and Pearl McGown. Hooked by Maryanne Lincoln, Wrentham, Massachusetts, 1973. In this version of the pattern, the bear is shaded but not sculptured.*

Both the Cushing and PRO Chemical & Dye companies sell brown dyes, such as Cushing's Seal Brown, Golden Brown, Medium Brown, and Dark Brown, and PRO Chem #504. Try dyeing them over yellow, apricot, beige, or natural wool. Also consider the browns discussed on page 28.

DYEING AND HOOKING BEARS

I hooked my shaded bear with a 6-value swatch, and the sculptured bears with dip-dyed wool. Because sculpturing requires you to pull the loops high and then clip them to shape, you must dye yard-long pieces of wool for the needed additional length. Dye much more wool than what you

FORMULAS FOR DIP DYEING

If you have some dyeing experience and would like to dip dye wool to hook the sculptured bear on page 121, at right, use wool measuring 36" x 24". Try white, natural, light beige, yellow, or apricot wool. Mix up one of the following formulas and then proceed with the dyeing instructions.

Note: The amounts in these formulas are doubled compared to what appears in my Country Colors booklet. In all cases dissolve the listed dyes in 1 cup of boiling water. Place the dry dyes in a 1-cup glass measure. Add a few teaspoons of tepid water to make a paste. Add boiling water to the 1-cup level and stir the solution briskly until the dyes are completely dissolved.

PRO Chem formulas

Golden Basket

Dye over Dorr's #83 yellow wool or any light yellow wool.
1/4 tsp #233 orange
1/16 tsp #490 blue

New Basket

Dye over any of the suggested wool colors.
1/2 tsp #233 orange
1/8 tsp #490 blue
1/32 tsp #672 black

Cushing formulas

Seasoned Basket

Dye over any of the suggested wool colors.
1 tsp Khaki Drab
1/8 tsp Maroon
1/16 tsp Light Brown

White Sand

Dye over white or natural wool.
3/4 tsp Ecru
9/64 tsp Silver Gray

Sand

Dye over any of the suggested wool colors.
1 1/4 tsp Medium Brown
1/32 tsp Navy Blue

would need for a regularly hooked version. Make sure to dip-dye enough material for the shirt as well, because it is also sculptured.

When dip-dyeing a piece of wool measuring 36" x 24", it is difficult to judge exactly how much of the dark, medium, and light areas to have on the strip. Try to allow enough dark for the areas in shadow (the ends of arms, the ears, the nose, and the dark leg) and enough light for the areas in light (the front leg, the tummy, the cheek, the eyebrows, and the arms). The largest area of the material will be medium to medium-light in value.

Once you dye the wool, take a good look at it before cutting it. Cut #3 strips lengthwise so each strip is 36" long and has dark values at one end and light values at the other. Don't tear the wool into shorter lengths; hook with the full length of the strip. Hook carefully to fill every hole in the backing so the loops will stand tightly together when they are clipped.

I hooked the background areas on the sculptured bear pictures with variations of the reverse stitch for the sky and the road, the chain stitch for the tree trunk, and high-and-low hooking to give dimension to the leafy areas of the tree. The leaves were not sculptured, however, and the grass and tipped honey pot were hooked normally

The browns I've included in the sidebar can be used in any project. But I may use them again to hook yet another bruin. That's because my bears have taken on an extra task: As of a couple of months ago they've been busy delighting not only me, but my new grandson, too.

Egg Yolk Yellow

Large Chicken, *10 1/2" x 10 3/4", #6-cut wool on linen. Designed and hooked by Maryanne Lincoln, Wrentham, Massachusetts, 2001. Maryanne used reverse stitching and Egg Yolk Yellow for this mat's background.*

THE SIMPLEST WAY TO DYE IS TO CREATE FORMULAS BY COMBINING THE THREE PRIMARY HUES—RED, BLUE, AND YELLOW. FROM THAT POINT WE CAN RELY ON THE INTERACTION OF COMPLEMENTARY COLORS AND OUR KNOWLEDGE OF THE COLOR WHEEL TO GUIDE US TO THE RIGHT FORMULAS FOR ANY COLOR WE DESIRE.

I created a new dye formula, Egg Yolk Yellow, to dye the background wool in the two chicken rugs seen above and on page 125. I used the primary hues plus some orange in the recipe. Egg Yolk Yellow required advanced dyeing skills to achieve the look I wanted for the background. The color is a very bright yellow; I wanted it to lean toward the red side of yellow, yet not be orange. I carefully added red dye to move the yellow in that direction. Since I didn't want it to be as bright as the yellow on the color wheel, I also added some blue dye to the recipe. I knew from experience that blue combines with red and makes purple (the complement of yellow) to create a slightly dulled color. I could have mixed blue

> *"Egg Yolk Yellow required advanced dyeing skills to achieve the look I wanted for the background. The color is a very bright yellow; I wanted it to lean toward the red side of yellow, yet not be orange."*

and red and then added the mixture to the yellow, but I chose not to because I have found that when working with yellow it is wise to add other dyes to it in small amounts. I added orange to the recipe because I wanted the result to be a slightly orange yellow.

The following formula uses PRO Chem wash-fast acid dyes. Combine the dyes in 2 cups of boiling water.

Egg Yolk Yellow

1 tsp #119 yellow
$^{1}/_{32}$ tsp #233 orange
$^{1}/_{64}$ tsp #338 red
$^{1}/_{128}$ tsp #490 blue

I used $^{1}/_{2}$ cup of dye and about $^{1}/_{2}$ yard of natural wool. I used a small bit of this wool to hook the background in the small chicken picture and the rest to hook the background behind the larger one. You probably recognize that the larger background is hooked with reverse stitching. The chickens are hooked with black and white hound's-tooth and no shading.

There is another way I could have dyed the background for my large chicken mat. I could have dip dyed the background in Egg Yolk Yellow and when the water cleared lifted the wool out of the dye bath. By adding a light mixture of red and blue to the dye bath and dipping the lighter areas

THE DYES THEY ARE A CHANGIN'

For many years veteran rug hookers weren't familiar with PRO Chem wash-fast acid dyes. If we dyed wool, most of us used Cushing or natural dyes, and some used Rit and Putnam.

My teacher, Edna Callis, used Cushing dyes, and all the formula books that I learned about from her had formulas written for that brand. I had read about natural dyeing, but it was mostly a mystery to me. Edna taught classes about dyeing 8-value gradation swatches with Cushing dyes. The formulas were from Lydia Hick's *Triple Over Dye (TOD) Books 1* and 2. We learned to hook these swatches to shade flowers, leaves, scrolls, and so forth. For the first five years of my hooking and dyeing life I knew about and used only Cushing dyes.

At that time Cushing dyes were available in two varieties, regular and all-fiber. The regular dyes came in familiar brown packages and were described as union dyes, meaning they were a combination of dyes that would allow you to dye other fabrics besides wool. Since there were about 100 different colors in published formulas, some of us accumulated a large number of dye packages.

Many rug hooking teachers did so much dyeing that they bought dye packages by the dozen (at least in the most popular colors). Many teachers retired before they used up all the dyes in their inventory. The dyes were sold to students and friends, and if they were carefully stored they are still usable.

Over the years there have been changes in the hues due to Cushing's reformulations. What's more, the dyes in the familiar brown packages have been changed to acid dyes and are now chemically different from what they used to be. And not too many years ago, Cushing discontinued selling their all-fiber dyes.

Some of us still have a sizable supply of all-fiber dyes as well as the older (pre-acid) regular Cushing dyes. When a formula calls for Cushing Aqua all-fiber dye, there are those of us who can still reach back on our shelves and find a package or two of Aqua. But if you are new to dyeing and don't have a stash, you cannot buy that particular color (or any of the old dyes) from Cushing any more. You can try to find a dyer who will part with her rare stock or you can use a different formula to get the same color.

During the latest changes at Cushing, I updated some of my Country Colors formulas that used the discontinued Cushing dyes. Maybe now you can understand why I occasionally publish adjusted formulations of my old favorite Country Color recipes.

Small Chicken, *5 1/4" x 5 1/4", #5-cut wool on burlap. Designed and hooked by Maryanne Lincoln, Wrentham, Massachusetts, 2001. Maryanne used her Egg Yolk Yellow recipe for this mat's background.*

of the dip-dyed yellow wool into this purple mixture, I could have created shadowy areas at one edge of the yellow background. Then I could have hooked the background so the shadowy areas would have been at the bottom of the piece. By hooking the background in rows, back and forth, the top third would have been totally yellow.

Egg Yolk Yellow, even with some of its complement added, is still quite bright. Dyeing over light textures, beige, light lavender, or camel can help tone it down. For a pleasing orange color, dye over light pink or coral wool with this formula. Use pale blue or green wool to create yellow-greens. Add the formula gradually until the wool is a pleasing color.

I have had several opportunities to obtain pieces of bright purple wool that were too garish to use in a background. I discovered I could tone down a bright purple with a small amount of Egg Yolk Yellow. The overdyed wool can then be used for hooking fruits and vegetables or as a pleasing background for flowers and leaves.

Uncle Sam at the Circus

Uncle Sam on Stilts, *9 3/4" x 18 1/4", #4-cut wool on open-weave linen. Designed and hooked by Maryanne Lincoln, Wrentham, Massachusetts, 1995. Maryanne explains how to dye wool for Sam's red, white, and blue outfit.*

IN THIS CHAPTER, I AM GOING TO EXPLAIN HOW TO DYE THE WOOL FOR *UNCLE SAM ON STILTS*, A HOOKED MAT BASED ON A LARGER *CIRCUS RUG* THAT I DESIGNED. THE FORMULAS FOR DYEING THE RED, WHITE, AND BLUE ARE INCLUDED BELOW.

As in previous chapters, these recipes are for jar dyeing, which will give you 6- or 8-value gradation swatches of each color (see page 44 for complete jar dyeing instructions). I used the same formulas in a different way (minus the salt and vinegar required for jar dyeing) to dip dye the red wool for Uncle Sam's pants and dye one piece of wool for his blue hat and jacket. I also dyed white wool with several light values of a warm (brown rather than gray) off-white. Here's how I dyed each of those colors.

Uncle Sam's Red

Use PRO Chem wash-fast acid dyes for this red.
1 cup boiling water
3/4 tsp #338 red
9/32 tsp #119 yellow
3/64 tsp #490 blue
two 3" x 24" pieces celery or beige wool
2 tsp salt in each jar
2 Tbsp white vinegar in each jar

After mixing the red formula, add dye solution by the spoonful to 1 quart of boiling water with white vinegar added (no salt), until you have a very strong red dye bath. Then dip dye two preset 3" x 24" strips of celery or beige wool. When the water clears, add more dye solution and dip about 3/4 of each strip again, Continue in this manner, dipping less of the strip each time you add dye solution, until you have red strips that go from the lightest value at one end to the darkest value at the other end. Then simmer the strips for a few minutes in the final dye bath to set the color. If you don't use all the dye solution, put the remainder in a labeled, tightly covered jar. Save it to dye other wool as needed.

Off-White Stripes and Accents

For this formula
use Cushing dyes.
1 cup boiling water
1/2 tsp Black
1/128 tsp Seal Brown
two 3" x 24" pieces white wool
2 tsp salt in each jar

Note how weak this formula is. Since you won't need any of the darker values for this project, dye only the lighter values. Mix the formula and dye a few 3" x 12" pieces of wool in a slightly mottled manner. Make a dye bath of 1 quart of water with 1/2 teaspoon of salt added and a few spoonfuls of the dye solution along with one of the preset strips of white wool. Experiment with the amount of dye solution to get the values you want. Use a pan that is too small for the wool or use less water so that the wool is not completely submerged. Stir occasionally to prevent polka dots; you want a softly mottled look when finished.

Double the dry dye for each of the colors to darken one value. Use four times the dry dye for two darker values.

True Blue Sam

Use PRO Chem wash-fast acid dyes for dyeing Sam's blue jacket.
1 cup boiling water
1/2 tsp #672 black
1/8 tsp #490 blue
one 6" x 24" beige wool
2 tsp salt
2 Tbsp white vinegar

Dye the blue piece in the same mottled manner as the off-white pieces. To determine how much water to use in the dye bath, put the wool in the pot with some water before adding the dye. You should be able to stir it around a little, but it should not be completely submerged.

If you want a blue that is less dull, dye over white or off-white wool. If you want it darker, double the amount of black and blue. If you want a brighter blue, increase the amount of blue and decrease the amount of black by the same amount. For example, increase the blue from 1/8 to 1/4 teaspoon and decrease the black from 1/2 to 3/8 teaspoon. If you want a greener blue, add 1/16 teaspoon of #119 yellow, or even more for a blue-green. For a purplish blue, add 1/16 teaspoon of #338 red.

MORE NOTES ON THE MAT

The red line of the border is different from Sam's pants, hat brim, and the flag. It is a piece of bright red new wool, overdyed with a little black. Use just enough black to dull the red and yet allow some of the brightness to shine through. Start with a small amount of black and add more until you like the results.

You can also use bits of Illusion Metallic Wool for the poles and the sparkling stars of Uncle Sam's walking sticks. Illusion Wool, a two-sided fabric with hooking wool on one side and a lively metallic finish on the other, is great for adding accents and sparkle. Hook the stars with silver on gray wool. Use metallic brown on black wool for the flag walking sticks. You can also use a bit of the brown on the edges of the soles of Sam's shoes. Clip some of the brown loops so that the black shows.

DYEING NOTES

Unless a formula gives you exactly the color you need, start with a formula that you are familiar with and then adjust the dye amounts to create the color that you want. I usually start with a formula that I already have and then make the color darker, duller, or brighter depending on what I want.

To make a color darker, double, triple, or quadruple the dry dye measurements in the formula, or add a small amount of its complement or black. Increasing the dye measurements will give you a deeper color and adding the complement or black will give you a duller color.

To brighten a color, decrease the part of the formula that is the complement. For example, the formula for Sam's pants has red, yellow, and blue dye in it. The blue and yellow form green, the complement of red. If you decrease the amount of yellow and blue, the red will be brighter. On the other hand, to make the formula duller, increase the amount of the complement, or dye the red formula over celery or mint-green wool instead of white or natural.

You can apply this same concept to other formulas. I was taught jar dyeing using *TOD Book I* formulas, which are grouped in families of three related formulas. Each of the three formulas uses the same dyes, but each has a different predominant dye. I learned quickly by experimenting that if I kept the amount of the predominant dye the same and decreased the amounts of the other two dyes, the new color would be brighter. You can also do this with other formulas. The best way to learn about what you can do with a dye formula is to experiment. Have fun, be adventurous, and you might be pleasantly surprised at what comes out of your dye pot.

Six Circus Colors

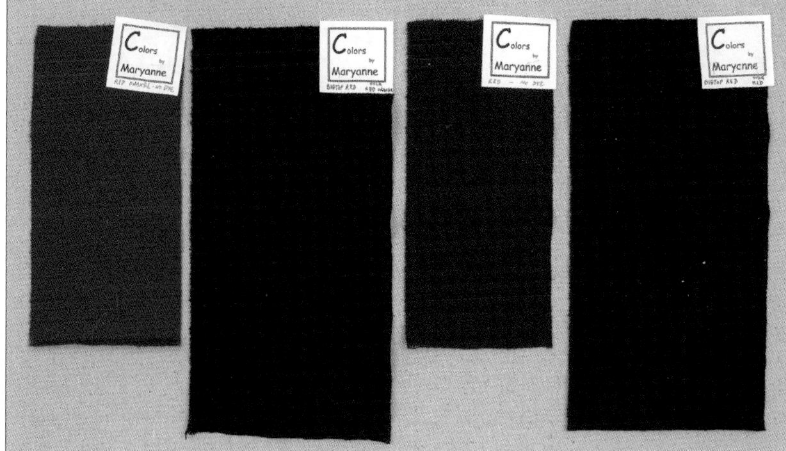

Top: *Three values of King Philip Red, dyed over oatmeal and beige wool.*
Bottom: *Maryanne overdyed red-orange wool with green and bright red wool with black to produce similar versions of Big Top Red.*

MANY OF MY STUDENTS WHO LIKE TO HOOK WIDE-CUT RUGS DO NOT WISH TO DYE 6- OR 8-VALUE SWATCHES OF MY SWATCH SAMPLES TO SEE IF THERE IS A VALUE OF A PARTICULAR COLOR THEY COULD DYE FOR THE YARDAGE THEY WANT.

To find the color and value that would be perfect for your project, first look through your favorite dye formulas. Also look over the dyed wools you have on hand to see if one or more might be overdyed to quickly get a particular color, instead of starting from scratch with white or natural wool. This saves not only time, but also dye.

In preparation for hooking a new circus-theme rug, I created formulas for red, gold, blue, and white wool in 1/4-yard, 1/2-yard, and 1-yard quantities. Amid my stash of wools waiting to be dyed I found a large piece of red-orange and a piece of bright red. I was interested in trying to get the red background I wanted by dyeing a little of the right color over the red-orange and bright red wools. By using a relatively small amount of dye I came up with a great background. If I had started with off-white wool, it would have taken much more dye to get the background color I needed. Another reason I overdyed the reds was to see if the color would bleed as reds so often do.

BIG TOP RED

Here's how I overdyed two red wools—and how you can, too. In a large, deep pan, soak a 1/2-yard piece of red-orange wool in hot tap water and a little Synthrapol or detergent. Then proceed to dye the wool, following the steps below.

Step 1

5/128 tsp PRO Chem wash-fast acid dye #728N green

Place the dye in a 1-cup glass measure cup and add a few teaspoons of tepid water to make a paste. Fill the measuring cup to the 1-cup level with boiling water and stir the water briskly until the dye is completely dissolved. Add the solution to a pot of heating water along with 1/4 cup of white vinegar. Add the red-orange wool and bring the dye bath to just under a boil. Stir it often and keep the wool submerged as best you can.

Cover the pan loosely with foil in between stirring to help maintain the water's temperature. When the water clears, remove the wool and proceed with **Step 2**.

Step 2

1 tsp #338 red

I added green dye in step 1 to dull some of the orange cast in the

Two values of Black & Blue, dyed over beige wool

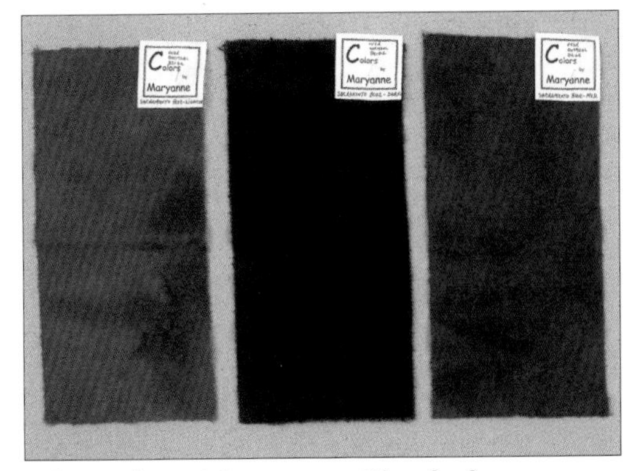

Three values of Sacramento Blue, dyed over oatmeal wool.

wool. (My other option would have been to use #490 blue.) In **Step 2** I'm adding red to the wool to swing its hue around the color wheel toward primary red.

Dissolve the red dye in 1 cup of boiling water and add the solution to the dye bath. Add the wool and simmer it until the water clears, remembering to cover the pan in between stirring. There may be a light red tinge in the water from dye that bled out of the wool; no amount of coaxing will put it back into the fabric. The wool should rinse clear after three good rinses in tepid water. If it doesn't, simmer the wool in water and vinegar for a while longer and rinse it again.

These colors did not bleed for me. However, if you have a piece of wool that just won't take the dye or won't stop bleeding even after you rinse it several times, you would be taking a risk to hook it into your rug. The world won't come to an end if you use it, but if you should ever have to clean the rug or it should get wet at some point, color would probably bleed onto other areas of your hooking. Bright red, especially, has a reputation for doing that.

To dye 1 yard of wool instead of the recommended 1/2 yard, double the formula and use a larger pot and more water in the dye bath. For 1/4 yard of wool, use half the formula, a smaller pot, and less water in the dye bath.

I produced a similar color by dyeing 1/2 yard of bright red wool with 1/32 teaspoon of PRO Chem #672 black. I could have added a little bit of #728N green or a weak mixture of #490 blue and #119 yellow, but I chose black because I wanted to smoke up the color a bit. It worked, and the results are much like the red-orange overdyed piece. I will use the similar wools together for the background of my circus piece.

Kentucky Moonshine

Recently my color class and I developed a beautiful gold called Kentucky Moonshine. I dyed 2 yards of a middle-light value of it for one of the backgrounds in my circus rug.

3/16 tsp + 3/64 tsp #119 yellow
1/32 tsp + 1/128 tsp #338 red
1/64 tsp #490 blue
1/128 tsp #672 black

Dissolve the dyes in 2 cups of boiling water and follow the procedure for Step 1 above to dye 2 yards of off-white wool. First soak the wool in hot water and a little Synthrapol or a detergent such as Ivory dish detergent. I soaked both yards at once, but split the amount during the dyeing process, dyeing 1 yard in half of the formula and then the other in the remaining formula. However, if you have a pot that will accommodate both yards, use the entire formula and dye both at once. I have a large enamel baby bathtub I sometimes use to dye 2 or 3 yards at a time.

Notice the small amounts of black and red in the Kentucky Moonshine formula. Because of those small amounts it is impossible to cut the dry dye formula in half to dye 1/2-yard pieces. However, you could prepare the formula as written for 2 yards and use 1/4 of the liquid (1/2 cup) to dye a 1/2-yard piece. For 1/3 or 1/4-yard pieces, mix up the formula as written and dye by eye to get the desired shade.

I also dyed a couple of darker values of Kentucky Moonshine over 1/2 yard of Dorr's #42 beige wool. Here are those formulas (follow the directions you did for the lighter value):

Medium

9/32 tsp #119 yellow
3/64 tsp #338 red
1/64 tsp #490 blue

Dark

9/16 tsp #119 yellow
3/32 tsp #338 red
1/32 tsp #490 blue

Sacramento Blue

Sacramento Blue was developed in a color course I presented in

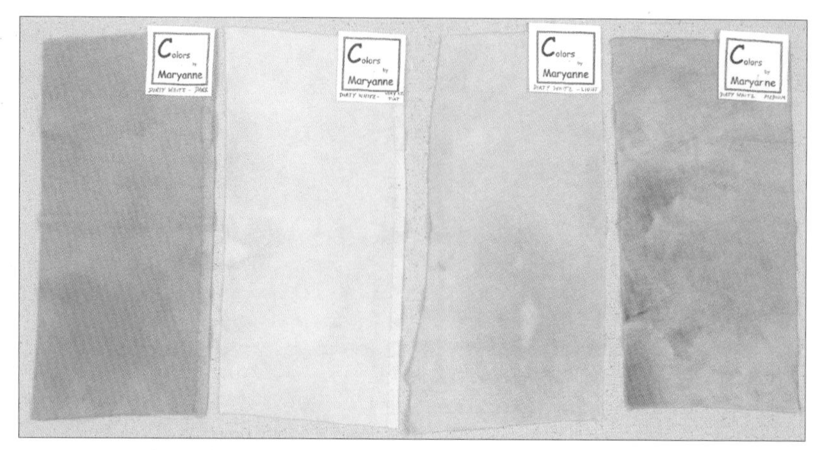

Maryanne's formula Winter Bark, dyed over off-white wool in four strengths, resulted in four values of Dirty White.

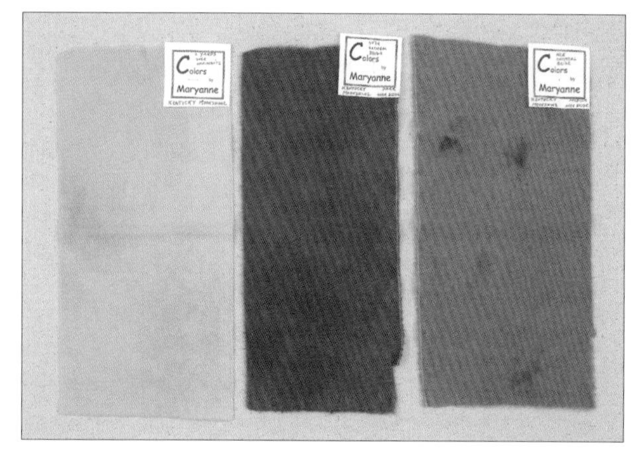

The lightest value of Kentucky Moonshine was dyed over off-white wool, and the others over beige wool.

Sacramento, California, many years ago. For each value dissolve the dyes in 1 cup of boiling water. Add to the dye bath this solution, 1/4 cup of white vinegar, and 1/4 yard of oatmeal or beige wool that has already been soaking in hot water and Synthrapol or detergent.

Dark

9/32 tsp #490 blue
3/32 tsp #338 red
3/32 tsp #119 yellow

Medium

9/64 tsp #490 blue
3/64 tsp #338 red
3/64 tsp #119 yellow

Light

9/128 tsp #490 blue
3/128 tsp ##338 red
3/128 tsp #119 yellow

Black & Blue

I dyed three shades of this mottled blue. For each value, dissolve the dyes in 1 cup of boiling water and add the solution to the dye bath with 1/4 cup of white vinegar and 1/4 yard of already wet beige wool.

Dark

3/32 tsp #490 blue
1/4 tsp #672 black

Medium

1/8 tsp #490 blue
1/4 tsp #672 black

Light

1/16 tsp #490 blue
1/16 tsp #672 black

Both Sacramento Blue and Black & Blue are great colors for Orientals, and they will help define the details and borders of my circus project. Dye these same blues over white or off-white wool for brighter colors.

Dirty White

The values of this appealing gray-to-white color are dyed with my formula Winter Bark.

1/64 tsp #490 blue
3/32 tsp #672 black
3/32 tsp #233 orange

Dissolve the dyes in 2 cups of boiling water and dye four values, each over 1/2 yard of off-white wool. Start with the lightest value, using about 1 tablespoon of the solution. Then use 1/8 cup of the solution for a light value, 1/4 cup for a medium one, and 1/2 cup for a dark.

King Philip Red

Dye this red over 1/2-yard pieces of oatmeal or beige wool, using the same procedure you did for the blue formulas.

Dark

9/16 tsp #338 red
9/16 tsp #119 yellow
1/32 tsp #490 blue

Medium

9/32 tsp #338 red
9/32 tsp #119 yellow
1/64 tsp #490 blue

Light

9/64 tsp #338 red
9/64 tsp #119 yellow
1/128 tsp #490 blue

These reds are softer than the background reds I dyed with Big Top Red. They will come in handy for detail work in my circus project.

I hope these formulas will fit into a project of your own. If they aren't quite what you need, try adjusting dye quantities or even adding new dyes until you achieve the color you desire. Experiment, try something new, and, above all, have fun.

Butterscotch Bears and More

Circus Parade: Bear on Unicycle, *10 3/8" x 19", #5-cut wool on burlap. Designed and hooked by Maryanne Lincoln, Wrentham, Massachusetts, 2001.*

IN THE FIRST SECTION I SHARED MY *UNCLE SAM ON STILTS* RUG WITH YOU. SAM IS THE LEADER OF A CIRCUS PARADE SERIES OF HOOKED RUGS I'M DOING. MY UNICYCLING BEAR, SHOWN HERE, IS ANOTHER OF SEVERAL UNITS IN THE PARADE. EACH UNIT IS HOOKED SEPARATELY WITH THE SAME RED, WHITE, AND BLUE LINE BORDERS. THEY'RE HUNG TOGETHER MARCHING ALONG MY FAMILY ROOM WALL.

There are several recipes I used for dyeing elements of this piece. Some of the formulas, such as Black & Blue, Dirty White, Sacramento Blue, and Big Top Red, appeared in the last section. Jar dyeing instructions are shown on page 44.

I hooked the bear's overalls with a couple of values of Black & Blue. For both values I used 1/4

"Keep in mind that when combining complementary colors it only takes a a small amount of added color to make a big difference in the color you are trying to adjust."

yard of beige wool. The dyes are PRO Chem wash-fast acid dyes. Here are the formulas:

Black & Blue Dark

3/32 tsp #490 blue
1/4 tsp #672 black

Black & Blue Light

1/16 tsp #490 blue
1/16 tsp #672 black

In both instances soak the wool beforehand. While it is soaking, dissolve the dyes in 1 cup of boiling water. Add the dye solution and 1/4 cup of white vinegar to the dye bath and add the wool. Bring the water to just under a rolling boil. As it heats, stir the wool to keep it submerged. When the wool has achieved the color you want, take it out of the pot and rinse it.

The unicycle tire and fishing rod were hooked with several values of Dirty White. I also used one value of Dirty White for the white stripe in the border. The blue stripe in the border is the dark value of Sacramento Blue and the red stripe is Big Top Red.

The bear's hat was hooked with three different dark purples. I relied on bits of colored wool from my odds and ends to hook the fish, the fishing lines, the spokes of the wheel, and the shadow of the bear's raised arm, as well as the other small details.

Kentucky Moonshine, a yellow-brown hue, was another dye formula introduced to you before. I wanted to use it in this piece, but it seemed too bright for the rest of the colors for the circus series. Therefore, before I hooked the next piece in the parade (a car full of clowns), I added a little purple to the recipe to tone it down. If we rely on an understanding of how complementary colors interact when combined, we can dull Kentucky Moonshine just a little without turning it completely brown.

Kentucky Moonshine, simply speaking, is a yellow. Here's the formula for it:

Kentucky Moonshine

3/16 tsp + 3/64 tsp #119 yellow
1/32 tsp + 1/128 tsp #338 red
1/64 tsp #490 blue
1/128 tsp #674 black

To dull yellow, add a small amount of purple. Start by mixing a weak solution of purple in 1 cup of boiling water:

1/64 tsp #338 red
1/128 tsp #490 blue

Add this dulling solution to the dye bath that already has Kentucky Moonshine in it. However, add only 1/4 cup at a time. Look at the bath each time to judge if it is dull enough for you. If you just dump the whole cup in at once, there is a chance it will dull the color too much. Therefore, to have some amount of control, add it 1/4 cup at a time. If that amount seems to change the color quite a bit, you may want to add less the next time. Keep in mind that when combining complementary colors it only takes a small amount of added color to make a big difference in the color you are trying to adjust. If you already have yellow or gold wool, but it is too bright, wet it and then dull it with this purple solution. Again, add just 1/4 cup at a time to the dye bath.

When it came to dyeing wool for the bear, I had a couple of recipes to choose from, which I'll mention to you. One is an adaptation of an existing PRO Chem formula that was developed as part of my Color Course. I changed it so the light values are lighter and brighter.

Golden Bear

Step 1

1/32 tsp #338 red
1/128 tsp #490 blue
1/8 tsp #119 yellow

Mix these 3 dyes together in 1 cup of boiling water and distribute the solution to 4 jars using the jar dyeing method. Now go on to step 2.

Step 2

1/4 tsp #119 yellow
1/16 tsp #338 red
1/64 tsp #490 blue

Mix these dyes together in 1 cup of boiling water. In this fashion add this dye solution to the 4 jars containing the **Step 1** solution: To the jar containing the lightest value, add 4 teaspoons of the **Step 2** solution. To the next lightest, add 8 teaspoons. To the middle-light value, add 14 teaspoons. To the middle-dark value, add 20 teaspoons. Place one 9" x 24" piece of natural wool in each jar. Then add 3 teaspoons of salt and a little extra water to each jar.

In my book *Recipes from the Dye Kitchen* (*Rug Hooking* magazine, 1999), there is a formula using Cushing dyes called Butterscotch that (with a few alterations) would make a nice bear color. I have changed the formula to make the color browner and more suitable for a bear by adjusting the amount of blue and red in it. The original recipe called for 1/128 teaspoon of Peacock and 1/64 teaspoon of Cherry.

Butterscotch Bear

1/2 tsp Canary
1/64 tsp Peacock
3/128 tsp Cherry

Mix the three dyes together in 1 cup of boiling water and use the jar dyeing procedure to distribute the solution to 4 jars. After adding 1 teaspoon of salt and extra water to each jar, place a 3" x 24" piece of natural, Dorr #42 beige, or Dorr #46 camel wool in each jar. Double the amounts of dye for 6" x 24" wool pieces and double the amount of salt added to each jar.

When you distribute the dye solution to the 4 jars, the first one that you pour is the darkest value, the second the next darkest, and so forth. Usually I dye 6 or 8 values of a color in jars, but for this bear I only needed the darkest values to get the look I wanted. The dye solution left after pouring the last value is strong enough to be worth saving. Put it in a tightly covered jar for use later.

There's yet another formula that would make a nice bear color. This one is called Golden Basket and uses PRO Chem dyes in a two-step jar dyeing process.

Golden Basket

Step 1

1/8 tsp # 233 orange
1/32 tsp #490 blue
3/128 tsp Cherry

Mix these dyes together in 1 cup of boiling water and distribute the mixture to 4 jars, following the jar dyeing method.

Step 2

1/64 tsp #119 yellow
1/128 tsp #233 orange
1/64 tsp #490 blue

Mix these dyes in 1 cup of boiling water. Add 4 tablespoons of the solution to the jars, starting with the darkest value. Stir; add 2 tablespoons of salt and 1 piece of 6" x 24" natural wool to each jar.

If this color is too bright for you, use Dorr #42 beige wool. If you like it as bright as mine, but you don't have any natural wool to dye over, use pale yellow or Dorr #83 yellow wool for beautiful results.

The background is hooked with the two darkest values of King Philip Red. I used 1/2-yard pieces of oatmeal or beige wool in each. The formula for the darkest value is:

Darkest Value

9/16 tsp #338 red
9/16 tsp #119 yellow
1/32 tsp #490 blue

You will notice that the top half of the background is a lighter red than the bottom. The formula for the lighter top area is:

Lighter Value

9/32 tsp #338 red
9/32 tsp #119 yellow
1/64 tsp #490 blue

Take a minute to look at this formula for the lighter value of King Philip Red. The denominators in each of the fractions for the lighter value are twice as large as the denominators in the formula for the darker value.

When you want to halve a fraction, just double the denominator and keep the numerator the same. In the formulas above, 9/32 teaspoon of dye is half as much dye as 9/16 teaspoon, and 1/64 teaspoon is half as much as 1/32 teaspoon. If you want to double the amount of dye, just cut the denominator in half and keep the numerator the same. As an example, look at the formula for the dark of King Philip Red: 9/16 teaspoon red + 9/16 teaspoon yellow + 1/32 teaspoon blue. To double the amount of dye the formula would be 9/8 teaspoon red + 9/8 teaspoon yellow + 1/16 teaspoon blue.

> *"When you want to halve a fraction, just double the denominator and keep the numerator the same."*

Baby Elephant Joins the Parade

Baby Elephant, *16 1/2" x 13 1/2", #5-cut wool on burlap. Designed and hooked by Maryanne Lincoln, Wrentham, Massachusetts, 2001.*

MY CIRCUS PARADE ARRAY OF HOOKED RUGS TOOK SHAPE WITH MY LATEST ADDITION, *BABY ELEPHANT*. MY PLAN WAS TO HOOK EACH UNIT OF THE PARADE SEPARATELY, ALL OF THEM HAVING THE SAME PATRIOTIC BORDER OF RED, WHITE, AND BLUE. READY AND WAITING TO BE HOOKED INTO RUGS ARE MATERIALS FOR A LION, A CAR FULL OF CLOWNS, A SEAL BALANCING A BALL, AND SOME SPECIAL BALLOONS. WHEN FINISHED THESE RUGS WILL BE HUNG TOGETHER TO FORM A COLORFUL PARADE.

There are several recipes I used for dyeing elements of this piece, and some may look familiar. I hooked the background of Baby Elephant in Big Top Red. The elephant's wool was dyed with my Dirty White recipe, and the blanket was hooked with Sacramento Blue. The dyes are PRO Chem wash-fast acid dyes, and I used the open pan dyeing method.

A more extensive version of the Big Top Red recipe appeared in the Six Circus Colors section, but I found I could get a similar color a little faster with the formula below.

Big Top Red

1/32 tsp #674 black

How can black dye create red wool? It can if the wool is red to begin with.

Soak 1/2 yard of bright red wool in Synthrapol wetting agent, and then place it in a pot of heating water. Dissolve the black dye in 1 cup of boiling water. Add the dye solution and 1/4 cup of white vinegar to the dye bath. Bring the water to just under a boil, stir in the wool and keep it submerged.

When the wool has achieved the color you want, remove it and rinse it.

Dirty White

$^3/_{32}$ tsp #672 black
$^1/_{64}$ tsp #490 blue
$^3/_{32}$ tsp #233 orange

For the elephant's outline I used a medium-dark value of my Dirty White formula and for its body a medium-light value. For all values I used $^1/_2$ yard of beige wool to dye over.

Dissolve the dyes in 2 cups of boiling water and dye four values. Start with the lightest value, using 1 tablespoon of the solution in a jar. Then use $^1/_8$ cup of the solution for a light value, $^1/_4$ cup for a medium one, and $^1/_2$ cup for a dark value.

Sacramento Blue

Many years ago I developed Sacramento Blue in a color course I presented in Sacramento, California. Presented below are the values I used for this parade panel. For each value dissolve the dyes in 1 cup of boiling water. Add to the dye bath this solution, $^1/_4$ cup of white vinegar, and $^1/_4$ yard of beige wool that has already been soaking in hot water and Synthrapol or detergent. (You can also use natural, oatmeal, or light gray wool.)

Medium

$^9/_{64}$ tsp #490 blue
$^3/_{128}$ tsp #338 red
$^3/_{128}$ tsp #119 yellow

Light

$^9/_{128}$ tsp #490 blue
$^3/_{128}$ tsp #338 red
$^3/_{128}$ tsp #119 yellow

The blanket on the elephant's back was hooked with blue wool along with a few strips of dull green, navy, and red from the background. I relied on my odds and ends of gold, green, and red to hook the topknot on the elephant's head. Bits of lighter gold wool were perfect for the toenails. I used plain black and white for the eye and a bit of white for the pompom in the topknot.

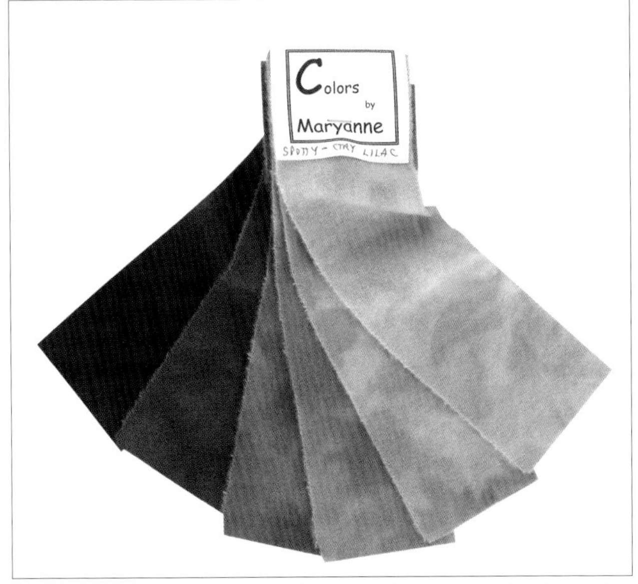

Notice the heavy spotting on these swatches, the result of not stirring the dye bath frequently.

MORE TIPS ON JAR DYEING

In chapter 3, I shared my instructions for jar dyeing with you. I'd like to add a few tips to those instructions that will help you achieve even better results.

Tip 1

After the dyes are dissolved I do not add any more boiling water to the jars at any time. Let me go back to the beginning. I start out with a pan (a roaster, canning, or refrigerator pan) and arrange six to eight wide-mouth (quart or pint) jars in it. I pour warm water in the pan around the outside of the jars until they begin to float. Then I prepare the dye solution by putting the dyes in a 1-cup glass measure cup and adding a teaspoon or two of tepid water to them, stirring them until they are well blended. I add boiling water to the 1-cup level and stir the solution briskly to completely dissolve the dyes. When I have to refill the cup after pouring out some in a jar, I use hot tap water, not boiling water. When I add extra water to each jar, again, it is not boiling.

Tip 2

I do not put the pan of jars on the stove to heat until after I get the dye solution, salt, wool, and extra water into the jars. Therefore, I do not have to worry about any spotting until later when I put the pan on the burner and turn up the heat. If I get interrupted during that first step of preparing my dye, not much can go wrong.

Once the pan is on the burner, I stir the wool carefully every 15 minutes to prevent heavy spotting. I gradually increase the heat to simmer the wool, and then I add vinegar to each jar.

Tip 3

Wool will not take on dye if it is above the surface of the dye bath.

If you add vinegar to the jars late in the jar dyeing process like I do, the water around the jars is at a simmer. The wool in the jars (although it gets cooled a bit when you add the cool vinegar) is also very hot. I stir the wool in each jar after 10 or 15 minutes and always make sure the wool is down in the solution with no part of it floating above the surface of the solution. If you wait too long between stirrings, the pieces of wool will bubble or balloon up to the surface. The part of the wool that is completely submerged will absorb the dye out of the solution, while the part above will not get any further dye.

Remember that when the pan heats, the water around and under the jars heats from bottom to top. This means that the dye solution on the bottom is hotter than at the top of the jars at any one time. The wool on the bottom that simmers first will begin to absorb the dye out of the solution first. Stirring brings better heat distribution so the wool becomes more evenly dyed. To summarize, if you want an entire piece of wool to absorb the dye evenly, gradually raise the heat under it, stir it often, and make sure it is completely submerged each time you finish stirring.

Everyone makes mistakes, and I am no exception. Looking at this swatch (on page 135) it occurred to me that others might benefit from seeing this failure. Recently, as I was dyeing wool I got interrupted right after I added the vinegar and put the wool back into the jars. It wasn't until an hour later that I got back to my kitchen and found the wool as you see it. All the dye was taken up, but the spotting was unacceptable.

A Perfect Background for a Circus Scene

MY CIRCUS PARADE OF HOOKED RUGS MARCHED ON WITH THE COMPLETION OF *CAR FULL OF CLOWNS*. THIS RUG WILL BE HUNG WITH *BEAR ON A UNICYCLE*, *BABY ELEPHANT*, AND *UNCLE SAM ON STILTS*. STILL ON MY HOOKING AGENDA FOR THIS SERIES ARE A RUG OF A LION AND A MONKEY TOGETHER AND ANOTHER OF A PERFORMING SEAL.

I shared the formulas and samples for my circus colors with you beginning on page 128. But there's always an exception, and in this case I made a new background color. My color plan for this rug changed from bright colors to more subdued ones, and I ended up dyeing it a duller hue than the original gold circus color I had used in previous rugs.

I originally intended to hook the clown car in rainbow stripes with brightly colored clowns. Soon after September 11, I began hooking this rug, and I just couldn't get started. That original color plan I had intended to use just didn't seem to work.

With all the patriotic feelings coming forth in this country following the tragedy, the stripes on the car, the star on the hood, and the wheels all stood out as a potential place for a flag motif to me. I changed my mind and decided to hook the car as a flag representation. I was content with my decision, but I also felt that I shouldn't hook all the clowns with happy, bright colors in order to preserve the theme of the rug.

Several weeks later, I began hooking the two clowns in the back of the car in subdued colors. After completing them, I could see that this color plan was working, and I quickly went ahead and finished all the other clowns. At this time I realized that the gold background also needed to be duller to fit into this new color scheme.

It may be helpful to read the sections in my book (*Recipes From the Dye Kitchen*, Stackpole Publishing, 1999) about background dyeing. Also, look up back issues of *Rug Hooking* in which I have given instructions on background dyeing.

For this recipe I used one yard of natural wool using the open pan dyeing method with the following PRO Chem wash-fast acid dyes.

Background for the Clown Rug

1/16 tsp #490 blue
1/16 tsp #233 orange
1/4 tsp #119 yellow
7/64 tsp #338 red
1/64 tsp #672 black

Car Full of Clowns, *25½" x 19", #3- and 5-cut wool on burlap. Designed and hooked by Maryanne Lincoln, Wrentham, Massachusetts, 2002.*

"I like to pre-wet the wool for background dyeing in the pot that I will be using. I always like to use shortcuts. This way, I will have one less pot cluttering up my tiny dye kitchen."

Measure all the dry dye together in a 1-cup glass measure. Add a teaspoon or two of tepid water to the dye, and stir it to make a paste. Add boiling water to bring the level to 1 cup. Stir briskly to make sure that all the dye particles are dissolved, and none are sticking to the bottom or sides of the glass cup.

Prepare a dye bath in a pan large enough to dye one yard at a time. Add hot tap water and a few drops of Synthrapol wetting agent to the pan, and then add the wool. Poke it around and under the water until it is thoroughly wet. If the wool has noticeably dry areas here and there, add another drop or two of Synthrapol and a bit more very hot tap water.

I like to pre-wet the wool for background dyeing in the pot that I will be using. I always like to use shortcuts. This way, I will have one less pot cluttering up my tiny dye kitchen.

Remove the wool to another pan while you add the dye solution to the bath. Set it aside for a minute or two, and do not rinse or wring it out.

Even though you will probably end up using all the dye, begin by adding only ¾ cup of the dye solution to the pan. Turn the heat under the pan to medium-low,

> "[After September 11] With all the patriotic feelings coming forth in this country following the tragedy, the stripes on the car, the star on the hood, and the wheels all stood out as a potential place for a flag motif to me."

SOME DYEING REMINDERS

1. To ensure even dyeing, add 2 teaspoons of plain salt when you add the dye solution in the beginning before you put the wool back in. Start the heat on low and stir constantly, gradually raising the heat to medium. Add a generous glug of white vinegar after the wool has taken up some or all of the dye. Continue to stir and process at this high heat until the dye bath has come to a simmer. When the dye bath clears, cover the pot loosely with foil, and process for a few minutes longer. These dyes do not activate until they reach temperatures at or just a few degrees below the boiling point. Consequently, if you don't care if your background is evenly dyed, you don't need to add salt in the beginning or stir constantly.
2. Always remember that the wool won't take up any dye if it bulges up above the water because you forgot to poke it under. Also, the dye will always attach in the spots that get the hottest first, so it is best to stir the wool and dye bath often so that there are no real hot spots.
3. Even when I do everything right, I am apt to get spots where I don't want them. My best advice for even dyeing is to be attentive, working slowly and deliberately. Don't hurry. This is definitely one time that haste makes waste.

and return the wool to the dye bath. Stir it around for a few minutes while tucking all the wool under the surface. The wool will have a tendency to rise to the surface if you don't occasionally work with it.

Stir often for the first 5 to 10 minutes, and then lift the wool out. To set the colors, add 1/4 cup of white vinegar for light backgrounds and 1/2 cup for medium and dark-colored backgrounds. Stir the dye bath and then put the wool back in, and stir again. Turn the heat up to medium. Then cover the pan loosely with foil, and stir after 5 minutes.

If the dye bath has started to clear somewhat, it is time to decide whether to add the rest of the dye solution from the 1-cup measure.

Maybe in your particular project, it won't matter whether it is a little lighter or darker than what I used for my background with the above amounts of dye. If this is the case, you could just dump all the dye in at once, as long as the color of the dye is close to what you see in my background.

You do have some control over the end result of your dyeing, however. You don't have to mix up the color and simply trust that when you dump it all in, the color will come out right. By gradually adding the color, you can get the background that is most pleasing to you.

Due to variations in water, as well as variations in the wool, your results may not match exactly what I get in my dye kitchen in Wrentham, Massachusetts, dyeing over Dorr natural wool. In fact, you may wish to dye this formula over different wools for a more textured look.

The Circus is Coming to Town

The Lion With Monkey, *20" x 16 1/4", #5-cut wool on burlap. Designed and hooked by Maryanne Lincoln, Wrentham, Massachusetts, 2005.*

THE LION WITH MONKEY HAS BEEN HOOKED WITH CIRCUS COLORS. FOR INSTANCE, THE RED BACKGROUND, BIG TOP RED, IS DYED OVER BRIGHT RED WOOL. THE LION'S BODY COLOR IS TWO VALUES OF KENTUCKY MOONSHINE DYED OVER OATMEAL-COLORED WOOL.

I used the darkest value to outline and the medium value to fill in the body. The lion's mane was dyed using some pieces of beige wool that had been dip-dyed in Cushing's Seal Brown so that one end of the wool was very dark brown and the other stayed quite light just on the last couple of inches of the strips. I also used some dark brown off the bolt (in other words, not hand-dyed) to add some darker brown in the mane and to hook the monkey. The monkey colors and the crown are hooked with wool from my odds and ends collection.

Big Top Red

1/32 tsp #672 black

I dyed 1/2 yard of bright red wool with 1/32 tsp #672 black PRO Chem wash-fast acid dye. Dissolve the dye in 1 cup boiling water. Prewet the wool in the pan you will be dyeing in. Use hot tap water with a few drops of PRO Chem's Synthrapol SP added. After the wool is thoroughly wet, lift it out and set it aside while you add 1/4 cup white vinegar and the dissolved dye. Have the heat under the dye pot on low. Stir and then add the red wool. Move the wool around in the dye bath—if you like it spotty, don't stir very much, if you like it even, stir constantly. (Make sure that the wool is poked under the water, as it has a tendency to balloon up as the dye bath heats.) Raise the heat under the dye pot gradually until the water clears.

> *"It all comes down to experimenting and keeping track of what you do. Eventually and without a large investment of time, wool, and dye, you will have gained the experience needed to be better able to judge which color of wool to use to dye colors that you want."*

When the dye bath is clear, remove the wool but don't discard the dye bath right away. Rinse the red wool in tepid water. If the water runs clear, wring the wool and dry it, and it is now ready to hook. If the water does not run clear after several rinses, add more white vinegar to the dye bath and put the wool back in. Simmer until the water runs clear when you rinse the wool.

Kentucky Moonshine

Dark

1/2 yard over oatmeal
3/16 tsp #119 yellow
3/32 tsp #338 red
1/32 tsp #490 blue

Medium

1/2 yard over oatmeal
9/32 tsp #119 yellow
3/64 tsp #338 red
1/64 tsp #490 blue

DYEING OVER COLORED WOOL

Most of the formulas that I have developed and shared with you have been dyed over Dorr white or natural wool. However, there are times when it is advantageous to dye over particular colors of wool other than those. For instance, the formula for the red background in *The Lion with Monkey* is dyed over bright red wool.

I dye over colors instead of white or natural to make use of colored wool that I already have and to save dye. I could have devised a formula to dye the same color over natural, but it would have taken a great deal of red dye and a lot more time in the dye kitchen. In fact, if you look at the formula for Big Top Red, you will see that I didn't use any red dye at all.

The lion color, Kentucky Moonshine, was dyed over oatmeal beige wool instead of natural because I wanted the color to be slightly duller (toned down), and the easiest way to do it was to dye over the beige wool. I had some oatmeal wool, so I came up with a color that I could use without trying to figure out what dyes to add to dull the basic formula. I have dyed beiges and other toned-down colors, but each one is a slightly different challenge. (Over natural wool, the Kentucky Moonshine is a beautiful color but wasn't suitable for what I wanted to use it for.)

After I dyed the two shades of Kentucky Moonshine I wanted to use for the lion, I tried to dye a lighter value over the oatmeal beige. Because the weaker dye was not strong enough to overcome the color of the wool itself, this lighter color did not look like it was dyed with the same formula as the other two shades. However, if you look at the light color on the lion's face, you will see that the light value, although duller than expected, worked out quite well when it came time to hook that area of the face.

There are some limitations when it comes to dyeing over colored and textured wool. Some things are obvious; for instance, if you want a bright color, you can't dye it over dull colored wool. If you want a light color, you can't dye over a medium or a dark color wool.

Remember the dye does not cover up the color of the wool. The final color is the sum of the wool color that you start with, plus the dye formula that you add.

ANOTHER DYE PROJECT

If you have a collection of colored wools, why don't you take one of the many lively formulas used for gradation dyeing over natural or white and dye it over colored wool instead? I would encourage you to especially try different greens over a variety of beige wool. Fairly bright strong formulas work best over medium colors of wool, such as, tweeds, checks, plaids, and so on.

Look at the wool that you want to overdye, and if it is medium grayish tweed, for example, look to see if there is a bit of red, green, or blue in it. If you see a tiny touch of red, you could dye it with a red formula to emphasize the red or you might try dyeing it with a green formula to cancel out the red (green is the complement of red). If you add enough green dye formula, the wool will turn a dark dull green. If instead of red, you see a tiny touch of blue, try dyeing the tweed with a blue formula to emphasize the blue or add an orange dye formula to cancel the blue (orange is the complement of blue). With the addition of orange the wool will become grayed orange, sort of a dull rust. If instead of red or blue you see a touch of green in the gray tweed, add a green formula to run the tweed to a dull green or add its complement, red, to cancel the green. If you add enough red the gray tweed will become a dull red.

ADDITIONAL THOUGHTS TO REMEMBER

The results you get depend on the color and the amount of dye that you add. When you are trying to dye over medium tweeds, plaids, and so on, it is necessary to add a strong dye formula to get satisfactory results. If after dyeing the wool, it still looks quite gray, mix up more of the same dye formula and re-dye the wool. Repeat as many times as necessary until the wool pleases you. Keep in mind that the wool looks darker when wet; therefore, don't stop adding dye until you think carefully about it. It takes a little experience, but before long it will be easier to judge when the color's okay for how you want to use it, or when you need to put it back in the dye bath with more dye.

It all comes down to experimenting and keeping track of what you do. Eventually and without a large investment of time, wool, and dye, you will have gained the experience needed to be better able to judge which color of wool to use to dye colors that you want.

Making the Most of Motifs

Sea Lion, *9 3/4" x 13 3/4", #5-cut wool on burlap. Designed and hooked by Maryanne Lincoln, Wrentham, Massachusetts, 2003.*

THE COLOR OF THE SEA LION IS BROWN HEATHER MATERIAL DYED IN PRO CHEM BLACK. I USED 1/32 TEASPOON #672 BLACK OVER 1/4 YARD WOOL. THE HAT, BALL, AND CART ARE HOOKED WITH ODDS AND ENDS OF DYED WOOL FROM MY WORKBASKET.

The background is Big Top Red, which was featured on page 128. Since I wanted to use Big Top Red for the background, I had to be careful where the values of all the colors touched it. I don't like when colors seem to blend into one another. I prefer a strong contrast between the motif and the background.

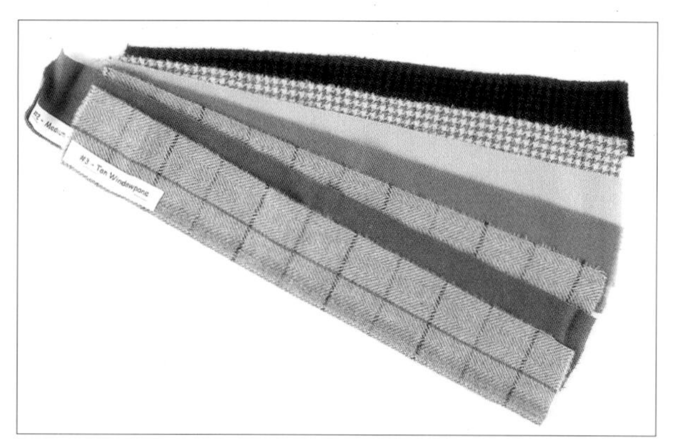

Swatches of wool before dyeing.

In my experience as a rug hooker, it is a common problem to have a leaf, scroll, or some other detail lost against the background of a rug. This is especially noticeable in rugs with medium backgrounds. I had this experience with my first rug, which had a camel colored background, and the edges of several flowers seem to fade into it. The challenge wouldn't have been as great if I had used a very light or dark background, or if a lighter or darker value has been used on the edges of some of the motifs to improve the contrast against the background.

When choosing very dark or very light background colors, it is fairly easy to keep an eye on the edges of all the motifs and remember to control the value of the color. For a light background avoid using light values on the edges of the flowers and leaves, and for a dark background avoid using dark values on the edges of the motifs.

A medium background, such as camel, requires more thought. Stay alert while hooking each motif and the background around it so that you avoid using values on the edges that are very similar to the background of the rug. (I am not talking about the color of the background but the lightness or darkness of it.)

OVERDYEING—A FUN CHALLENGE

To dye a satisfactory color for my sea lion, I overdyed brown heather wool with black dye. Overdyeing colored wools and textures is a great way to come up with lots of beautiful colors. At random I went into my wool storage area and chose a handful of different wools in $\frac{1}{2}$-yard pieces as you see here.

Because I wasn't dyeing this wool for any particular project, I chose colors out of my collection of PRO Chem formulas that you might be familiar with. Then I had to make some decisions as to which formula to overdye each $\frac{1}{2}$ yard of wool. I have left the black out of several of the formulas because I wanted to simplify the formula, and the colors would be slightly duller if black was included.

All formulas are dyed with PRO Chem wash-fast acid dyes in an open pan with enough water for the wool to move freely about as it is agitated. The only additions to the dye bath are Synthrapol SP to wet the wool and then $\frac{1}{4}$ cup white vinegar as the dye assistant. Bring the dye bath to a very high heat—a boil, but not rolling—and then cover loosely. Turn heat down to simmer and process until the water clears. Let the wool cool a few minutes in the dye bath, then rinse.

1. The black and green check (houndstooth) was dyed in Seafoam Green with black left out of the formula. I used three times the formula found in the *PRO Chem Dye* booklet, and also in *Recipes from the Dye Kitchen*, because the check is such dark wool to begin with. Because of this, I knew I would need a strong dye solution to have any effect on the basic color of the check.

   The formula for the $\frac{1}{2}$ yard is:

   $\frac{1}{8}$ tsp #490 blue
   $\frac{3}{8}$ tsp #119 yellow
2. The next wool that I worked with was medium purple. A splotchy periwinkle can be created over this purple by adding blue. The formula is $\frac{1}{16}$ teaspoon #490 blue over $\frac{1}{2}$ yard wool, which I didn't agitate very much because I wanted some of the purple to show through. After it was dyed, the color made me think of delphinium flowers.
3. I dyed two pieces of the tan texture with blue lines through it. The first $\frac{1}{2}$ yard was dyed with $\frac{1}{16}$ teaspoon #490 blue.
4. The other $\frac{1}{2}$ yard of tan texture was dyed in the Old Clay Pots formula found in my

Swatches of overdyed wool.

PRO Chem Dye booklet and *Recipes from the Dye Kitchen*. Because the wool is not very dark, I mixed it up just as it is written but without the black and then dyed the wool.

5. The orange was dyed with 1/32 teaspoon #490 blue. I knew that the color would become dull rusty orange, since complements dull each other. Adding some red will change the color to redder rust, a color more pleasing to my eye.
6. The 1/2 yard of (Dorr's #42) beige was dyed in Princess Pine, another formula from my *PRO Chem Dye* booklet. As before, I left out the black dye but mixed the dyes just as the formula is written in the booklet:

   3/64 tsp #490 blue
   9/32 tsp #119 yellow
   3/128 tsp #338 red

   If this is dyed over a camel color, the results would look duller and the green would look more yellow.
7. The last 1/2 yard is a gray and white check, which I dyed in a variation of my Country Blue formula:

   1/16 tsp #672 black
   1/32 tsp #490 blue

   This soft blue is very easy on the eye, yet it still has character.

Many of you have stacks and stacks of wool in all colors, textures, and plaids. If you seem puzzled about how to zip them up or calm them down, take some time to experiment and dye some with your favorite formulas.

Keep in mind that to change a dark color, use a lot of dye because the wool is already dark. To quiet down a very bright color, remember that it takes very little of the complement of a color to dull and darken it. A plaid can be made more pleasing if it has white/ light areas and dark areas. Look at it to determine if it already has a predominant color, or a color you would like to see more. If it does, overdye the plaid with more of that color. The white areas will become colored, and the end result will probably be more compatible with other wool that you have.

When you overdye colored, textured, or plaid wool, it doesn't cover up the color of the wool but becomes part of the dyed color. For instance, if you dye blue over gold or yellow wool, the color that you get will be in the green family. Blue and yellow combine to make green. Just what green it ends up looking like depends on the amount of blue used, as well as the depth of color in the yellow/gold wool.

There are a couple of other points to consider when you are trying to decide what color to overdye those textures that don't really seem to have a color.

Maybe if you look closely, you will find a bright colored thread running through it or some bright colored flecks scattered over it. Consider dyeing the wool one of those colors.

If it is a brownish texture, overdye with warm colors like reds, yellows, oranges, and even more brown.

If it is a gray, overdye with cool colors like greens, blues, blue greens, and even some red purples, such as plum.

I am usually pleased with the dyeing that I do. However, occasionally when overdyeing textures, if I don't like what I get the first time, it is because the dye wasn't strong enough. Back in the pot it goes with more dye, and in a matter of just a few minutes, the color comes to life and I am pleased. Sometimes, it takes a great deal of dye to make a difference over the medium-to-dark wool colors.

DYEING SUPPLIERS

- **Grey Dye Spoons**
  4877 Ashworth Rd.
  Mariposa, CA 95338
  (209) 966-5888
  Dye spoons
- **Maryanne Lincoln**
  10 Oak Point
  Wrentham, MA 02093
  (508) 384-8188
- **PRO Chemical & Dye, Inc.**
  P.O. Box 14
  Somerset, NJ 02726
  (800) 2-BUY-DYE (orders only)
  Dyes, supplies, free catalog
- **Triple Over Dye**
  187 Jane Dr.
  Syracuse, NY 13219
  (315) 468-2616
  Dye spoons, dye-formula books
- **W. Cushing & Company**
  P.O. Box 351
  Kennebunkport, ME 04046
  (800) 626-7847
  Dyes, dyeing books, dyed wools, spoons, color wheels

METRIC EQUIVALENTS

Keep this chart handy for converting metric measurements (milliliters) to teaspoons, tablespoons, and cups, and vice versa.

- 1.25 ml = 1/4 teaspoon
- 2.5 ml = 1/2 teaspoon
- 5 ml = 1 teaspoon
- 15 ml = 1 tablespoon
- 60 ml = 1/4 cup
- 80 ml = 1/3 cup
- 120 ml = 1/2 cup
- 160 ml = 2/3 cup
- 180 ml = 3/4 cup
- 240 ml = 1 cup

GLOSSARY OF TERMS

- **Acid dye—**A type of dye that requires an acid (such as vinegar or citric acid crystals) in the dye bath in order to activate and attach to fibers.
- **Analogous colors—**Colors adja cent to each other on the color wheel.
- **Complementary colors—**Colors opposite each other on the color wheel.
- **Dye assistant—**A chemical added to a dye bath to create an environment in which dye and fiber will more easily bond. Vinegar is a dye assistant.
- **Dye bath—**The solution of dyes, dye assistants, and water in which fabrics are dyed.
- **Exhaust—**To cause a color to be totally absorbed by a fabric, thus clearing the dye bath.
- **Gradation—**A step-by-step group of a color's values ranging from light to dark.
- **Hue—**The color-wheel name of a color.
- **Intensity—**The saturation or strength of a color, referred to as brightness or dullness. Also known as *chroma*.
- **Light-fast dye—**A dye that can hold its hue when exposed to light and not fade or discolor.
- **Migration—**The spreading or bleeding of a color outside the area where it was applied.
- **Mordant—**A substance that becomes part of the bond between dye and fiber. We often refer to white vinegar as a mordant, but it is really a dye assistant because it does not become part of the bond.
- **Overdyeing—**Dyeing over colored wool, or dyeing over previously dyed areas with another color.
- **Primary colors—**The basic colors red, yellow, and blue that connot be mixed by combining other colors and from which all other colors are mixed.
- **Retardant—**A chemical, such as salt, that delays the absorption of the dye by a fiber.
- **Saturation—**The strength of a color; the amount of pure hue in a color.
- **Swatch—**A packet of pieces of colored wool. The pieces are usually all of the same hue and in gradation.
- **Synthrapol SP—**See wetting agent.
- **Value—**The lightness or darkness of a color.
- **Wash-fast dye—**A dye that can withstand washing without bleeding or washing out of a fabric.
- **Wetting agent—**A substance that, when added to a hot-water bath in which fabric is soaking, enhances the ability of the fabric to absorb dye. Synthrapol SP is a wetting agent.